Knit and Purl

CW0040β456

W0006525

Welcome to The Stitch Collection—a set of handy little guides to knit stitches that are as portable as can be; pick and choose which ones to throw into your knitting bag when you're on the go, and leave the others at home in the case. By design, they are not complete guides to knitting; instead, they are mini-encyclopedias of the stitches themselves. Their purpose is to help you choose the best stitch pattern for your projects.

Like most stitch guides, these books are written in terms of knitting flat—knitting back and forth on the needles, turning after each row. The set is divided into five volumes. Book 1 covers the knit and purl stitches; Book 2 focuses on rib stitches; Book 3 contains lace stitches; Book 4 is all about cables; and Book 5 is a compilation of specialty stitches. Each booklet has some common introductory material to help you determine which pattern you want to use, followed by text that is specific to that book's category of stitch. Each individual stitch pattern is ranked according to its level of difficulty, its drape, and offers suggestions as to its best function in a project (as an overall stitch, a filler stitch, a panel stitch, or an edge stitch).

CHOOSING A STITCH PATTERN

The following sections give you suggestions on how to best use the guides in the set.

Look Before You Swatch

When choosing a stitch pattern to use for a project, be sure to look through all the books. Some patterns are included in one category, but have traits that overlap with the others. It's important to read through a pattern before starting it, too. Often an instruction can seem confusing or intimidating on paper, but will make complete sense when you have the knitting in hand and are ready to work that portion of the pattern.

fingering

Next, make a swatch. The swatches in this book are knit in varying weights of wool (worsted, sport, and fingering) provided by Lorna's Laces. In general, the patterns with small stitch multiples (less than 8 or 10) and panels are knit with Shepherd Worsted; the larger stitch multiples are done in Shepherd Sport. A few of the very large stitch repeats in Book 1 and Book 3 are worked in Shepherd Sock. The swatches have been blocked minimally for photography, and thus you may occasionally note irregularities that are inherent in hand knitting.

sport

worsted

The appearance and drape of the stitch pattern will depend on the yarn chosen—color, style of spinning, fiber content, and weight—and on the gauge used. Keep in mind that large stitch motifs can overwhelm small projects, and small stitch motifs might be lost on a large project. Scale is important. Changing the weight of yarn and gauge it is knit at can help reduce or enlarge a motif as desired. The photos on this page show an example of the Tulip lace pattern knit with three different weights of yarn at three different gauges. The appearance of the pattern changes in each case and stresses the importance of swatching.

Knit and Purl

Follow the Organization

Each book is organized from smallest stitch multiple to largest, making it easier to find the pattern that best suits the project you have in mind. A small-scale lace pattern is better for a baby sweater than a large-scale one, for instance.

Match the Pattern to the Purpose

The descriptions included with each stitch pattern also suggest the type of project for which it is best suited. Many of the descriptions also indicate whether it works well as an overall stitch, a filler stitch, a panel stitch, or an edge stitch. An overall stitch pattern is used throughout the full project rather than in just a small area. You can convert patterns presented as panels into an overall stitch pattern by simply working one or more stitches (usually Stockinette or Reverse Stockinette) between repeats of the panel.

Filler stitches are worked in small areas of a larger project to fill open space. Filler stitches appear in between panels of other stitches or as a panel themselves. Filler stitches often have a small multiple and are easier to use in sizing and shaping. When combining filler stitches with other stitches (panels or overall patterns), always check the gauge of each stitch pattern. They can vary widely, even on the same needles with the same yarn.

A panel pattern is intended to be a section of a larger project. Most often, panels are just the stitch pattern itself, and the knitter needs to add border or background stitches. Panels can be worked as either a stitch multiple, by themselves, or combined with other panels or stitch patterns. Cables are very often written as a panel, for instance.

Lastly, edge or border stitch patterns can be used as filler stitches or overall patterns, but they lie flat and look tidy along the edges, making them suitable for hems, cuffs, or edges on other patterns.

Understand the Ratings

Each stitch pattern in this collection has a skill level and a drape rating. The skill level ratings include easy (basic knitting knowledge required), advanced beginner, intermediate, and experienced. Remember what looks difficult on paper is often easier to understand with the knitting on needles in front of you.

All knitting has at least some amount of drape, so the ratings are relative and are based on using wool at the recommended gauge for the yarn. The ratings are: low (a firmer fabric), medium (reasonable amount of drape), and high (a flowing fabric). In general, the denser the fabric (e.g., more stitches per inch) is with stitches, the less drape it will have. The more open the fabric is (e.g., fewer stitches per inch), the more drape it will have. Cable patterns, for instance, will have less drape than lace patterns. However, drape also depends on the yarn chosen for a project and on the gauge used. Some fibers have more drape than others, and the finer the yarn, the more drape the fabric will have. A tighter gauge will have less drape than a looser gauge.

Understand Stitch Multiples and Balancing Stitches

Stitch patterns are presented with information about the number of stitches required to complete one pattern repeat. For panels, the information is simply how many stitches wide the panel is. For all other patterns, this information is presented as a multiple of stitches, plus any balancing stitches needed. For example, if you want to work six repeats of a pattern, and it requires four stitches and one balancing stitch (multiple of 4 + 1), you would cast on 24 stitches plus one balancing stitch, for a total of 25 stitches.

level

    easy

    advanced beginner

    intermediate

    experienced

drape

    low

    medium

    high

Knit and Purl

Add Selvage Stitches

The patterns in these books do not include selvage stitches, which are one or more spare stitches included at the edge of your knitting for seaming or for tidying the edge. Some knitters don't even use selvage stitches unless specifically directed to do so in a pattern. If you are a knitter who likes to use selvage stitches, you will need to add them to the edges of your projects.

Work Increases and Decreases

These guides use a variety of increases and decreases. It is important to use the correct technique for the increases and decreases called for in the pattern instructions; this insures that your stitch pattern has the proper appearance, as the various techniques create different effects, such as slants or holes. Perhaps the most common increase used in the patterns is done by knitting into the front and back of a single stitch. There are several decreases used in the patterns—some decrease one stitch at a time (single decreases), some decrease two stitches at a time (double decreases), some decrease even more! When a pattern says simply to decrease one stitch, but doesn't say which decrease to use, the assumption is that you will use a k2tog (knit two stitches together) or a p2tog (purl two stitches together), depending on whether you are on the right or wrong side of your work. Consult the Abbreviations and Glossary section (page 62) for explanations of each type of increase or decrease.

Knit and Purl

CHOOSING THE BEST YARN

How do you choose the most suitable yarn for a stitch pattern or a project? The first thing to consider is the pattern itself. The busier the stitch pattern is, the simpler the yarn should be, and vice versa. If you want to work a lace pattern or an elaborate cable pattern, choose a smooth, plain-colored yarn. A subtly variegated or kettle-dyed solid yarn might work with a fancy pattern stitch, but a yarn with extreme color changes or striping will detract from the pattern stitch.

Fiber content makes a difference, too. Plant fibers (cotton, linen, hemp, rayon) are inelastic, as is silk. When you work with plant fibers, your knitting tends to be what-you-see-is-what-you-get. Blocking will not improve it.

In contrast, animal fibers are almost magical to knit with, and a good blocking hides a multitude of sins. The fiber has memory and will retain its shape until the next time it gets wet.

Consider Yarn Requirements

Knitting a swatch before beginning a project is important, of course. But when choosing stitch patterns for a project you design, it is useful to consult a reference to see what the estimated yardage requirements are for the size and type of project you are creating at the gauge you are knitting. Yardage requirement tables are usually based on Stockinette stitch, but keep in mind that different stitch patterns require different amounts of yarn. For instance, Garter stitch has a very compressed row gauge, so it will take more yarn than Stockinette stitch. Lace is very open, so it can use less yarn than Stockinette stitch. Cables and many fancy patterns are very dense and can use *much* more yarn than Stockinette stitch.

Knit and Purl

INTRODUCTION TO KNIT AND PURL

Knit-purl pattern stitches are exactly as they sound—stitch motifs composed of knit stitches and purl stitches. The visual interest in knit-purl stitch patterns comes from the variation in texture between the two stitches. Because the patterns rely on this texture to show well, knit-purl patterns are typically most effective when knit at a firm gauge—the recommended gauge for the yarn or slightly firmer. Smooth yarns and solid color yarns also help the stitch patterns stand out. There are exceptions to the rule where a looser gauge or fancier yarn works just fine. But the stitch patterns that are the exceptions tend to be the simplest of patterns—Stockinette, Reverse Stockinette, and Garter stitch, for instance.

Many knit-purl stitch patterns have small stitch multiples yet retain strong textures, making them well suited to serve as filler stitches in projects such as Aran sweaters. Others are made up of larger stitch multiples that work as stand-alone panels. They are a particularly appealing group of patterns for any projects where the wrong side of the work might show, as the patterns, if not completely reversible, usually have an attractive wrong side.

Knit-purl pattern stitches are extremely versatile. They can usually be substituted in any pattern calling for Stockinette stitch. The reason for this is that the knit stitches and purl stitches in knit-purl patterns are reasonably balanced so the resulting fabric has many of the same characteristics as Stockinette stitch. Knit-purl patterns work well in just about any type of project in any weight of yarn.

Knit and Purl

These patterns are also a great way to create pictures in knitting without having to do colorwork. Using knitter's graph paper, you can easily chart out your own pictures composed of nothing more than knit and purl stitches. Generally speaking, purl stitches stand out more strongly on a Stockinette stitch background than the reverse. Horizontal lines of purl stitches on a Stockinette stitch background will cause a welt, or compression, of the row gauge. Vertical lines of purl stitches on a Stockinette stitch background cause a rib effect, so that the fabric starts to pull in. A roughly even distribution of knits and purls will lie flat.

The first four stitch patterns—Garter stitch, Stockinette stitch, Reverse Stockinette stitch, and Twisted Stockinette stitch—form the basis for all knitting patterns. Add in increases, decreases, and some cable twists, and you can create just about any knitted stitch motif possible.

Knit and Purl

GARTER STITCH

Garter stitch is interesting because it is a perfectly balanced stitch. This means that you can truly knit a square with Garter stitch by casting on *n* stitches and working *2n* rows. Garter stitch is very compressed—two rows is equivalent in height to the width of one stitch—and elastic. It will lie flat, making it perfect for edgings. Many people consider Garter stitch to be a beginner's stitch because it is simply knit every row. However, its applications are great, and it is used in a great number of patterns.

THE PATTERN

Multiple of any number of stitches

Row 1 (WS): Knit.

Row 2: Knit.

Repeat rows 1 and 2.

level
drape

STOCKINETTE STITCH

Stockinette stitch is what most people think of when they think of knitting. It works up rectangular rather than square. (This is why knitter's graph paper has a rectangular grid rather than a square grid.) There are more rows per inch than stitches per inch, the exact ratio varying with the knitter. Stockinette stitch curls at both edges, so it is best when worked with another stitch at the edges. However, the natural curl of Stockinette stitch can make an attractive rolled edge at a hem or cuff. Stockinette stitch is suitable for just about any knitted project.

THE PATTERN

Multiple of any number of stitches

Row 1 (WS): Purl.

Row 2: Knit.

Repeat rows 1 and 2.

level

drape

REVERSE STOCKINETTE STITCH

Reverse Stockinette stitch is simply the back side of Stockinette stitch—the purl stitches are on the right side rather than the knit stitches. All of the characteristics of Stockinette stitch also hold true with Reverse Stockinette stitch. Reverse Stockinette stitch is often used as a background for stitch patterns, especially cables, as the simple fabric makes other stitches stand out.

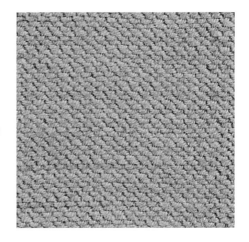

level
drape

THE PATTERN

Multiple of any number of stitches

Row 1 (WS): Knit.

Row 2: Purl.

Repeat rows 1 and 2.

Knit and Purl

TWISTED STOCKINETTE STITCH

Twisted Stockinette stitch is Stockinette stitch with the knit stitches (worked on the right side of the knitting) being knit through the back loop. This technique twists the stitch, giving the resulting fabric an interesting texture.
The characteristics of Stockinette stitch are also applicable to Twisted Stockinette stitch.

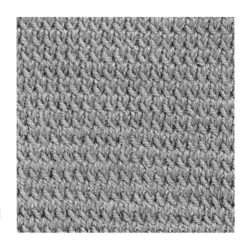

level
drape

THE PATTERN

Multiple of any number of stitches

Row 1 (WS): Purl.

Row 2: K tbl.

Repeat rows 1 and 2.

SAND STITCH

Sand stitch is a particularly nice pattern stitch for several reasons. It has a simple, but nice, texture; it lies flat, so no border pattern is needed; and while it is written as a right and wrong side pattern, both sides are attractive, so Sand stitch works well for projects where reversibility is important. Sand stitch would be appropriate for just about any project.

level
drape ▥ ▥

THE PATTERN

Multiple of 2

Row 1 (WS): Knit.

Row 2: * K1, p1. Repeat from * to end of row.

Row 3: Knit.

Row 4: * P1, k1. Repeat from * to end of row.

Repeat rows 1–4.

SEED STITCH

Seed stitch is a wonderful stitch pattern—it lies completely flat and works up almost square. As long as you remember to cast on an odd number of stitches, the pattern is simply knitting the purl stitches and purling the knit stitches. The texture of Seed stitch makes it perfect for almost any purpose. It makes a great edge treatment for projects, but is also attractive for the main fabric. Because of its small multiple, Seed stitch also works well as a filler panel in projects that combine stitch motifs.

level

drape

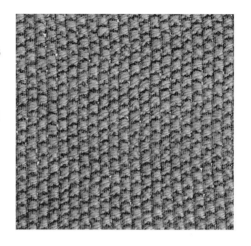

THE PATTERN

Multiple of 2 + 1

Row 1 (WS): K1, * p1, k1. Repeat from * to end of row.

Row 2: K1, * p1, k1. Repeat from * to end of row.

Repeat rows 1 and 2.

MOSS STITCH

Moss stitch is very similar to Seed stitch (page 15) in appearance and characteristics. It is basically a 1 x 1 rib that is offset every other row. Moss stitch is highly textured like Seed stitch, but has a more elongated appearance. It is suitable for use in any project for which you would use Seed stitch. Traditionally, Moss stitch is frequently used as a filler stitch in Aran sweater patterns.

level ◑

drape ▥ ▥

THE PATTERN

Multiple of 2 + 1

Row 1 (WS): K1, * p1, k1. Repeat from * to end of row.

Row 2: P1, * k1, p1. Repeat from * to end of row.

Row 3: P1, * k1, p1. Repeat from * to end of row.

Row 4: K1, * p1, k1. Repeat from * to end of row.

Repeat rows 1–4.

RICE STITCH

Rice stitch has a bumpy texture resembling grains of rice on the right side of the work. The twisted knit stitch enhances the texture. The wrong side of this pattern resembles a ribbing pattern without pulling in the fabric. Rice stitch is an excellent filler stitch in larger projects. It also makes an attractive overall pattern on its own for sweaters or blankets. Rice stitch lies flat, so no additional edge stitch is required.

level

drape

THE PATTERN

Multiple of 2 + 1

Row 1 (WS): Knit.

Row 2: P1, * k tbl, p1. Repeat from * to end of row.

Repeat rows 1 and 2.

Knit and Purl

17

OFFSET RICE STITCH

Offset rice stitch has the same bumpy texture as Rice stitch (page 17), but the stitches are offset every other row, so the fabric has less of a linear appearance. The characteristics of the fabric are similar to Rice stitch. Offset rice stitch can be used in any project where you would use Rice stitch.

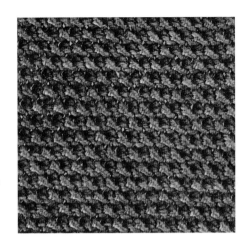

level ◉

drape ▦ ▦

THE PATTERN

Multiple of 2 + 1

Row 1 (WS): Knit.

Row 2: P1, * k tbl, p1. Repeat from * to end of row.

Row 3: Knit.

Row 4: K tbl * p1, k tbl. Repeat from * to end of row.

Repeat rows 1–4.

LINEN STITCH

Linen stitch produces a knitted fabric that resembles a woven fabric. It is very dense and not terribly elastic. It does lie very flat, though. Linen stitch is excellent for garments like knitted jackets, where not as much elasticity is needed. When knit at a slightly looser gauge, the drape greatly improves.

level
drape

THE PATTERN

Multiple of 2 + 1

Row 1 (WS): K1, p1, * sl 1 wyib, p1. Repeat from * to last stitch, end k1.

Row 2: K1, * sl 1 wyif, k1. Repeat from * to end of row.

Repeat rows 1 and 2.

WOVEN STITCH

Woven stitch is similar to Linen stitch (page 19), but the fabric produced has more drape and is not as dense because the yarn is only slipped every other row, instead of every row. Unlike Linen stitch, Woven stitch has one side that looks more woven (the right side) and one side that looks more knitted (the wrong side). Woven stitch works well in vests, cardigans, and jackets.

level ● ●
drape ▦ ▦

THE PATTERN

Multiple of 2 + 1

Row 1 (WS): Purl.

Row 2: K1, * sl 1 wyif, k1. Repeat from * to end of row.

Row 3: Purl.

Row 4: K2, * sl 1 wyif, k1. Repeat from * to last stitch, end k1.

Repeat rows 1–4.

TEXTURED SLIP STITCH

Textured slip stitch is a basic Garter stitch pattern where every other stitch is slipped on rows 2 and 3 of the pattern. Slipping the stitches gives the appearance of Stockinette stitch v's nested in purl bumps; it looks more complex than it is. Because the pattern is based in Garter stitch, it lies flat and works well as an edge stitch. However, the fabric created is also an excellent filler stitch or overall pattern for a sweater. Textured slip stitch is also attractive when worked in more than one color; simply change colors on right-side rows.

level ● ●
drape ● ○

THE PATTERN

Multiple of 2 + 1

Row 1 (WS): Knit.
Row 2: K1, * sl 1 wyib, k1. Repeat from * to end of row.
Row 3: K1, * sl 1 wyif, k1. Repeat from * to end of row.
Row 4: Knit.
Repeat rows 1–4.

OFFSET TEXTURED SLIP STITCH

Offset textured slip stitch is the same as Textured slip stitch (page 21), but is worked over twice as many rows so that the slipped stitches are offset. The end result is a rich texture with a complex appearance that is actually quite simple and quick to work. The fabric lies flat and works well as an edge stitch because it is based in Garter stitch. However, the fabric created is also an excellent filler stitch or overall pattern for a classic sweater or cardigan. Offset textured slip stitch can be worked in more than one color by changing colors on right-side rows.

level
drape

THE PATTERN

Multiple of 2 + 1

Row 1 (WS): Knit.

Row 2: K1, * sl 1 wyib, k1. Repeat from * to end of row.

Row 3: K1, * sl 1 wyif, k1. Repeat from * to end of row.

Row 4: Knit.

Row 5: Knit.

Row 6: K2, * sl 1 wyib, k1. Repeat from * to last stitch, end k1.

Row 7: K2, * sl 1 wyif, k1. Repeat from * to last stitch, end k1.

Row 8: Knit.

Repeat rows 1–8.

Knit and Purl

ROSE GARDEN STITCH

Rose garden stitch is a brioche-style stitch where stitches are knit into the row below. This creates a thick, fluffy fabric with a honeycomb-like appearance. Because stitches are knit into the row below, rose garden stitch can work well with variegated yarns. Rose garden stitch is a good pattern for sweaters or blankets and it also works well as a filler stitch.

level

drape

THE PATTERN

Multiple of 2 + 1

Row 1 (WS): K2, * p1, k1. Repeat from * to last stitch, end k1.

Row 2: K1, * k1b, k1. Repeat from * to end of row.

Row 3: K1, * p1, k1. Repeat from * to end of row.

Row 4: K2, * k1b, k1. Repeat from * to last stitch, end k1.

Repeat rows 1–4.

Knit and Purl

23

LITTLE RIPPLE

Little ripple uses a simple technique of working a twist by knitting two stitches together, then knitting the first stitch again. It appears as if the knit stitches are rippling across the purl stitches. Little ripple is a nice filler stitch, or an overall stitch for small projects like socks, accessories, or baby sweaters.

level ⏸ ⏸
drape ⫼ ⫼

THE PATTERN

Multiple of 3

Rows 1 and 3 (WS): Purl.

Row 2: * K2tog, k the first stitch again, k1. Repeat from * to end of row.

Row 4: * K1, k2tog, k the first stitch again. Repeat from * to end of row.

Repeat rows 1–4.

KNIT-PURL DIAMOND CHECKERBOARD

Knit-purl diamond checkerboard is a checkerboard pattern turned on end. Although it is a small stitch motif, it works well as either a filler stitch or an overall pattern. It can be used in small projects, like socks or other accessories, or in larger projects like sweaters and blankets.

level

drape

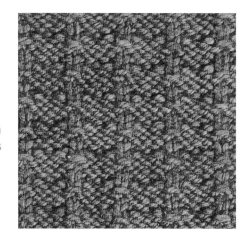

THE PATTERN

Multiple of 4 + 1

Row 1 (WS): P1, * p1, k1, p2. Repeat from * to end of row.

Row 2: K1, * p3, k1. Repeat from * to end of row.

Row 3: Knit.

Row 4: K1, * p3, k1. Repeat from * to end of row.

Repeat rows 1–4, ending after working row 1.

DOUBLE MOSS STITCH

Double moss stitch is a classic Aran filler stitch pattern. It is simply Moss stitch (page 16) worked double wide. Double moss stitch has the same characteristics as Seed stitch (page 15) and Moss stitch. It appears bumpier because of the increased width of the motif. It can be used anywhere you would normally use Seed stitch or Moss stitch.

level

drape

THE PATTERN

Multiple of 4 + 2

Row 1 (WS): K2, * p2, k2. Repeat from * to end of row.

Row 2: P2, * k2, p2. Repeat from * to end of row.

Row 3: P2, * k2, p2. Repeat from * to end of row.

Row 4: K2, * p2, k2. Repeat from * to end of row.

Repeat rows 1–4.

WAFFLE PATTERN

Waffle pattern is a mixture of a basket weave-style pattern and a rib. While it is not quite reversible, the wrong side of the pattern is attractive. It lies flat without pulling in a lot, making it a nice edge stitch. The small stitch multiple and nice texture make Waffle pattern good for use as a filler pattern. The stitch motif is suitable for just about any project.

level

drape

THE PATTERN

Multiple of 4 + 2

Row 1 (WS): Purl.

Row 2: Knit.

Row 3: P2, * k2, p2. Repeat from * to end of row.

Row 4: K2, * p2, k2. Repeat from * to end of row.

Repeat rows 1–4.

DOT STITCH

Dot stitch is basically Stockinette stitch with an occasional purl bump on the right side of the work. Its characteristics are very similar to those of Stockinette stitch, but there is more visual interest. Dot stitch can be used anywhere you would use Stockinette stitch. It is great to use with yarns like cotton, where any discrepancy in tension shows. The occasional purl bump draws the eye away from any flaws.

level
drape

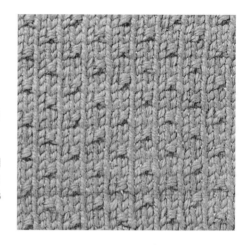

THE PATTERN

Multiple of 4 + 3
Row 1 (WS): Purl.
Row 2: * K3, p1. Repeat from * to last 3 stitches, end k3.
Row 3: Purl.
Row 4: K1, * p1, k3. Repeat from * to last 2 stitches, end p1, k1.
Repeat rows 1–4.

SMALL BASKETWEAVE

Small basketweave is a stitch pattern that resembles latticework or a woven basket. It is a small-multiple, highly textured motif. Small basketweave is perfect for smaller projects like accessories, or as a filler stitch in a larger project. It is also a nice stitch pattern for children's sweaters.

level

drape

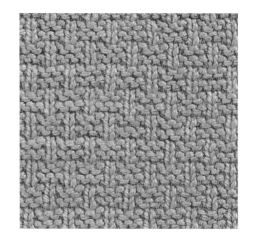

THE PATTERN

Multiple of 4 + 3

Row 1 (WS): K1, p1, * k3, p1. Repeat from * to last stitch, end k1.

Row 2: Knit.

Row 3: K3, * p1, k3. Repeat from * to end of row.

Row 4: Knit.

Row 5: K3, * p1, k3. Repeat from * to end of row.

Row 6: Knit.

Row 7: K1, p1, * k3, p1. Repeat from * to last stitch, end k1.

Row 8: Knit.

Repeat rows 1–8.

LOZENGE STITCH

Lozenge stitch is a traditional Italian stitch pattern. Like many of the knit-purl stitch motifs, it is reversible. The small triangle motifs form larger rectangles. This motif is perfect for unisex projects. Lozenge stitch works well as a filler stitch, or as the main pattern for socks, other accessories, and sweaters.

level *

drape *** ***

THE PATTERN

Multiple of 5

Row 1 (WS): * P1, k4. Repeat from * to end of row.

Row 2: * P3, k2. Repeat from * to end of row.

Row 3: * P3, k2. Repeat from * to end of row.

Row 4: * P1, k4. Repeat from * to end of row.

Row 5: * K4, p1. Repeat from * to end of row.

Row 6: * K2, p3. Repeat from * to end of row.

Row 7: * K2, p3. Repeat from * to end of row.

Row 8: * K4, p1. Repeat from * to end of row.

Repeat rows 1–8.

Knit and Purl

LITTLE DIAMONDS

Little diamonds is made up of small Moss stitch (page 16) diamonds on a Stockinette stitch background. The small stitch multiple makes this pattern appropriate as an overall pattern or as a filler stitch. Little diamonds is perfect for accessories, like hats and mittens, socks, or sweaters for the whole family.

level

drape

THE PATTERN

Multiple of 6

Row 1 (WS): * P1, k1, p4. Repeat from * to end of row.
Row 2: * K1, p1, k4. Repeat from * to end of row.
Row 3: * P4, k1, p1. Repeat from * to end of row.
Row 4: * P1, k1, p1, k3. Repeat from * to end of row.
Row 5: * P3, k1, p1, k1. Repeat from * to end of row.
Row 6: * K1, p1, k4. Repeat from * to end of row.
Row 7: * P4, k1, p1. Repeat from * to end of row.
Row 8: * K4, p1, k1. Repeat from * to end of row.
Row 9: * P1, k1, p4. Repeat from * to end of row.
Row 10: * K3, p1, k1, p1. Repeat from * to end of row.
Row 11: * K1, p1, k1, p3. Repeat from * to end of row.
Row 12: * K4, p1, k1. Repeat from * to end of row.
Repeat rows 1–12.

PURL ZIGZAGS

Purl zigzags are jagged stripes of purl stitches across a Stockinette stitch background. There is a nice linear appearance to the pattern. Purl zigzags is a good motif to use for most projects. The small multiple fits smaller projects well, but the vertical lines are flattering in larger projects. The balance of knits and purls help keep the fabric from curling at the cast-on edge, so no additional edge stitch is required.

level //)

drape //// ///

THE PATTERN

Multiple of 6

Row 1 (WS): * P1, k2, p3. Repeat from * to end of row.

Row 2: * K2, p2, k2. Repeat from * to end of row.

Row 3: * P3, k2, p1. Repeat from * to end of row.

Row 4: * P2, k4. Repeat from * to end of row.

Row 5: * P3, k2, p1. Repeat from * to end of row.

Row 6: * K2, p2, k2. Repeat from * to end of row.

Row 7: * P1, k2, p3. Repeat from * to end of row.

Row 8: * K4, p2. Repeat from * to end of row.

Repeat rows 1–8.

WAVING BLOCKS

Waving blocks is a particularly nice pattern where the wrong side is just as nice as the right side. The blocks of knit and purl stitches gently wave as if they are floating in water. Because the knits and purls are balanced, the fabric lies flat and doesn't pull in. Waving blocks is a perfect blanket motif. It is also attractive in accessories like hats, mittens, or socks, and in sweaters.

level

drape

THE PATTERN

Multiple of 6

Row 1 (RS): * P4, k2. Repeat from * to end of row.

Row 2: * P2, k4. Repeat from * to end of row.

Row 3: * P3, k3. Repeat from * to end of row.

Row 4: * P3, k3. Repeat from * to end of row.

Row 5: * P2, k4. Repeat from * to end of row.

Row 6: * P4, k2. Repeat from * to end of row.

Row 7: P1, * k4, p2. Repeat from * to last 5 stitches, end k4, p1.

Row 8: K1, p4, * k2, p4. Repeat from * to last stitch, end k1.

Row 9: P1, * k3, p3. Repeat from * to last 5 stitches, end k3, p2.

Row 10: K2, p3, * k3, p3. Repeat from * to last stitch, end k1.

Row 11: P1, * k2, p4. Repeat from * to last 5 stitches, end k2, p3.

Row 12: K3, p2, * k4, p2. Repeat from * to last stitch, end k1.

Repeat rows 1–12.

Knit and Purl

PENNANTS

Pennants is a cheerful pattern that is reminiscent of a sailing regatta with flags blowing in the breeze. The pattern is reversible, making it appealing for projects where both sides might be visible. Pennants would be a cute pattern to use in projects for babies or children. The low stitch multiple is good for other small projects, too.

level

drape

THE PATTERN

Multiple of 7

Row 1 (WS): Purl.
Row 2: * K6, p1. Repeat from * to end of row.
Row 3: * K2, p5. Repeat from * to end of row.
Row 4: * K4, p3. Repeat from * to end of row.
Row 5: * K4, p3. Repeat from * to end of row.
Row 6: * K2, p5. Repeat from * to end of row.
Row 7: * K6, p1. Repeat from * to end of row.
Row 8: * K1, p6. Repeat from * to end of row.
Row 9: * K5, p2. Repeat from * to end of row.
Row 10: * K3, p4. Repeat from * to end of row.
Row 11: * K3, p4. Repeat from * to end of row.
Row 12: * K5, p2. Repeat from * to end of row.
Row 13: * K1, p6. Repeat from * to end of row.
Row 14: Knit.
Repeat rows 1–14.

SEED STITCH LIGHTNING BOLTS

Seed stitch lightning bolts are zigzag bolts of Seed stitch (page 15) across a Stockinette stitch background. The effect is nice vertical lines that don't look like stripes. The mixture of knits and purls is sufficient to keep the cast-on edge from curling so no edge stitch is required. Seed stitch lightning bolts looks best used as an overall pattern in projects of any size, from accessories to blankets.

level
drape

THE PATTERN

Multiple of 7

Row 1 (WS): * P3, [k1, p1] twice. Repeat from * to end of row.
Row 2: * P1, k1, p1, k4. Repeat from * to end of row.
Row 3: * P4, k1, p1, k1. Repeat from * to end of row.
Row 4: * [K1, p1] twice, k3. Repeat from * to end of row.
Row 5: * P3, [k1, p1] twice. Repeat from * to end of row.
Row 6: * K2, [p1, k1] twice, k1. Repeat from * to end of row.
Row 7: * P2, [k1, p1] twice, p1. Repeat from * to end of row.
Row 8: * K3, [p1, k1] twice. Repeat from * to end of row.
Row 9: * [P1, k1] twice, p3. Repeat from * to end of row.
Row 10: * K4, p1, k1, p1. Repeat from * to end of row.
Row 11: * [K1, p1] twice, p3. Repeat from * to end of row.
Row 12: * K3, [p1, k1] twice. Repeat from * to end of row.
Row 13: * [P1, k1] twice, p3. Repeat from * to end of row.
Row 14: * K2, [p1, k1] twice, k1. Repeat from * to end of row.
Row 15: * P2, [k1, p1] twice, p1. Repeat from * to end of row.
Row 16: * [K1, p1] twice, k3. Repeat from * to end of row.
Repeat rows 1–16.

DIAMOND BROCADE

Diamond brocade is a very dainty knit-purl pattern composed of purl diamond outlines on a Stockinette stitch background. This stitch motif is an attractive overall motif for blankets or sweaters. It would make a nice stitch pattern for a girl's dress. Because diamond brocade has a relatively small stitch multiple, it is also good for small projects like socks or mittens.

level ◍
drape ▥ ▥

THE PATTERN

Multiple of 8 + 1

Row 1 (RS): K4, * p1, k7. Repeat from * to last 5 stitches, end p1, k4.

Row 2: P3, * k1, p1, k1, p5. Repeat from * to end of row, ending last repeat p3.

Row 3: K2, * p1, k3. Repeat from * to end of row, ending last repeat k2.

Row 4: P1, * k1, p5, k1, p1. Repeat from * to end of row.

Row 5: * P1, k7. Repeat from * to last stitch, end p1.

Row 6: P1, * k1, p5, k1, p1. Repeat from * to end of row.

Row 7: K2, * p1, k3. Repeat from * to end of row, ending last repeat k2.

Row 8: P3, * k1, p1, k1, p5. Repeat from * to end of row, ending last repeat p3.

Repeat rows 1–8.

FLYING X'S

Flying X's is made up of purl stitch X's on a background of knit stitches. The combination of knit and purl stitches cause the fabric to lie flat. However, trimmed with a simple edge stitch, this motif would make an attractive blanket. It would also work well in sweaters, either as an overall pattern or as a panel surrounded by other motifs.

level

drape

Multiple of 8 + 1

THE PATTERN

Row 1 (WS): P1, * k1, p5, k1, p1. Repeat from * to end of row.
Row 2: K1, * p2, k3, p2, k1. Repeat from * to end of row.
Row 3: P1, * k3, p1, k3, p1. Repeat from * to end of row.
Row 4: K1, * k1, p2, k1, p2, k2. Repeat from * to end of row.
Row 5: P1, * p2, k1, p1, k1, p3. Repeat from * to end of row.
Row 6: K1, * k3, p1, k4. Repeat from * to end of row.
Row 7: P1, * p2, k1, p1, k1, p3. Repeat from * to end of row.
Row 8: K1, * k3, p1, k4. Repeat from * to end of row.
Row 9: P1, * p2, k1, p1, k1, p3. Repeat from * to end of row.
Row 10: K1, * k1, p2, k1, p2, k2. Repeat from * to end of row.
Row 11: P1, * k3, p1, k3, p1. Repeat from * to end of row.
Row 12: K1, * p2, k3, p2, k1. Repeat from * to end of row.
Row 13: P1, * k1, p5, k1, p1. Repeat from * to end of row.
Row 14: Knit.
Repeat rows 1–14.

GANSEY DIAMONDS

Gansey diamonds is a classic knit-purl pattern that is commonly used as a panel in a Gansey or Aran sweater. It is most striking when worked in a smooth, solid-colored yarn. While traditionally used as a panel, Gansey diamonds also works nicely as an overall pattern. It is a good motif for sweaters, socks, hats, mittens, or gloves.

level ◉

drape ▥ ▥

THE PATTERN

Multiple of 8 + 1

Row 1 (RS): K1, * [k1, p1] 3 times, k2. Repeat from * to end of row.

Row 2: P1, * p2, k1, p1, k1, p3. Repeat from * to end of row.

Row 3: K1, * k3, p1, k4. Repeat from * to end of row.

Row 4: Purl.

Row 5: K1, * k3, p1, k4. Repeat from * to end of row.

Row 6: P1, * p2, k1, p1, k1, p3. Repeat from * to end of row.

Row 7: K1, * [k1, p1] 3 times, k2. Repeat from * to end of row.

Row 8: P1, * k1, p1. Repeat from * to end of row.

Row 9: P1, * k1, p1. Repeat from * to end of row.

Row 10: P1, * k1, p1. Repeat from * to end of row.

Row 11: K1, * [k1, p1] 3 times, k2. Repeat from * to end of row.

Row 12: P1, * p2, k1, p1, k1, p3. Repeat from * to end of row.

Row 13: K1, * k3, p1, k4. Repeat from * to end of row.

Row 14: Purl.

Row 15: K1, * k3, p1, k4. Repeat from * to end of row.

Row 16: P1, * p2, k1, p1, k1, p3. Repeat from * to end of row.

Repeat rows 1–16.

BASKETWEAVE

Basketweave is a stitch pattern that resembles latticework or a woven basket. It is a highly textured motif that is larger than its Small basketweave (page 29) counterpart. Basketweave is perfect for accessories or as a filler stitch in a larger project. It is also a nice stitch pattern for sweaters or blankets of all sizes. The combination of knit and purl stitches is enough to make the fabric lie flat, but an edge stitch makes Basketweave look more refined.

level
drape

THE PATTERN

Multiple of 8 + 4

Row 1 (WS): P4, * k4, p4. Repeat from * to end of row.
Row 2: K4, * p4, k4. Repeat from * to end of row.
Row 3: P4, * k4, p4. Repeat from * to end of row.
Row 4: K4, * p4, k4. Repeat from * to end of row.
Row 5: K4, * p4, k4. Repeat from * to end of row.
Row 6: P4, * k4, p4. Repeat from * to end of row.
Row 7: K4, * p4, k4. Repeat from * to end of row.
Row 8: P4, * k4, p4. Repeat from * to end of row.
Repeat rows 1–8.

Knit and Purl

THE STITCH COLLECTION | knit and purl

PARALLELOGRAM CHECK

Parallelogram check is
a completely reversible
knit-purl pattern of small
parallelograms drifting
across the fabric. As long
as it is knit at a firm
gauge so the pattern
stands out, it will work
in any weight of yarn.
Parallelogram check
is well suited for small
projects like socks and
baby sweaters to large
projects like adult sweaters and blankets.

level
drape ▥ ▥

THE PATTERN

Multiple of 10

Row 1 (WS): * P5, k5. Repeat from * to end of row.

Row 2: * K5, p5. Repeat from * to end of row.

Row 3: K4, * p5, k5. Repeat from * to last 6 sts, end p5, k1.

Row 4: P2, * k5, p5. Repeat from * to last 8 sts, end k5, p3.

Row 5: K2, * p5, k5. Repeat from * to last 8 sts, end p5, k3.

Row 6: P4, * k5, p5. Repeat from * to last 6 sts, end k5, p1.

Repeat rows 1–6.

FLYING GEESE

Flying geese is a classic Gansey motif of Seed-stitch geese flying across a Stockinette-stitch sky. The pattern should be knit at a firm gauge in a smooth yarn for the stitches to show. Flying geese can be used as a panel in a Gansey or Aran sweater, but it is also an attractive overall stitch pattern.

level
drape

THE PATTERN

Multiple of 10

Row 1 (WS): * K1, p9. Repeat from * to end of row.

Row 2: * K8, p1, k1. Repeat from * to end of row.

Row 3: * K1, p1, k1, p7. Repeat from * to end of row.

Row 4: * K2, [p1, k1] 4 times. Repeat from * to end of row.

Row 5: * [K1, p1] 4 times, p2. Repeat from * to end of row.

Row 6: * P1, k3, [p1, k1] 3 times. Repeat from * to end of row.

Row 7: * [K1, p1] 3 times, p2, k1, p1. Repeat from * to end of row.

Row 8: * [P1, k1] twice, k2, [p1, k1] twice. Repeat from * to end of row.

Row 9: * [K1, p1] twice, p2, [k1, p1] twice. Repeat from * to end of row.

Row 10: * K6, [p1, k1] twice. Repeat from * to end of row.

Row 11: * P2, k1, p7. Repeat from * to end of row.

Row 12: * K6, p1, k3. Repeat from * to end of row.

Repeat rows 1–12.

TUMBLING BLOCKS

Tumbling blocks is a knit-purl stitch pattern with an almost three-dimensional appearance—are the cubes coming out of the knitting or retreating in? It is an almost whimsical motif that looks good knit in any weight of yarn. Tumbling blocks is a fun pattern for blankets or sweaters in heavier yarns, but would make stunning socks or mittens knit in a fine gauge.

level

drape

THE PATTERN

Multiple of 10

Row 1 (WS): * [P1, k1] 5 times. Repeat from * to end of row.
Row 2: * P2, [k1, p1] 3 times, k2. Repeat from * to end of row.
Row 3: * P3, [k1, p1] twice, k3. Repeat from * to end of row.
Row 4: * P4, k1, p1, k4. Repeat from * to end of row.
Row 5: * P5, k5. Repeat from * to end of row.
Row 6: * P5, k5. Repeat from * to end of row.
Row 7: * K1, p4, k4, p1. Repeat from * to end of row.
Row 8: * P1, k1, p3, k3, p1, k1. Repeat from * to end of row.
Row 9: * K1, p1, k1, p2, k2, p1, k1, p1. Repeat from * to end of row.
Row 10: * [P1, k1] 5 times. Repeat from * to end of row.
Row 11: * [K1, p1] 5 times. Repeat from * to end of row.
Row 12: * [P1, k1] twice, k1, p2, k1, p1, k1. Repeat from * to end of row.
Row 13: * K1, p1, k3, p3, k1, p1. Repeat from * to end of row.
Row 14: * P1, k4, p4, k1. Repeat from * to end of row.
Row 15: * K5, p5. Repeat from * to end of row.
Row 16: * K5, p5. Repeat from * to end of row.

there's more >

Knit and Purl

TUMBLING BLOCKS

more >

Row 17: * K4, p1, k1, p4. Repeat from * to end of row.

Row 18: * K3, [p1, k1] twice, p3. Repeat from * to end of row.

Row 19: * K2, [p1, k1] 3 times, p2. Repeat from * to end of row.

Row 20: * [K1, p1] 5 times. Repeat from * to end of row.

Repeat rows 1–20.

CHUTES AND LADDERS

This knit-purl stitch pattern forms columns of diagonal slashes that are reminiscent of chutes and ladders. The overall effect is vertical lines, making a very flattering pattern for use in garments. Chutes and ladders is unisex and ageless in appearance, making it a good motif for use in projects for the entire family.

level ◑

drape ▥ ▥

THE PATTERN

Multiple of 10

Row 1 (RS): * P4, k1, p1, k4. Repeat from * to end of row.

Row 2: * P3, k2, p2, k3. Repeat from * to end of row.

Row 3: * P2, k2, p1, k1, p2, k2. Repeat from * to end of row.

Row 4: * P1, k2, p2, k2, p2, k1. Repeat from * to end of row.

Row 5: * K2, p3, k3, p2. Repeat from * to end of row.

Row 6: * K1, p4, k4, p1. Repeat from * to end of row.

Repeat rows 1–6.

KNIT-PURL PLAID

Knit-purl plaid is simply a plaid pattern created in texture rather than color. It is unisex and would work well in most any project, but it would be a particularly attractive boy's or men's sweater. Knit-purl plaid isn't quite reversible, but the wrong side is nice looking, so the pattern could be used in a project like an afghan or throw.

level

drape

THE PATTERN

Multiple of 10 + 1

Row 1 (WS): P1, * p3, k1, p1, k1, p4. Repeat from * to end of row.

Row 2: K1, * k3, p3, k4. Repeat from * to end of row.

Row 3: P1, * p3, k1, p1, k1, p4. Repeat from * to end of row.

Row 4: K1, * k3, p3, k4. Repeat from * to end of row.

Row 5: P1, * p3, k1, p1, k1, p4. Repeat from * to end of row.

Row 6: Purl.

Row 7: * K1, p1. Repeat from * to last stitch, end k1.

Row 8: Purl.

Row 9: P1, * p3, k1, p1, k1, p4. Repeat from * to end of row.

Row 10: K1, * k3, p3, k4. Repeat from * to end of row.

Row 11: P1, * p3, k1, p1, k1, p4. Repeat from * to end of row.

Row 12: K1, * k3, p3, k4. Repeat from * to end of row.

Repeat rows 1–12.

Knit and Purl

EYELET BASKETWEAVE

Eyelet basketweave is a variation on Basketweave (page 39) that adds a touch of openwork. The knitted fabric has the same characteristics as Small basketweave (page 29) and Basketweave, with additional lightness and drape. Eyelet basketweave can be used in any project for which you would consider using Basketweave; it is particularly well suited to feminine socks and summer sweaters.

level
drape

THE PATTERN

Multiple of 10 + 5

Row 1 (WS): P5, * k5, p5. Repeat from * to end of row.

Row 2: K2tog, yo, k1, yo, ssk, * p5, k2tog, yo, k1, yo, ssk. Repeat from * to end of row.

Row 3: P5, * k5, p5. Repeat from * to end of row.

Row 4: Ssk, yo, k1, yo, k2tog, * p5, ssk, yo, k1, yo, k2tog. Repeat from * to end of row.

Row 5: P5, * k5, p5. Repeat from * to end of row.

Row 6: K5, * p5, k5. Repeat from * to end of row.

Row 7: K5, * p5, k5. Repeat from * to end of row.

Row 8: P5, * k2tog, yo, k1, yo, ssk, p5. Repeat from * to end of row.

Row 9: K5, * p5, k5. Repeat from * to end of row.

Row 10: P5, * ssk, yo, k1, yo, k2tog, p5. Repeat from * to end of row.

Row 11: K5, * p5, k5. Repeat from * to end of row.

Row 12: P5, * k5, p5. Repeat from * to end of row.

Repeat rows 1–12.

GARTER STRIPED CHEVRON

Garter striped chevron is a classic chevron pattern that is interrupted by bands of Garter stitch that wave across the surface of the fabric. This pattern is suitable for use with variegated yarns and can be worked in stripes. Garter striped chevron is perfect for blanket patterns. It would also be nice in a woman's top or in socks.

level

drape

THE PATTERN

Multiple of 11

Rows 1, 2, 3, 4, and 5: Knit.

Row 6 (RS): * K2tog, k2, knit into the front and back of each of the next 2 stitches, k3, ssk. Repeat from * to end of row.

Rows 7, 9, and 11: Purl.

Row 8: * K2tog, k2, knit into the front and back of each of the next 2 stitches, k3, ssk. Repeat from * to end of row.

Row 10: * K2tog, k2, knit into the front and back of each of the next 2 stitches, k3, ssk. Repeat from * to end of row.

Row 12: * K2tog, k2, knit into the front and back of each of the next 2 stitches, k3, ssk. Repeat from * to end of row.

Repeat rows 1–12.

STOCKINETTE STITCH CHEVRON

Stockinette stitch chevron uses a paired increase and decrease to create the motif. The column of decreases is taller than the rest of the knitting, so the cast-on edge develops points. This pattern works well with variegated yarns because the knitting naturally zigzags, which helps break up the variegation. Stockinette stitch chevron also works well as a striped pattern, with changing colors every four to six rows on a right-side row. As long as you have not cast on too tightly, Stockinette stitch chevron will lie flat along the cast-on edge. It is a good pattern to use for any project where you want to have a decorative edge.

level ⦸ ⦸
drape ▥ ▥

THE PATTERN

Multiple of 11

Row 1: Purl.

Row 2: * K2tog, k2, knit into the front and the back of each of the next 2 stitches, k3, sl 1, k1, psso. Repeat from * to end of row.

Repeat rows 1 and 2.

Knit and Purl

KING CHARLES BROCADE

King Charles brocade is very similar to Diamond brocade (page 36), except that the purl bands forming the diamonds are wider. It should be worked at a firm gauge for maximum visibility. This stitch motif is a pretty overall motif for blankets or sweaters. King Charles brocade would also make a nice stitch pattern for a girl's dress.

level
drape

THE PATTERN

Multiple of 12 + 1

Row 1 (RS): K1, * p1, k9, p1, k1. Repeat from * to end of row.

Row 2: K1, * p1, k1, p7, k1, p1, k1. Repeat from * to end of row.

Row 3: K1, * p1, k1, p1, k5, [p1, k1] twice. Repeat from * to end of row.

Row 4: P1, * [p1, k1] twice, p3, k1, p1, k1, p2. Repeat from * to end of row.

Row 5: K1, * k2, [p1, k1] three times, p1, k3. Repeat from * to end of row.

Row 6: P1, * p3, [k1, p1] twice, k1, p4. Repeat from * to end of row.

Row 7: K1, * k4, p1, k1, p1, k5. Repeat from * to end of row.

Row 8: P1, * p3, [k1, p1] twice, k1, p4. Repeat from * to end of row.

Row 9: K1, * k2, [p1, k1] three times, p1, k3. Repeat from * to end of row.

Row 10: P1, * [p1, k1] twice, p3, k1, p1, k1, p2. Repeat from * to end of row.

Row 11: K1, * p1, k1, p1, k5, [p1, k1] twice. Repeat from * to end of row.

Row 12: K1, * p1, k1, p7, k1, p1, k1. Repeat from * to end of row.

Repeat rows 1–12.

Knit and Purl

49

DIAMOND JACQUARD

The observant knitter will notice that on the wrong-side rows of Diamond jacquard, the pattern works out to simply knit the knit stitches and purl the purl stitches. Both sides of the work are equally attractive and this reversibility makes it an ideal stitch to use for anything where both sides might show. Because the pattern is based in Stockinette stitch, it would benefit from having an edge stitch added to prevent curling. The stitch is suitable for just about any weight of yarn or any fiber. Because the pattern relies on the knits and purls to form a picture, it is best worked at a stitch gauge no looser than recommended for the yarn used.

level 🔾
drape ▦ ▦

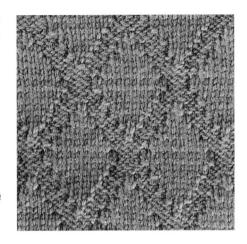

THE PATTERN

Multiple of 12 + 1

Row 1 (WS): P5, * k3, p9. Repeat from * to end of row, end last repeat p5.

Row 2: K4, * p5, k7. Repeat from * to end of row, end last repeat k4.

Row 3: P4, * k5, p7. Repeat from * to end of row, end last repeat p4.

Row 4: K3, * p3, k1, p3, k5. Repeat from * to end of row, end last repeat k3.

Row 5: P3, * k3, p1, k3, p5. Repeat from * to end of row, end last repeat p3.

Row 6: K2, * p3, k3. Repeat from * to end of row, end last repeat k2.

Row 7: P2, * k3, p3. Repeat from * to end of row, end last repeat p2.

Row 8: K1, * p3, k5, p3, k1. Repeat from * to end of row.

Row 9: P1, * k3, p5, k3, p1. Repeat from * to end of row.

Row 10: P3, * k7, p5. Repeat from * to end of row, end last repeat p3.

Row 11: K3, * p7, k5. Repeat from * to end of row, end last repeat k3.

there's more >

Knit and Purl

DIAMOND JACQUARD

more >

Row 12: P2, * k9, p3. Repeat from * to end of row, end last repeat p2.

Row 13: K2, * p9, k3. Repeat from * to end of row, end last repeat k2.

Row 14: P3, * k7, p5. Repeat from * to end of row, end last repeat p3.

Row 15: K3, * p7, k5. Repeat from * to end of row, end last repeat k3.

Row 16: K1, * p3, k5, p3, k1. Repeat from * to end of row.

Row 17: P1, * k3, p5, k3, p1. Repeat from * to end of row.

Row 18: K2, * p3, k3. Repeat from * to end of row, end last repeat k2.

Row 19: P2, * k3, p3. Repeat from * to end of row, end last repeat p2.

Row 20: K3, * p3, k1, p3, k5. Repeat from * to end of row, end last repeat k3.

Row 21: P3, * k3, p1, k3, p5. Repeat from * to end of row, end last repeat p3.

Row 22: K4, * p5, k7. Repeat from * to end of row, end last repeat k4.

Row 23: P4, * k5, p7. Repeat from * to end of row, end last repeat p4.

Row 24: K5, * p3, k9. Repeat from * to end of row, end last repeat k5.

Repeat rows 1–24.

CONCENTRIC SQUARES

Concentric squares is a fun little knit-purl pattern where the stitches form square after square. It is best worked in a smooth yarn at the recommended gauge or slightly firmer. Concentric squares can be used in children's sweaters or in blanket patterns. It would also knit into an attractive unisex sock.

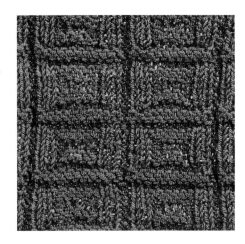

level ◑

drape ▦ ▦

THE PATTERN

Multiple of 12 + 2

Row 1 (WS): Knit.

Row 2: Purl.

Row 3: K2, * p10, k2. Repeat from * to end of row.

Row 4: P2, * k10, p2. Repeat from * to end of row.

Row 5: K2, * p2, k6, p2, k2. Repeat from * to end of row.

Row 6: P2, * k2, p6, k2, p2. Repeat from * to end of row.

Row 7: K2, * p2, k2, p2, k2, p2, k2. Repeat from * to end of row.

Row 8: P2, * k2, p2, k2, p2, k2, p2. Repeat from * to end of row.

Row 9: K2, * p2, k6, p2, k2. Repeat from * to end of row.

Row 10: P2, * k2, p6, k2, p2. Repeat from * to end of row.

Row 11: K2, * p10, k2. Repeat from * to end of row.

Row 12: P2, * k10, p2. Repeat from * to end of row.

Repeat rows 1–12. End after working rows 1 and 2 once more.

KNIT-PURL CHEVRON

Unlike the other chevron patterns included here, the Knit-purl chevron uses the placement of knit and purl stitches to form the chevron rather than increases and decreases. This composition also means that the cast-on edge remains straight rather than scalloped. As a result, this chevron pattern would not work well with variegated yarns. However, the knit-purl chevron is reversible, which makes it a good stitch motif for blankets or scarves.

level

drape

THE PATTERN

Multiple of 14 + 1

Row 1 (WS): K1, * k1, p2, k2, p1, k1, p1, k2, p2, k2. Repeat from * to end of row.

Row 2: P1, * k2, p2, k2, p1, k2, p2, k2, p1. Repeat from * to end of row.

Row 3: K1, * p1, k2, p2, k3, p2, k2, p1, k1. Repeat from * to end of row.

Row 4: P1, * p2, k2, p5, k2, p3. Repeat from * to end of row.

Repeat rows 1–4.

Knit and Purl

UP AND DOWN TRIANGLES

Up and down triangles forms an interesting pattern of right-side up and upside-down triangles through a combination of knit and purl stitches, paired with decreases and increases. Because the decreases and increases shift the stitches, Up and down triangles will work well with many variegated yarns. It is a good stitch motif for socks or sweaters, especially for children.

level ◐ ◐
drape ▦ ▦

THE PATTERN

Multiple of 16

Row 1 (WS): Purl.

Row 2: Knit.

Row 3: * K4, p8, k4. Repeat from * to end of row.

Row 4: * P3, k2tog, k3, M2, k3, ssk, p3. Repeat from * to end of row.

Row 5: * K3, p10, k3. Repeat from * to end of row.

Row 6: * P2, k2tog, k3, M1, k2, M1, k3, ssk, p2. Repeat from * to end of row.

Row 7: * K2, p12, k2. Repeat from * to end of row.

Row 8: * P1, k2tog, k3, M1, k4, M1, k3, ssk, p1. Repeat from * to end of row.

Row 9: * K1, p14, k1. Repeat from * to end of row.

Row 10: * K2tog, k3, M1, k6, M1, k3, ssk. Repeat from * to end of row.

Repeat rows 1–10.

STAIRCASE STITCH

Staircase stitch is a
simple knit-purl motif
that creates a step-like
motif across the fabric.
It will look good knit
in any weight of yarn,
as long as the gauge
is the recommended
gauge or firmer so the
stitches really stand out.
Staircase stitch is a
good pattern for unisex
sweaters or socks, and
would work well in a
blanket. Note that
Staircase stitch com-
presses vertically and
requires a good blocking.

level
drape

THE PATTERN

Multiple of 18

Row 1 (RS): * K15, p3. Repeat from * to end of row.

Row 2 and all even-numbered rows: Knit the knit sts and purl the purl sts.

Row 3: * K15, p3. Repeat from * to end of row.

Row 5: * K3, p15. Repeat from * to end of row.

Row 7: * K3, p15. Repeat from * to end of row.

Row 9: * K3, p3, k12. Repeat from * to end of row.

Row 11: * K3, p3, k12. Repeat from * to end of row.

Row 13: * P6, k3, p9. Repeat from * to end of row.

Row 15: * P6, k3, p9. Repeat from * to end of row.

Row 17: * K9, p3, k6. Repeat from * to end of row.

Row 19: * K9, p3, k6. Repeat from * to end of row.

Row 21: * P12, k3, p3. Repeat from * to end of row.

Row 23: * P12, k3, p3. Repeat from * to end of row.

Repeat rows 1-24.

PARQUET

Parquet is reminiscent of an elaborate hardwood or tile floor. The stitch pattern appears complex, but the wrong side rows are simply knitting the knit stitches and purling the purl stitches. Because Parquet is a large motif, it is most effective used in larger projects like sweaters or blankets.

level
drape

THE PATTERN

Multiple of 18

Row 1 (WS): * P2, k1, p5, k1, p1, [k1, p3] twice. Repeat from * to end of row.

Row 2: * K2, p1, k5, p7, k3. Repeat from * to end of row.

Row 3: * P3, k7, p5, k1, p2. Repeat from * to end of row.

Row 4: * [K1, p1] twice, k5, p5, k4. Repeat from * to end of row.

Row 5: * P4, k5, p5, [k1, p1] twice. Repeat from * to end of row.

Row 6: * P1, k3, p1, k5, p3, k5. Repeat from * to end of row.

Row 7: * P5, k3, p5, k1, p3, k1. Repeat from * to end of row.

Row 8: * K5, p1, k5, p7. Repeat from * to end of row.

Row 9: * K7, p5, k1, p5. Repeat from * to end of row.

Row 10: * [P1, k5] twice, p5, k1. Repeat from * to end of row.

Row 11: * P1, k5,[p5, k1] twice. Repeat from * to end of row.

Row 12: * K1, [p1, k5] twice, p3, k2. Repeat from * to end of row.

Row 13: * P2, k3, [p5, k1] twice, p1. Repeat from * to end of row.

Row 14: K2, * p1, k5. Repeat from * to end of row, ending last repeat p1, k3.

there's more >

Knit and Purl

PARQUET

more >

Row 15: P3, k1, * p5, k1. Repeat from * to last 2 stitches, end p2.

Row 16: * K3, p1, k5, p1, k3, p1, k1, p1, k2. Repeat from * to end of row.

Row 17: * P2, k1, p1, k1, p3, k1, p5, k1, p3. Repeat from * to end of row.

Row 18: * K4, p1, k5, p1, k1, p1, k3, p1, k1. Repeat from * to end of row.

Row 19: * P1, k1, p3, k1, p1, k1, p5, k1, p4. Repeat from * to end of row.

Row 20: * K5, p7, k5, p1. Repeat from * to end of row.

Row 21: * K1, p5, k7, p5. Repeat from * to end of row.

Row 22: * P1, k5, p5, k5, p1, k1. Repeat from * to end of row.

Row 23: * P1, k1, p5, k5, p5, k1. Repeat from * to end of row.

Row 24: * K1, p1, k5, p3, k5, p1, k2. Repeat from * to end of row.

Row 25: * P2, k1, p5, k3, p5, k1, p1. Repeat from * to end of row.

Row 26: * K2, p7, k5, p1, k3. Repeat from * to end of row.

Row 27: * P3, k1, p5, k7, p2. Repeat from * to end of row.

Row 28: * K1, p1, k1, p5, k5, p1, k4. Repeat from * to end of row.

Row 29: * P4, k1, p5, k5, p1, k1, p1. Repeat from * to end of row.

Row 30: * P1, k3, p3, k5, p1, k5. Repeat from * to end of row.

Row 31: * P5, k1, p5, k3, p3, k1. Repeat from * to end of row.

Row 32: * K5, p1. Repeat from * to end of row.

Row 33: * K1, p5. Repeat from * to end of row.

Row 34: * K4, p1, k1, p1, k3, p1, k5, p1, k1. Repeat from * to end of row.

Row 35: * P1, k1, p5, k1, p3, k1, p1, k1, p4. Repeat from * to end of row.

Row 36: * [K3, p1] twice, k1, p1, k5, p1, k2. Repeat from * to end of row.

Repeat rows 1–36.

PINNACLE CHEVRON

Pinnacle chevron is essentially a rib pattern where the columns of knits and purls shift. As a result, the knitted fabric is very elastic, lies flat, and pulls in. Pinnacle chevron also has the characteristic of being reversible. The stitch pattern would make an elegant close-fitting sweater or unisex socks.

level ⬤ ⬤

drape ▥ ▥

THE PATTERN

Multiple of 18 + 1

Row 1 (WS): P1, * [k2, p2] twice, k1, [p2, k2] twice, p1. Repeat from * to end of row.

Row 2: K1, * [p2, k2] twice, p1, [k2, p2] twice, k1. Repeat from * to end of row.

Row 3: P1, * [k2, p2] twice, k1, [p2, k2] twice, p1. Repeat from * to end of row.

Row 4: K1, * [p2, k2] twice, p1, [k2, p2] twice, k1. Repeat from * to end of row.

Row 5: P1, * p1, k2, p2, k2, p3, [k2, p2] twice. Repeat from * to end of row.

Row 6: K1, * k1, p2, k2, p2, k3, [p2, k2] twice. Repeat from * to end of row.

Row 7: P1, * p1, k2, p2, k2, p3, [k2, p2] twice. Repeat from * to end of row.

Row 8: K1, * k1, p2, k2, p2, k3, [p2, k2] twice. Repeat from * to end of row.

Row 9: K1, * [p2, k2] twice, p1, [k2, p2] twice, k1. Repeat from * to end of row.

Row 10: P1, * [k2, p2] twice, k1, [p2, k2] twice, p1. Repeat from * to end of row.

there's more >

Knit and Purl

PINNACLE CHEVRON

more >

Row 11: K1, * [p2, k2] twice, p1, [k2, p2] twice, k1. Repeat from * to end of row.

Row 12: P1, * [k2, p2] twice, k1, [p2, k2] twice, p1. Repeat from * to end of row.

Row 13: K1, * k1, p2, k2, p2, k3, [p2, k2] twice. Repeat from * to end of row.

Row 14: P1, * p1, k2, p2, k2, p3, [k2, p2] twice. Repeat from * to end of row.

Row 15: K1, * k1, p2, k2, p2, k3, [p2, k2] twice. Repeat from * to end of row.

Row 16: P1, * p1, k2, p2, k2, p3, [k2, p2] twice. Repeat from * to end of row.

Repeat rows 1–16.

SEED STITCH STARS

Seed stitch stars is Seed stitch (page 15) worked on a background of Stockinette stitch. The pattern will show best when knit with a smooth yarn at the recommended gauge or slightly tighter. Seed stitch stars would make an excellent panel on an Aran or Gansey style sweater. It would also be a cute motif for a child's sweater or baby blanket.

level ▥ ▥

drape ▦ ▦

THE PATTERN

Multiple of 19 + 1

Row 1 (WS): Purl.

Row 2: K1 * k11, p1, k7. Repeat from * to end of row.

Row 3: P1, * p7, k1, p11. Repeat from * to end of row.

Row 4: K1, * k9, p1, k1, p1, k7. Repeat from * to end of row.

Row 5: P1, * p7, k1, p1, k1, p9. Repeat from * to end of row.

Row 6: K1, * k7, [p1, k1] twice, p1, k7. Repeat from * to end of row.

Row 7: P1, * p7, [k1, p1] 5 times, k2. Repeat from * to end of row.

Row 8: K1, * [k1, p1] 6 times, k7. Repeat from * to end of row.

Row 9: P1, * p5, [k1, p1] 5 times, k1, p3. Repeat from * to end of row.

Row 10: K1, * k3, [p1, k1] 5 times, p1, k5. Repeat from * to end of row.

Row 11: P1, * p3, [k1, p1] 5 times, k1, p5. Repeat from * to end of row.

Row 12: K1, * k5, [p1, k1] 5 times, p1, k3. Repeat from * to end of row.

Row 13: P1, * [p1, k1] 6 times, p7. Repeat from * to end of row.

there's more >

SEED STITCH STARS

more >

Row 14: K1, * k7, [p1, k1] 5 times, p1, k1. Repeat from * to end of row.

Row 15: P1, * p7, [k1, p1] twice, k1, p7. Repeat from * to end of row.

Row 16: K1, * k7, p1, k1, p1, k9. Repeat from * to end of row.

Row 17: P1, * p9, k1, p1, k1, p7. Repeat from * to end of row.

Row 18: K1, * k7, p1, k11. Repeat from * to end of row.

Row 19: P1, * p11, k1, p7. Repeat from * to end of row.

Row 20: Knit.

Repeat rows 1–20.

Needle Size Chart

Metric (mm)	US	UK/CAN
2	0	14
2.25	1	13
2.5		
2.75	2	12
3		11
3.25	3	10
3.5	4	
3.75	5	9
4	6	8
4.5	7	7
5	8	6
5.5	9	5
6	10	4
6.5	10 ½	3
8	11	0
9	13	00
10	15	000
12.75	17	
15	19	
19	35	

Abbreviations and Glossary

C3 over 4: Slip 4 stitches to the cable needle and hold to the back of the work. Knit the next 3 stitches, then purl 1 stitch from the cable needle, then knit the remaining stitches from the cable needle.

C6: Slip 2 stitches onto the cable needle and hold to the front of the work, slip 2 stitches onto a second cable needle and hold to the back of the work, k2, p2 from the second cable needle, k2 from the first cable needle.

CB2: Slip 1 stitch to the cable needle and hold to the back of the work. Knit the next stitch, then knit the stitch from the cable needle.

CB3: Slip 1 stitch to the cable needle and hold to the back of the work. Knit the next 2 stitches, then knit the stitch from the cable needle.

CB4: Slip 2 stitches to the cable needle and hold to the back of the work. Knit the next 2 stitches, then knit the stitches from the cable needle.

CB5: Slip 3 stitches to the cable needle and hold to the back of the work. Knit the next 2 stitches, then knit the stitches from the cable needle.

CB6: Slip 3 stitches to the cable needle and hold to the back of the work. Knit the next 3 stitches, then knit the stitches from the cable needle.

CB8: Slip 4 stitches to the cable needle and hold to the back of the work. Knit the next 4 stitches, then knit the stitches from the cable needle.

CF2 over 3: Slip the next 3 stitches to the cable needle and hold to the back of the work. Knit the next 2 stitches, then p1, k2 from the cable needle.

CF2: Slip 1 stitch to the cable needle and hold to the front of the work. Knit the next stitch, then knit the stitch from the cable needle.

CF3: Slip 2 stitches to the cable needle and hold to the front of the work. Knit the next stitch, then knit the stitches from the cable needle.

Yarn Chart

YARN WEIGHT SYMBOL & CATEGORY NAMES	0 lace	1 super fine	2 fine	3 light	4 medium	5 bulky	6 super bulky
TYPE OF YARNS IN CATEGORY	Fingering, 10-count crochet thread	Sock, Fingering, Baby	Sport, Baby	DK, Light Worsted	Worsted, Afghan, Aran	Chunky, Craft, Rug	Bulky, Roving

Source: Craft Yarn Council of America's www.YarnStandards.com

CF4: Slip 2 stitches to the cable needle and hold to the front of the work. Knit the next 2 stitches, then knit the stitches from the cable needle.

CF6: Slip 3 stitches to the cable needle and hold to the front of the work. Knit the next 3 stitches, then knit the stitches from the cable needle.

CF8: Slip 4 stitches to the cable needle and hold to the front of the work. Knit the next 4 stitches, then knit the stitches from the cable needle.

Cn: Cable needle.

DI: Double increase as follows: [k1 tbl, k1] into the next stitch, then insert the left-hand needle behind the vertical strand that runs downward from between the 2 stitches just made and k1 tbl into this strand to create the third stitch.

Inc 1 pwise: Increase 1 stitch purlwise by purling into the front and the back of the next stitch.

Inc 1: Increase 1 stitch by knitting into the front and the back of the next stitch.

K: Knit.

K1b: Knit the next stitch in the row below.

K2tog: Knit 2 stitches together.

K3tog: Knit 3 stitches together.

K4tog: Knit 4 stitches together.

K tbl: Knit through the back of the loop. If the k is followed by a number, knit that many stitches through the back loop. For example, k3 tbl means knit 3 stitches (1 at a time) through the back loops.

Kwise: Knitwise.

LH: Left hand.

LT: Left twist. Knit into the back of the second stitch on the left-hand needle. Do not drop it from the left-hand needle. Knit into the front of the first stitch on the left-hand needle. Drop off both stitches from the left-hand needle. For a left twist on the wrong side of the work, simply purl the stitches instead of knitting them.

LTP: Purl through the back of the second stitch on the left-hand needle without removing it from the needle, then knit the first stitch on the left-hand needle, slipping both stitches off of the needle at the same time. If this is difficult to work, you can use a T1L1 in its place.

M1: Pick up the horizontal strand of yarn lying between the stitch just worked and the next stitch on the left-hand needle from front to back and knit into the back of it. Also referred to as M1 kwise because the new stitch is a knit stitch.

M2: Pick up the horizontal strand of yarn lying between the stitch just worked and the next stitch on the left-hand needle from front to back and knit into the back and the front of it, creating 2 new stitches.

MB (make bobble): [K1, yo, k1, yo, k1] into the next stitch on the left-hand needle. Turn work. Purl 5. Turn work. Knit 5. Turn work. P2tog, k1, p2tog. Turn work. Sl 1, k2tog, psso. Bobble is complete.

P: Purl.

P2sso: Pass 2 slipped stitches over.

P tbl: Purl through the back loop. If the p is followed by a number, purl that many stitches through the back loop. For example, p3 tbl means purl 3 stitches (1 at a time) through the back loops.

P2tog tbl: Purl 2 stitches together through the back loops. If your knitting is too tight to comfortably purl 2 stitches together through the back loops, try working an ssp in place of p2tog tbl. While it is not exactly the same decrease, it is very close.

P2tog: Purl 2 stitches together.

P3tog: Purl 3 stitches together.

Psso: Pass slipped stitch over.

Pwise: Purlwise.

RH: Right hand.

RS: Right side.

RT: Right twist. Knit into the second stitch on the left-hand needle. Do not drop it from the left-hand needle. Knit into the first stitch on the left-hand needle. Drop both stitches from the left-hand needle. For a right twist on the wrong side of the work, simply purl the stitches instead of knitting them.

RTP: Knit into the front of the second stitch on the left-hand needle without removing it from the needle, then purl the first stitch on the left-hand needle, slipping both stitches off the needle at the same time.

Knit and Purl

63

S5: Slip the next 5 stitches onto a cable needle (or short double-pointed needle) and hold to the front of the work. Wind the yarn counter-clockwise twice around the stitches on the cable needle, then work the stitches from the cable needle as k1, p3, k1.

Sl 1: Slip 1 stitch. When slipping stitches, it is customary to slip them purlwise unless working a decrease, when they are normally slipped knitwise. Individual instructions should indicate which direction to slip stitches.

Sl 2: Slip 2 stitches as if to k2tog.

Ssk: Working 1 stitch at a time, slip 2 stitches from the left-hand needle to the right-hand needle as if to knit. Insert the left-hand needle into the back of the 2 slipped stitches on the right-hand needle and knit the stitches together.

Ssp: Working 1 stitch at a time, slip 2 stitches from the left-hand needle to the right-hand needle as if to knit. Insert the left-hand needle into the back of the 2 slipped stitches on the right-hand needle and purl the stitches together.

Sssk: Working 1 stitch at a time, slip 3 stitches from the left-hand needle to the right-hand needle as if to knit. Insert the left-hand needle into the back of the 3 slipped stitches on the right-hand needle and knit the stitches together.

T1L1 (travel 1 stitch to the left 1 stitch): Slip 1 stitch to the cable needle and hold to the front of the work. Purl the next stitch, then knit the stitches from the cable needle.

T1L2 (travel 1 stitch to the left 2 stitches): Slip 1 stitch to the cable needle and hold to the front of the work. Knit the next 2 stitches, then knit the stitch from the cable needle.

T1R1 (travel 1 stitch to the right 1 stitch): Slip 1 stitch to the cable needle and hold to the back of the work. Knit the next stitch, then purl the stitch from the cable needle.

T1R2 (travel 1 stitch to the right 2 stitches): Slip 2 stitches to the cable needle and hold to the back of the work. Knit the next stitch, then knit the stitches from the cable needle.

T2L1 (travel 2 stitches to the left 1 stitch): Slip 2 stitches to the cable needle and hold to the front of the work. Purl the next stitch, then knit the stitches from the cable needle.

T2L2 (travel 2 stitches to the left 2 stitches): Slip 2 stitches to the cable needle and hold to the front of the work. Purl the next 2 stitches, then knit the stitches from the cable needle.

T2R1 (travel 2 stitches to the right 1 stitch): Slip 1 stitch to the cable needle and hold to the back of the work. Knit the next 2 stitches, then purl the stitch from the cable needle.

T2R2 (travel 2 stitches to the right 2 stitches): Slip 2 stitches to the cable needle and hold to the back of the work. Knit the next 2 stitches, then purl the stitches from the cable needle.

T3L1 (travel 3 stitches to the left 1 stitch): Slip 3 stitches to the cable needle and hold to the front of the work. Purl the next stitch, then knit the stitches from the cable needle.

T3L2 (travel 3 stitches to the left 2 stitches): Slip 3 stitches to the cable needle and hold to the front of the work. Purl the next 2 stitches, then knit the stitches from the cable needle.

T3R1 (travel 3 stitches to the right 1 stitch): Slip 1 stitch to the cable needle and hold to the back of the work. Knit the next 3 stitches, then purl the stitches from the cable needle.

T3R2 (travel 3 stitches to the right 2 stitches): Slip 2 stitches to the cable needle and hold to the back of the work. Knit the next 3 stitches, then purl the stitches from the cable needle.

T4L2 (travel 4 stitches to the left 2 stitches): Slip 4 stitches to the cable needle and hold to the front of the work. Purl the next 2 stitches, then knit the stitches from the cable needle.

T4R2 (travel 4 stitches to the right 2 stitches): Slip 2 stitches to the cable needle and hold to the back of the work. Knit the next 4 stitches, then purl the stitches from the cable needle.

T8B RIB: Slip the next 4 stitches onto the cable needle and hold to back of the work, k1, p2, k1 from the left-hand needle, then k1, p2, k1 from the cable needle.

T8F RIB: Slip the next 4 stitches onto the cable needle and hold to front of the work, k1, p2, k1 from the left-hand needle, then k1, p2, k1 from the cable needle.

WS: Wrong side.

Wyib: With yarn in back of work.

Wyif: With yarn in front of work.

Yo: Yarn over.

Rib

Stitches

Welcome to The Stitch Collection—a set of handy little guides to knit stitches that are as portable as can be; pick and choose which ones to throw into your knitting bag when you're on the go, and leave the others at home in the case. By design, they are not complete guides to knitting; instead, they are mini-encyclopedias of the stitches themselves. Their purpose is to help you choose the best stitch pattern for your projects.

Like most stitch guides, these books are written in terms of knitting flat—knitting back and forth on the needles, turning after each row. The set is divided into five volumes. Book 1 covers the knit and purl stitches; Book 2 focuses on rib stitches; Book 3 contains lace stitches; Book 4 is all about cables; and Book 5 is a compilation of specialty stitches. Each booklet has some common introductory material to help you determine which pattern you want to use, followed by text that is specific to that book's category of stitch. Each individual stitch pattern is ranked according to its level of difficulty, its drape, and offers suggestions as to its best function in a project (as an overall stitch, a filler stitch, a panel stitch, or an edge stitch).

CHOOSING A STITCH PATTERN

The following sections give you suggestions on how to best use the guides in the set.

Look Before You Swatch

When choosing a stitch pattern to use for a project, be sure to look through all the books. Some patterns are included in one category, but have traits that overlap with the others. It's important to read through a pattern before starting it, too. Often an instruction can seem confusing or intimidating on paper, but will make complete sense when you have the knitting in hand and are ready to work that portion of the pattern.

fingering

Next, make a swatch. The swatches in this book are knit in varying weights of wool (worsted, sport, and fingering) provided by Lorna's Laces. In general, the patterns with small stitch multiples (less than 8 or 10) and panels are knit with Shepherd Worsted; the larger stitch multiples are done in Shepherd Sport. A few of the very large stitch repeats in Book 1 and Book 3 are worked in Shepherd Sock. The swatches have been blocked minimally for photography, and thus you may occasionally note irregularities that are inherent in hand knitting.

sport

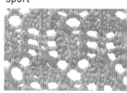

worsted

The appearance and drape of the stitch pattern will depend on the yarn chosen—color, style of spinning, fiber content, and weight—and on the gauge used. Keep in mind that large stitch motifs can overwhelm small projects, and small stitch motifs might be lost on a large project. Scale is important. Changing the weight of yarn and gauge it is knit at can help reduce or enlarge a motif as desired. The photos on this page show an example of the Tulip lace pattern knit with three different weights of yarn at three different gauges. The appearance of the pattern changes in each case and stresses the importance of swatching.

Rib

Follow the Organization

Each book is organized from smallest stitch multiple to largest, making it easier to find the pattern that best suits the project you have in mind. A small-scale lace pattern is better for a baby sweater than a large-scale one, for instance.

Match the Pattern to the Purpose

The descriptions included with each stitch pattern also suggest the type of project for which it is best suited. Many of the descriptions also indicate whether it works well as an overall stitch, a filler stitch, a panel stitch, or an edge stitch. An overall stitch pattern is used throughout the full project rather than in just a small area. You can convert patterns presented as panels into an overall stitch pattern by simply working one or more stitches (usually Stockinette or Reverse Stockinette) between repeats of the panel.

Filler stitches are worked in small areas of a larger project to fill open space. Filler stitches appear in between panels of other stitches or as a panel themselves. Filler stitches often have a small multiple and are easier to use in sizing and shaping. When combining filler stitches with other stitches (panels or overall patterns), always check the gauge of each stitch pattern. They can vary widely, even on the same needles with the same yarn.

A panel pattern is intended to be a section of a larger project. Most often, panels are just the stitch pattern itself, and the knitter needs to add border or background stitches. Panels can be worked as either a stitch multiple, by themselves, or combined with other panels or stitch patterns. Cables are very often written as a panel, for instance.

Lastly, edge or border stitch patterns can be used as filler stitches or overall patterns, but they lie flat and look tidy along the edges, making them suitable for hems, cuffs, or edges on other patterns.

Rib

Understand the Ratings

Each stitch pattern in this collection has a skill level and a drape rating. The skill level ratings include easy (basic knitting knowledge required), advanced beginner, intermediate, and experienced. Remember what looks difficult on paper is often easier to understand with the knitting on needles in front of you.

All knitting has at least some amount of drape, so the ratings are relative and are based on using wool at the recommended gauge for the yarn. The ratings are: low (a firmer fabric), medium (reasonable amount of drape), and high (a flowing fabric). In general, the denser the fabric (e.g., more stitches per inch) is with stitches, the less drape it will have. The more open the fabric is (e.g., fewer stitches per inch), the more drape it will have. Cable patterns, for instance, will have less drape than lace patterns. However, drape also depends on the yarn chosen for a project and on the gauge used. Some fibers have more drape than others, and the finer the yarn, the more drape the fabric will have. A tighter gauge will have less drape than a looser gauge.

level

   easy
   advanced beginner
   intermediate
   experienced

drape

   low
   medium
   high

Understand Stitch Multiples and Balancing Stitches

Stitch patterns are presented with information about the number of stitches required to complete one pattern repeat. For panels, the information is simply how many stitches wide the panel is. For all other patterns, this information is presented as a multiple of stitches, plus any balancing stitches needed. For example, if you want to work six repeats of a pattern, and it requires four stitches and one balancing stitch (multiple of 4 + 1), you would cast on 24 stitches plus one balancing stitch, for a total of 25 stitches.

Add Selvage Stitches

The patterns in these books do not include selvage stitches, which are one or more spare stitches included at the edge of your knitting for seaming or for tidying the edge. Some knitters don't even use selvage stitches unless specifically directed to do so in a pattern. If you are a knitter who likes to use selvage stitches, you will need to add them to the edges of your projects.

Work Increases and Decreases

These guides use a variety of increases and decreases. It is important to use the correct technique for the increases and decreases called for in the pattern instructions; this insures that your stitch pattern has the proper appearance, as the various techniques create different effects, such as slants or holes. Perhaps the most common increase used in the patterns is done by knitting into the front and back of a single stitch. There are several decreases used in the patterns—some decrease one stitch at a time (single decreases), some decrease two stitches at a time (double decreases), some decrease even more! When a pattern says simply to decrease one stitch, but doesn't say which decrease to use, the assumption is that you will use a k2tog (knit two stitches together) or a p2tog (purl two stitches together), depending on whether you are on the right or wrong side of your work. Consult the Abbreviations and Glossary section (page 61) for explanations of each type of increase or decrease.

CHOOSING THE BEST YARN

How do you choose the most suitable yarn for a stitch pattern or a project? The first thing to consider is the pattern itself. The busier the stitch pattern is, the simpler the yarn should be, and vice versa. If you want to work a lace pattern or an elaborate cable pattern, choose a smooth, plain-colored yarn. A subtly variegated or kettle-dyed solid yarn might work with a fancy pattern stitch, but a yarn with extreme color changes or striping will detract from the pattern stitch.

Fiber content makes a difference, too. Plant fibers (cotton, linen, hemp, rayon) are inelastic, as is silk. When you work with plant fibers, your knitting tends to be what-you-see-is-what-you-get. Blocking will not improve it.

In contrast, animal fibers are almost magical to knit with, and a good blocking hides a multitude of sins. The fiber has memory and will retain its shape until the next time it gets wet.

Consider Yarn Requirements

Knitting a swatch before beginning a project is important, of course. But when choosing stitch patterns for a project you design, it is useful to consult a reference to see what the estimated yardage requirements are for the size and type of project you are creating at the gauge you are knitting. Yardage requirement tables are usually based on Stockinette stitch, but keep in mind that different stitch patterns require different amounts of yarn. For instance, Garter stitch has a very compressed row gauge, so it will take more yarn than Stockinette stitch. Lace is very open, so it can use less yarn than Stockinette stitch. Cables and many fancy patterns are very dense and can use *much* more yarn than Stockinette stitch.

Rib

INTRODUCTION TO RIB

Rib stitches are characterized by columns of knits and purls. Unlike the knit-purl stitch patterns, these columns are often combined with other techniques, like increases, decreases, or twists, to add variety. Generally speaking, ribbing is used to provide a firm elastic edge to a knitted project—the hem or neck band of a sweater, or the cuffs of socks or mittens. If the ribbing is intended to provide stability for the project, work the rib using a knitting needle one to two sizes smaller than the needle used to work the main fabric.

Some rib patterns, though, are more decorative than functional. All rib stitches are perfect edge stitches. Because of the way the knit and purl stitches are combined, rib stitches don't curl along the bottom and top edges. Some ribs may curl slightly along the side edges.

Rib stitches are also perfect for any project for which you want some negative ease, meaning the knitting is slightly smaller than the body part for which is intended, so the fit is snug. They are also perfect for any project requiring a lot of elasticity. (Typically, you want elasticity in anything that is knit with negative ease in mind.) In these projects, rib stitches may be used as the overall stitch motif.

Rib stitches pull in to varying degrees. All of them, though, stretch out easily. The degree to which a rib pattern will stay stretched out with blocking varies with the pattern stitch and with the yarn used. Rib patterns do not have a lot of drape, and they tend to be fairly dense. (Some of the rib patterns with bits of lace work are an exception.) Rib patterns usually look best knit at a firm gauge—the recommended gauge for the yarn or tighter. When knit too loosely, rib stitches often look sloppy.

The most basic style of rib stitch is a combination of plain columns of knits and purls. I refer to these rib patterns here as *m x n* rib, where, on the right side of the work, *m* is the number of knit stitches per column and *n* is the number of purl stitches per column. For example, 2 x 2 rib consists of two knit stitches alternating with two purl stitches.

This book begins with five different *m x n* rib patterns, to give you an idea of what it looks like to combine different numbers of knit and purl stitches into a rib. Notice that the ratio does not need to be 1 knit stitch to 1 purl stitch. In fact, having more knits or more purls is often more attractive or can change the pull of the fabric. Also take note that the number of knit or purl stitches in the columns can vary, so that the rib varies in thickness across the fabric. There are no rules in creating an *m x n* rib; however, if you're knitting flat (instead of in the round, as is typical for rib) and want your pattern to be symmetrical, add one more set of *m* stitches for balance.

Rib

2 X 2 RIB

2 x 2 rib is one of the most basic and widely used rib patterns. It is composed of columns of 2 knit stitches alternating with columns of 2 purl stitches, and is completely reversible. 2 x 2 rib, like most rib stitch patterns, is best worked at the recommended gauge for a yarn or firmer. 2 x 2 rib is suitable for use anywhere you would normally use a rib stitch—edges of sweaters, socks, mittens, hats, gloves—or for any project requiring a close fit.

level
drape

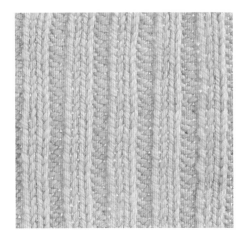

THE PATTERN

Multiple of 4 + 2

Row 1 (WS): P2, * k2, p2. Repeat from * to end of row.

Row 2: K2, * p2, k2. Repeat from * to end of row.

Repeat rows 1 and 2.

3 X 2 RIB

Another classic pattern, the balance of more knits than purls gives 3 x 2 rib a bit more visual interest. 3 x 2 rib is extremely elastic and pulls in a great deal—so much so that it could be mistaken for Stockinette stitch when not stretched or blocked. Like 2 x 2, it is the perfect pattern to use to trim a sweater or hat, or in the cuff of socks or mittens. It would work well for a close-fitting sweater as well.

level

drape

THE PATTERN

Multiple of 5 + 3

Row 1 (WS): P3, *k2, p3. Repeat from * to end of row.
Row 2: K3, * p2, k3. Repeat from * to end of row.
Repeat rows 1 and 2.

4 X 1 RIB

From the right side (as written), 4 x 1 rib looks almost like Stockinette stitch. From the wrong side, it looks almost like the Slip stitch rib (page 43). Either side can be used as the right side for your project. 4 x 1 rib behaves a lot like Stocki-nette stitch, with the exception that the one column of purl stitches keeps the fabric from curling along the cast-on edge. 4 x 1 rib would be great in a project where you want the Stockinette stitch appearance, but don't want to include a different edge stitch.

THE PATTERN

Multiple of 5 + 4

Row 1 (WS): P4, * k1, p4. Repeat from * to end of row.
Row 2: K4, * p1, k4. Repeat from * to end of row.
Repeat rows 1 and 2.

level
drape

4 X 2 RIB

This rib is a traditional choice for edging a sweater or sock cuff because it is elastic and lies flat, but can also work well as an overall stitch pattern. The resulting fabric will tend to pull in and not have a great deal of drape, which helps keep the hem of a sweater from looking sloppy, for instance. The pattern creates a reversible fabric, either of which can be considered the right side. The stitch is suitable for just about any weight of yarn or any fiber. It is often advisable to go down one or two needle sizes from what you would use for Stockinette stitch when working this pattern.

level
drape

THE PATTERN

Multiple of 6 + 4

Row 1 (WS): P4, * k2, p4. Repeat from * to end of row.

Row 2: K4, * p2, k4. Repeat from * to end of row.

Repeat rows 1 and 2.

K2P2K4P2 RIB

K2P2K4P2 rib is an excellent example of how you can mix up the number of knits and purls in the ribbed columns of an *m* x *n* rib to give the fabric a new appearance. It has all of the traits of an *m* x *n* rib in terms of drape, pull, and elasticity, but the unevenness of the columns adds visual interest. K2P2K4P2 rib can be used in any project where you would normally use a rib stitch.

level ◉
drape ▦

THE PATTERN

Multiple of 10 + 2

Row 1 (WS): P2, * k2, p4, k2, p2. Repeat from * to end of row.

Row 2: K2, * p2, k4, p2, k2. Repeat from * to end of row.

Repeat rows 1 and 2.

BRIOCHE RIB

Brioche rib is one of the classic brioche stitch patterns. This class of stitches uses knitting into the row below to create a puffy stitch. Brioche rib has the appearance of being dense, but the feel of being airy. It lies flat and doesn't pull in very much. Brioche rib is a suitable edge stitch for any project where you would normally use a standard *m x n* rib pattern.

level

drape

THE PATTERN

Multiple of 2

Row 1 (WS): Knit.

Row 2: * K1, k1b. Repeat from * to last 2 sts, end k2.

Repeat rows 1 and 2.

NOT QUITE A RIB

This pattern is basically Stockinette stitch that is interrupted by a 1 x 1 rib stitch every few rows. This stitch is nice because it looks almost like a broken rib from a distance, but the fabric doesn't pull in like a rib stitch. It can be used as an edge stitch because it doesn't curl, but it also works as an overall pattern in projects like blankets, socks, or sweaters.

level ◉
drape ▥

THE PATTERN

Multiple of 2 + 1

Rows 1 and 3 (WS): Purl.

Row 2: K1, * p1, k1. Repeat from * to end of row.

Row 4: Knit.

Repeat rows 1–4.

BROKEN RIB

Broken rib is a 1 x 1 rib that is "broken" by a plain knit row. The right side appearance is highly textured with pronounced purl stitches. The wrong side is columns of knit stitches separated by columns of Seed stitch (Book 1, page 15). Broken rib lies flat and doesn't pull in much. It is a great rib pattern for unisex scarves or for use anywhere requiring an edge or rib stitch.

level

drape

THE PATTERN

Multiple of 2 + 1

Row 1 (WS): Knit.

Row 2: K1 * p1, k1. Repeat from * to end of row.

Repeat rows 1 and 2.

FISHERMAN'S RIB

Fisherman's rib is a
dense rib stitch with
pronounced knit veins.
It doesn't pull in very
much and lies very flat.
The right side looks like
a knit-purl rib, but the
wrong side looks more
like a Reverse Stocki-
nette stitch. Fisherman's
rib is perfect as an
overall pattern for hats,
mittens, or sweaters. It
is also an excellent edge
finish.

level ◑ ◑
drape ▥

THE PATTERN

Multiple of 2 + 1

Row 1 (WS): Purl.

Row 2: P1, * k1b, p1. Repeat from * to end of row.

Repeat rows 1 and 2.

SHAKER RIB

Shaker rib is a very fluffy, spongy rib that is completely reversible. It would knit into a very cozy, yet lightweight, blanket or sweater. It is also a nice edge stitch to use with other stitch patterns. If used in this way, it is advisable to go down one to two needle sizes from that used for the main stitch motif.

level
drape

THE PATTERN

Multiple of 2 + 1

Row 1 (WS): K1, * p1, k1. Repeat from * to end of row.
Row 2: P1, * k1b, p1. Repeat from * to end of row.
Repeat rows 1 and 2.

MOCK RIB

Mock rib is very similar to Rice stitch (Book 1, page 17) in construction, except that there are no twisted stitches. The "ribbed" side is the right side. Mock rib is nice because it neither curls nor pulls in. The appearance is like a very tidy 1 x 1 rib. The small stitch repeat is great for smaller projects like accessories and baby sweaters, but the pleasing texture is perfect for larger projects like adult sweaters.

level ●
drape ▦

THE PATTERN

Multiple of 2 + 1

Row 1 (WS): Purl.

Row 2: K1, * p1, k1. Repeat from * to end of row.

Repeat rows 1 and 2.

WAVY RIB

Wavy rib is character-
ized by lots of tiny cable
twists that create a
wave-like appearance
in the knit columns.
The twists make the rib
slower to work, but the
results are worth the
effort! Wavy rib can be
used in any project where
you would normally use a
rib stitch. It would make
an elegant motif for a
close-fitting sweater.

level ⬚ ⬚ ⬚
drape ⬚

THE PATTERN

Multiple of 3 + 1

Rows 1 and 3 (WS): K1, * p2, k1. Repeat from * to end of row.
Row 2: P1, * CB2, p1. Repeat from * to end of row.
Row 4: P1, * CF2, p1. Repeat from * to end of row.
Repeat rows 1–4.

RICKRACK RIB

Rickrack rib is a highly textured rib stitch that resembles rickrack trim. It uses a modified twist maneuver to create the jagged columns. Rickrack rib is a more interesting rib to use in place of a plain *m x n* rib as an edge finish. It would add fabulous texture to socks or close-fitting sweaters, too.

level ● ● ●
drape ▦

THE PATTERN

Multiple of 3 + 1

Row 1 (RS): P1, * knit into the back of the second stitch on the LH needle without slipping it from the needle, knit into the first stitch on the LH needle as usual, slipping both stitches from the needle together, p1. Repeat from * to end of row.

Row 2: K1, * wyif purl the second stitch on the LH needle without slipping it from the needle, purl the first stitch on the LH needle as usual, slipping both stitches from the needle together, k1. Repeat from * to end of row.

Repeat rows 1 and 2.

TWISTED RIB

Twisted rib is a very dense rib based on a 2 x 1 rib stitch. The columns of knits are twisted to the right and to the left in a miniature cable pattern. Twisted rib is the perfect fancy edge stitch for any project that requires a rib stitch, such as socks, hats, mittens, or sweaters. The motif would be beautiful for a close-fitting top.

level ⊕ ⊕ ⊕
drape ▦

THE PATTERN

Multiple of 3 + 1 stitches

Row 1 and all odd numbered rows (WS): K1, *p2, k1. Repeat from * to end of row.

Row 2 and 4: P1, * RT, p1. Repeat from * to end of row.

Row 6: P1, * k2, p1. Repeat from * to end of row.

Rows 8 and 10: P1, * LT, p1. Repeat from * to end of row.

Row 12: P1, * k2, p1. Repeat from * to end of row.

Repeat rows 1–12.

SHIFTING COLUMNS RIB

Although this pattern is a rib pattern, it doesn't pull in quite as much as something like the 4 x 2 rib, nor is it reversible. However, it will lie flat and hold firm, making it perfect for edgings. The pattern also works as an overall fabric, although it will not have a great deal of drape, and will look best worked at a firmer gauge.

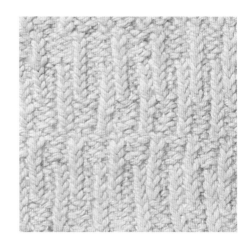

level ●
drape ▥

THE PATTERN

Multiple of 3 + 1

Row 1 (WS): K1, * p tbl, k2. Repeat from * to end of row.
Row 2: P1, * p1, k tbl, p1. Repeat from * to end of row.
Row 3: K1, * p tbl, k2. Repeat from * to end of row.
Row 4: P1, * p1, k tbl, p1. Repeat from * to end of row.
Row 5: K1, * p tbl twice, k1. Repeat from * to end of row.
Row 6: P1, * k tbl twice, p1. Repeat from * to end of row.
Row 7: K1, * p tbl twice, k1. Repeat from * to end of row.
Row 8: P1, * k tbl twice, p1. Repeat from * to end of row.
Row 9: K1, * k1, p tbl, k1. Repeat from * to end of row.
Row 10: P1, * k tbl, p2. Repeat from * to end of row.
Row 11: K1, * k1, p tbl, k1. Repeat from * to end of row.
Row 12: P1, * k tbl, p2. Repeat from * to end of row.
Repeat rows 1–12.

SHADOW RIB

Shadow rib is attractive on both the right and wrong sides. The right side is columns of knits separated by recessed columns of Twisted seed stitch. The wrong side is Reverse Stockinette with pronounced twisted purl bumps. Shadow rib does not curl along the cast-on edge or pull in. It does, however, curl along the side edges. Shadow rib would be a good edge stitch for just about any project.

level ◉ ◉
drape ▥

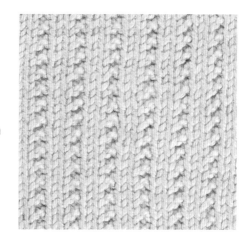

THE PATTERN

Multiple of 3 + 2
Row 1 (RS): Knit.
Row 2: P2, * k tbl, p2. Repeat from * to end of row.
Repeat rows 1 and 2.

PUFFED RIB

Puffed rib is character-
ized by little lacy puffs
created by adding extra
stitches on row 1 and
removing them on row
4. While the stitch motif
lies flat and makes a
perfect edge stitch (a
lovely finish for a fancy
project), it doesn't have a
classic rib stitch appearance. It would also look
very nice in a sweater or
cardigan, and could be
used as an overall stitch
for a blanket.

level ● ●
drape ▦

THE PATTERN

Multiple of 3 + 2

Row 1 (RS): P2, * yo, k1, yo, p2. Repeat from * to end of row.

Row 2: K2, * p3, k2. Repeat from * to end of row.

Row 3: P2, * k3, p2. Repeat from * to end of row.

Row 4: K2, * p3tog, k2. Repeat from * to end of row.

Repeat rows 1–4.

Note: On row 1, there are two extra stitches per repeat. The
stitches return to the original count on row 4.

DIAGONAL RIB

Diagonal rib is a very striking rib pattern with strong diagonal lines. It is a great pattern because it lies flat, is elastic, doesn't pull in, and doesn't shift, as tends to happen with many diagonal motifs. It is also reversible. Diagonal rib can be used as an edge stitch, but is perfect for larger projects, too. Try it as a flattering stitch in a cardigan or in a cozy afghan.

level
drape

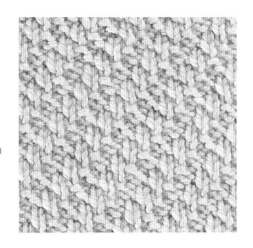

THE PATTERN

Multiple of 4

Row 1 (WS): * K2, p2. Repeat from * to end of row.
Row 2: Repeat row 1.
Row 3: K1, * p2, k2. Repeat from * to last 3 stitches, end p2, k1.
Row 4: P1, * k2, p2. Repeat from * to last 3 stitches, end k2, p1.
Row 5: * P2, k2. Repeat from * to end of row.
Row 6: Repeat row 5.
Row 7: Repeat row 4.
Row 8: Repeat row 3.

Repeat rows 1–8.

Rib

27

GARTER STITCH RIB

Garter stitch rib combines the appearance of Garter stitch with the characteristics of rib. The result is a dense elastic fabric that doesn't pull in very much, but has the linear appearance of rib. Garter stitch rib can be used as an edge stitch, but would also work well for projects like a blanket or a men's sweater.

level ●
drape ▦

THE PATTERN

Multiple of 4 + 2

Row 1 (WS): K2, * p2, k2. Repeat from * to end of row.

Row 2: K2, * p2, k2. Repeat from * to end of row.

Repeat rows 1 and 2.

Rib

28

RIDGED RIB

Ridged rib is very simple to work, yet has a striking texture. A basic 2 x 2 rib pattern is interrupted by rows of Garter stitch, creating a fabric that is less rib-like in appearance. This pattern can be used anywhere a 2 x 2 rib would be used—socks, accessories, or sweaters. Ridged rib doesn't pull in as much as 2 x 2 rib, which means it is also suitable for blankets or unisex scarves.

level

drape

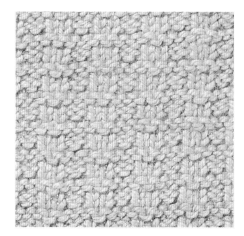

THE PATTERN

Multiple of 4 + 2

Row 1 (WS): Knit.

Row 2: Knit.

Row 3: K2, * p2, k2. Repeat from * to end of row.

Row 4: P2, * k2, p2. Repeat from * to end of row.

Repeat rows 1–4.

Rib

KNOTTED RIB

Knotted rib uses an increase on row 1 and a decrease on row 2 to create a knot in the knit column of this pattern. It is an interesting sub-stitution for a plain rib stitch, and would work well as an edge stitch for a heavily textured sweater design. Knotted rib can also be used in unisex sock patterns or other accessories.

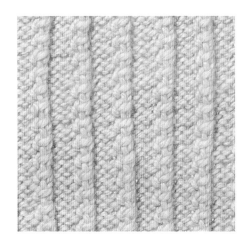

level
drape

THE PATTERN

Multiple of 4 + 3

Row 1: P3, * inc 1, p3. Repeat from * to end of row.

Row 2: K3, * p2tog, k3. Repeat from * to end of row.

Repeat rows 1 and 2.

Note: On row 1, there is one extra stitch added per repeat. On row 2, you will return to the original stitch count.

CORDED RIB

Corded rib is a traditional Italian stitch pattern. It is made up of dense areas of twisted decreases and lighter areas of increases. The increase pulls the cast-on edge gently, giving it a slight picot appearance. The resulting fabric is highly textured and very beautiful. Corded rib would be a very elegant edge stitch. If used for socks, avoid carrying the corded rib down the instep, as the heavy texture might be uncomfortable inside a shoe.

level ⬤ ⬤ ⬤
drape ▦

THE PATTERN

Multiple of 4 + 2

Row 1 (WS): K1, * k2tog tbl, M1 kwise, p2. Repeat from * to last st, end k1.

Row 2: K1, * k2tog tbl, M1 kwise, p2. Repeat from * to last st, end k1.

Repeat rows 1 and 2.

BELLFLOWER RIB

Bellflower rib is a 2 x 2 rib where stitches are crossed every few rows to create bell-shaped flowers. Although tricky to work at first, it is worth the effort. This pattern pulls in dramatically unless it is blocked because of the crossing of stitches on rows 6 and 12. Bellflower rib is a good replacement for any project in which you would normally use a 2 x 2 rib pattern.

level ◉ ◉ ◉ ◉
drape ▥

THE PATTERN

Multiple of 4 + 2

Row 1 (WS): P2, * k2, p2. Repeat from * to end of row.

Row 2: K2, * p2, k2. Repeat from * to end of row.

Row 3: P2, * k2, p2. Repeat from * to end of row.

Row 4: K2, * p2, k2. Repeat from * to end of row.

Row 5: P2, * k2, p2. Repeat from * to end of row.

Row 6: K1, * sl 1 to cn and hold to front of work, p1, knit the second stitch on the LH needle and slip it off of the needle over the top of the first stitch while leaving the first stitch on the LH needle, bring the yarn to the front of work and knit the stitch from cn, p1. Repeat from * to last stitch, end k1.

Row 7: K2, * p2, k2. Repeat from * to end of row.

Row 8: P2, * k2, p2. Repeat from * to end of row.

Row 9: K2, * p2, k2. Repeat from * to end of row.

Row 10: P2, * k2, p2. Repeat from * to end of row.

Row 11: K2, * p2, k2. Repeat from * to end of row.

there's more >

BELLFLOWER RIB

more >   **Row 12:** K1, knit the second stitch on the LH needle and slip it off of the needle over the top of the first stitch while leaving the first stitch on the LH needle, bring the yarn to the front of work, p1. * Sl 1 to cn and hold to front of work, p1, knit the second stitch on the LH needle and slip it off of the needle over the top of the first stitch while leaving the first stitch on the LH needle, bring the yarn to the front of work and knit the stitch from cn, p1. Repeat from * to last 3 stitches, end sl 1 to cn and hold to the front of work, p1, k1 from cn, k1.

Repeat rows 1–12.

Note: Working this pattern requires the use of a cable needle or short double-pointed needle.

Rib

MOCK CABLE RIB

Mock cable rib uses a twisted-stitch technique to create the appearance of miniature cables. Because no cable needle is involved, it is quicker to work than true cables. The result is a very elastic fabric that pulls in like any other rib. Mock cable rib is an attractive edge stitch for accessories or sweaters. It is also well suited as an overall pattern in close-fitting garments.

level ● ◐
drape ▥

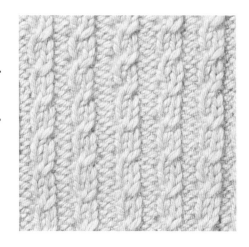

THE PATTERN

Multiple of 4 + 2

Rows 1 and 3 (WS): K2, * p2, k2. Repeat from * to end of row.

Row 2: P2, * RT, p2. Repeat from * to end of row.

Row 4: P2, * k2, p2. Repeat from * to end of row.

Repeat rows 1–4.

MISTAKE STITCH RIB

Mistake stitch rib is a favorite rib stitch pattern for many knitters. Its creator was probably trying to knit a 2 x 2 rib, but had one too few stitches, which disrupted the alignment of the knit and purl stitches. This pattern lies flat and does not pull in quite as much as many other rib patterns. Mistake stitch rib is the perfect edge treatment for just about any sweater or accessories project.

level ▥
drape ▥

THE PATTERN

Multiple of 4 + 3

Row 1 (WS): * K2, p2. Repeat from * to last 3 stitches, end k2, p1.

Row 2: *K2, p2. Repeat from * to last 3 stitches, end k2, p1.

Repeat rows 1 and 2.

RIGHT SLANTING DIAGONAL RIB

Right slanting diagonal
rib is basically a standard
knit-purl rib where the
knit stitches travel to the
right to create a diagonal
slant. This pattern can be
used as an edge stitch
or as a rather striking
side panel in a sweater or
blanket design. Try creating a sweater where right
and left slanting diagonal
ribs meet in the middle!

level ● ● ●
drape ▦

THE PATTERN

Multiple of 4 + 3

Row 1 (WS): K5, p1, * k3, p1. Repeat from * to the last stitch,
end k1.

Row 2: P4, RTP, * p2, RTP. Repeat from * to the last stitch,
end p1.

Row 3: K2, p1, * k3, p1. Repeat from * to last the 4 stitches,
end k4.

Row 4: P3, * RTP, p2. Repeat from * to end of row.

Row 5: K3, * p1, k3. Repeat from * to end of row.

Row 6: * P2, RTP. Repeat from * to the last 3 stitches, end p3.

Row 7: K4, p1, * k3, p1. Repeat from * to the last 2 stitches,
end k2.

Row 8: P1, * RTP, p2. Repeat from * to the last 2 stitches,
end p2.

Repeat rows 1–8.

LEFT SLANTING DIAGONAL RIB

Left slanting diagonal rib creates the opposite effect of Right slanting diagonal rib (page 36), so the knit stitches travel to the left to create a diagonal slant. Use it as you would Right slanting diagonal rib (page 36).

level

drape

THE PATTERN

Multiple of 4 + 3

Row 1 (WS): K1, p1, * k3, p1. Repeat from * to the last 5 stitches, end k5.

Row 2: P1, LTP, * p2, LTP. Repeat from * to the last 4 stitches, end p4.

Row 3: K4, p1, * k3, p1. Repeat from * to the last 2 stitches, end k2.

Row 4: * P2, LTP. Repeat from * to the last 3 stitches, end p3.

Row 5: K3, * p1, k3. Repeat from * to end of row.

Row 6: P3, * LTP, p2. Repeat from * to end of row.

Row 7: K2, p1, * k3, p1. Repeat from * to the last 4 stitches, end k4.

Row 8: P4, LTP, * p2, LTP. Repeat from * to the last 5 stitches, end p5.

Repeat rows 1-8.

Rib

SINGLE EYELET RIB

Single eyelet rib is a simple lace pattern divided by columns of Reverse Stockinette stitch. The eyelet portion has an almost cable-like appearance, but is simple to work. Single eyelet rib makes an elegant edge finish, but it also works nicely as an overall pattern in scarves, knit tops, or baby blankets.

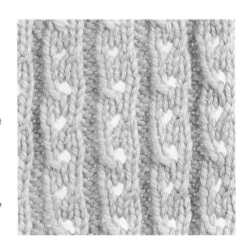

level ● ●
drape ▥

THE PATTERN

Multiple of 5 + 2

Row 1 and all odd numbered rows (WS): K2, * p3, k2. Repeat from * to end of row.

Row 2: P2, * k3, p2. Repeat from * to end of row.

Row 4: P2, * k2tog, yo, k1, p2. Repeat from * to end of row.

Row 6: P2, * k3, p2. Repeat from * to end of row.

Row 8: P2, * k1, yo, ssk, p2. Repeat from * to end of row.

Repeat rows 1–8.

LACY RIB

Lacy rib is delicate little rib pattern that incorporates a very simple lace pattern against Reverse Stockinette stitch columns. It is very straightforward to work. Lacy rib is the perfect edge stitch on any fancy sweater, mitten, or hat design, or overall pattern for a summer cardigan. Because both sides of the fabric are attractive, lacy rib would make a nice scarf.

level

drape

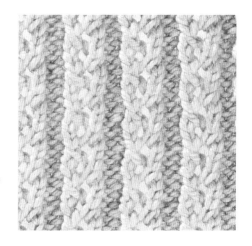

THE PATTERN

Multiple of 5 + 2

Row 1 (WS): K2, * p3, k2. Repeat from * to end of row.

Row 2: P2, * k1, yo, ssk, p2. Repeat from * to end of row.

Row 3: K2, * p3, k2. Repeat from * to end of row.

Row 4: P2, * k2tog, yo, k1, p2. Repeat from * to end of row.

Repeat rows 1–4.

LITTLE SHELL RIB

Little shell rib is a fancy rib stitch where dainty seashells are created by removing stitches on row 2 and adding them back on row 3. The pattern is particularly pretty when worked in a finer gauge yarn because it takes on a delicate look. Little shell rib is the perfect edge stitch for sophisticated sweaters. It is also a beautiful motif for use in socks.

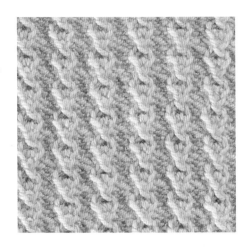

level
drape ▦

THE PATTERN

Multiple of 5 + 2

Row 1 (WS): K2, * p3, k2. Repeat from * to end of row.

Row 2: P2, * sl 1, k2tog, psso, p2. Repeat from * to end of row.

Row 3: K2, * (p1, k1, p1) into the next stitch on LH needle, k2. Repeat from * to last stitch.

Row 4: P2, * k3, p2. Repeat from * to last stitch.

Repeat rows 1–4.

Note: On row 2, you will be decreasing two stitches per pattern repeat. On row 3, you will increase back to the original number of stitches.

DIAGONAL GARTER STITCH RIB

Diagonal Garter stitch rib gives the impression of diagonal lines without actually traveling the stitches. Instead, the knits and purls are shifted as they are worked. While Diagonal Garter stitch is an attractive and different edge stitch, it should also be considered as an overall stitch for projects like blankets or scarves.

level

drape

THE PATTERN

Multiple of 5 + 2

Row 1 (WS): P2, *k3, p2. Repeat from * to end of row.

Row 2 and all even numbered rows: Knit.

Row 3: K1, * p2, k3. Repeat from * to last stitch, end p1.

Row 5: K2, * p2, k3. Repeat from * to end of row.

Row 7: * K3, p2. Repeat from * to last 2 stitches, end k2.

Row 9: P1, * k3, p2. Repeat from * to last stitch, end k1.

Row 10: Knit.

Repeat rows 1–10.

Rib

RAINDROP RIB

Raindrop rib is composed of lacy raindrop motifs falling in columns separated by Reverse Stockinette stitch. It is not difficult to work, but it adds a special something to your knitted project. Raindrop rib is a nice edge stitch for fancier stitch patterns. It would work well in socks or as a nice overall motif for a summer sweater.

level ◍ ◍
drape ▥

THE PATTERN

Multiple of 5 + 3

Row 1 and all odd numbered rows (WS): K3, * p2, k3. Repeat from * to end of row.
Row 2: P3, * k2, p3. Repeat from * to end of row.
Row 4: P3, * k2tog, yo, p3. Repeat from * to end of row.
Row 6: P3, * k2, p3. Repeat from * to end of row.
Row 8: P3, * yo, ssk, p3. Repeat from * to end of row.
Repeat rows 1–8.

Rib

SLIP STITCH RIB

Slip stitch rib is characterized by pronounced
slip stitch columns on
a Reverse Stockinette
background. It is not
reversible and curls
at the side edges. Slip
stitch rib, however, does
not curl along the bottom
edge or pull in. It has a
strong linear appearance
that is very clean. Slip
stitch rib is an attractive
pattern as the hem of
a sweater or an overall
sweater pattern.

level ⊕ ⊕
drape ▦

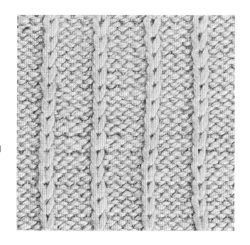

THE PATTERN

Multiple of 5 + 4

Row 1 (WS): K4, * p1, k4. Repeat from * to end of row.

Row 2: P4, * sl 1 pwise, p4. Repeat from * to end of row.

Repeat rows 1 and 2.

ELONGATED SLIP STITCH RIB

Elongated slip stitch rib has very pronounced ribs against a Reverse Stockinette stitch background. The slipped stitches prevent the bottom edge of the fabric from curling, although the sides of the fabric will still curl. The motif has a strong graphic appearance. It is appropriate for the same uses as Slip stitch rib (page 43).

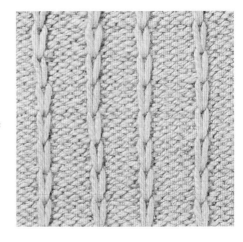

level ⊕ ⊕
drape ▥

THE PATTERN

Multiple of 5 + 4

Row 1 (WS): K4, * p1, k4. Repeat from * to end of row.

Row 2: P4, * sl 1 pwise wyib, p4. Repeat from * to end of row.

Row 3: K4, * sl 1 pwise wyif, k4. Repeat from * to end of row.

Row 4: P4, * sl 1 pwise wyib, p4. Repeat from * to end of row.

Repeat rows 1–4.

CLOVERLEAF RIB

Cloverleaf rib is a little cloverleaf lace pattern separated by columns of purl stitches. It is easy enough for even the beginning lace knitter to knit. The knitted fabric will lie flat and not pull in a great deal. Cloverleaf rib would be nice for use as a fancy edge stitch. It also is attractive in socks or a knitted top.

level

drape

THE PATTERN

Multiple of 6 + 1

Row 1 and all odd numbered rows (WS): K1, * p5, k1. Repeat from * to end of row.

Row 2: P1, * k1, yo, sl 1, k2tog, psso, yo, k1, p1. Repeat from * to end of row.

Row 4: P1, * k2, yo, ssk, k1, p1. Repeat from * to end of row.

Row 6: P1, * k5, p1. Repeat from * to end of row.

Repeat rows 1–6.

ITALIAN CHAIN RIB

Italian chain rib is a pretty rib stitch pattern where columns of open-work create a chain-like appearance. The finished fabric lies perfectly flat after blocking and has more drape than most rib patterns. Italian chain rib should be considered as an overall stitch motif for scarves or dressy sweaters in addition to being used as a special edge treatment.

level
drape

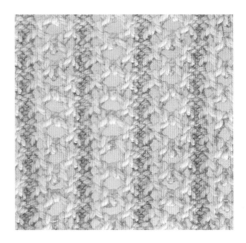

THE PATTERN

Multiple of 6 + 2

Row 1 (WS): K2, * p4, k2. Repeat from * to end of row.

Row 2: P2, * k2tog, yo twice, ssk, p2. Repeat from * to end of row.

Row 3: K2, * p1, p1 into first yo, k1 into second yo, p1, k2. Repeat from * to end of row.

Row 4: P2, * yo, ssk, k2tog, yo, p2. Repeat from * to end of row.

Repeat rows 1–4.

Rib

TWISTED COLUMNS RIB

Twisted columns is a rib stitch best reserved for use with smooth, tightly spun yarns, as that will best accentuate the pattern. The columns are created by working twists every other row, resulting in a braided effect. Twisted columns would make an attractive fitted top, in addition to being a very sleek edge stitch on most any project.

level ⊕ ⊕ ⊕
drape ▦

THE PATTERN

Multiple of 6 + 2

Row 1 (WS): K2, * p4, k2. Repeat from * to end of row.

Row 2: P2, * LT, RT, p2. Repeat from * to end of row.

Repeat rows 1 and 2.

WIDE LEFT SLANTING DIAGONAL RIB

Wide left slanting diagonal rib is basically a standard knit-purl rib where the knit stitches travel to the left to create a diagonal slant to the rib. Wide left slanting diagonal rib can be used as an edge stitch or as a rather striking side panel in a sweater or blanket design.

level
drape

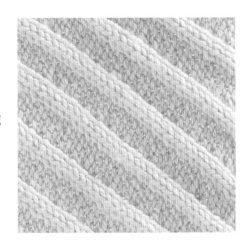

THE PATTERN

Multiple of 6 + 4

Row 1 (WS): K1, * p2, k4. Repeat from * to the last 3 stitches, end k3.

Row 2: P1, * T2L1, p3. Repeat from * to the last 3 stitches, end p3.

Row 3: K6, p2, * k4, p2. Repeat from * to the last 2 stitches, end k2.

Row 4: P2, * T2L1, p3. Repeat from * to the last 2 stitches, end p2.

Row 5: K5, p2, * k4, p2. Repeat from * to the last 3 stitches, end k3.

Row 6: * P3, T2L1. Repeat from * to the last 4 stitches, end p4.

Row 7: K4, * p2, k4. Repeat from * to end of row.

Row 8: P4, * T2L1, p3. Repeat from * to end of row.

Row 9: K3, * p2, k4. Repeat from * to the last stitch, end k1.

Row 10: P5, T2L1, * p3, T2L1. Repeat from * to the last 2 stitches, end p2.

there's more >

WIDE LEFT SLANTING DIAGONAL RIB

more >

Row 11: K2, * p2, k4. Repeat from * to the last 2 stitches, end k2.

Row 12: P6, T2L1, * p3, T2L1. Repeat from * to the last stitch, end p1.

Repeat rows 1–12.

WIDE RIGHT SLANTING DIAGONAL RIB

Wide right slanting diagonal rib has the opposite effect of Wide left slanting diagonal rib (page 48), as the knit stitches travel to the right to create a diagonal slant. It can be used similarly to Wide left slanting diagonal rib.

level
drape

THE PATTERN

Multiple of 6 + 4

Row 1 (WS): K7, p2, * k4, p2. Repeat from * to the last stitch, end k1.

Row 2: P6, T2R1, * p3, T3R1. Repeat from * to the last stitch, end p1.

Row 3: K2, * p2, k4. Repeat from * to the last 2 stitches, end k2.

Row 4: P5, T2R1, * p3, T3R1. Repeat from * to the last 2 stitches, end p2.

Row 5: K3, * p2, k4. Repeat from * to the last stitch, end k1.

Row 6: P4, * T2R1, p3. Repeat from * to end of row.

Row 7: K4, * p2, k4. Repeat from * to end of row.

Row 8: * P3, T2R1. Repeat from * to the last 4 stitches, end p4.

Row 9: K5, p2, * k4, p2. Repeat from * to the last 3 stitches, end k3.

Row 10: P2, * T2R1, p3. Repeat from * to the last 2 stitches, end p2.

there's more >

WIDE RIGHT SLANTING DIAGONAL RIB

more >   Row 11: K6, p2, * k4, p2. Repeat from * to the last 2 stitches, end k2.

Row 12: P1, * T2R1, p3. Repeat from * to the last 3 stitches, end p3.

Repeat rows 1–12.

ANOTHER LACE RIB

Another lace rib is a very elegant rib stitch with a few benefits. Because of the lace, it has more drape than most rib stitches and doesn't pull in very much. On the other hand, it lies flat like other rib stitches and is very elastic. Another lace rib is a sophisticated edge stitch for any project and can also be used as an overall pattern in a garment such as a cardigan.

level ● ● ●
drape ▧ ▧ ▧

THE PATTERN

Multiple of 7 + 3

Rows 1 and 3 (WS): K1, p1, k1, * p4, k1, p1, k1. Repeat from * to end of row.

Row 2: P1, k tbl, p1, *k2tog, yo, k2tog, yo, p1, k tbl, p1. Repeat from * to end of row.

Row 4: P1, k tbl, p1, * yo, ssk, yo, ssk, p1, k tbl, p1. Repeat from * to end of row.

Repeat rows 1–4.

DOUBLE EYELET RIB

Double eyelet rib is a simple mirrored lace pattern divided by columns of Reverse Stockinette stitch. The eyelet portion has an almost cable-like appearance, but is simple to work. Double eyelet rib makes an elegant edge finish, but it also works nicely as an overall pattern in scarves, knit tops, or baby blankets. Consider this pattern for a special summer top.

level

drape

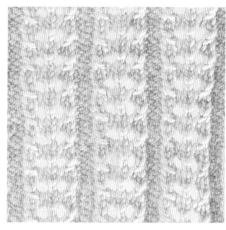

THE PATTERN

Multiple of 7 + 2

Rows 1 and 3 (WS): K2, * p5, k2. Repeat from * to end of row.

Row 2: P2, * k5, p2. Repeat from * to end of row.

Row 4: P2, * k2tog, yo, k1, yo, ssk, p2. Repeat from * to end of row.

Repeat rows 1-4.

WIDE RIB

Wide rib is another example of an *m x n* rib pattern done over a larger number of stitches. It pulls in dramatically, but is very elastic. It will lie flat along the cast-on edge, but will tend to curl along the side edges. Wide rib is appropriate to use in any project in which you would normally use an *m x n* rib, especially those over a larger number of stitches.

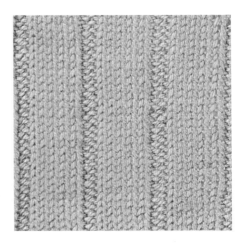

level ●
drape ▦

THE PATTERN

Multiple of 7 + 5

Row 1 (WS): P5, * k2, p5. Repeat from * to end of row.

Row 2: K5, * p2, k5. Repeat from * to end of row.

Repeat rows 1 and 2.

SLIP STITCH CABLE RIB

Slip stitch cable rib is made up of wide cable panels separated by columns of purl stitches. The cables are created by carrying a slipped stitch over two knit stitches without the use of a cable needle. Because the stitches have been slipped over four rows, the slipped stitches remain stable when dropped off of the needles. Slip stitch cable rib does not curl and does not pull in very much. It is a good pattern for use as an edge, as on a sweater, or throughout a project such as a sock.

level ⊕ ⊕ ⊕
drape ⊕

THE PATTERN

Multiple of 8 + 2

Row 1 (WS): K2, * p6, k2. Repeat from * to end of row.

Row 2: P2, * sl 1 wyib, k4, sl 1 wyib, p2. Repeat from * to end of row.

Row 3: K2, * sl 1 wyif, p4, sl 1 wyif, k2. Repeat from * to end of row.

Row 4: P2, * sl 1 wyib, k4, sl 1 wyib, p2. Repeat from * to end of row.

Row 5: K2, * sl 1 wyif, p4, sl 1 wyif, k2. Repeat from * to end of row.

Row 6: P2, * drop the slipped stitch off the needle to the front of work, k2, then pick up the slipped stitch on to LH needle and knit it, sl 2, drop the slipped stitch to the front of work, pass the 2 slipped stitches from the RH needle back to the LH needle, pick up the dropped slipped stitch and knit it, k2, p2. Repeat from * to end of row.

Repeat rows 1–6.

SPIRALING RIB

At first glance, Spiraling rib appears to be a heavily twisted cable. In reality, the spiraling effect is the result of working small twists by knitting two stitches together, then knitting into the first stitch again. Spiraling rib is a beautiful edge stitch for sweaters, hats, mittens, or socks. With its cable-like appearance, it would also make an elegant pullover.

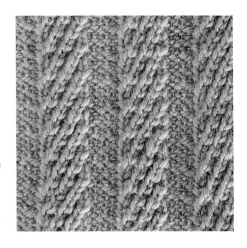

level
drape

THE PATTERN

Multiple of 9 + 3

Rows 1 and 3 (WS): K3, * p6, k3. Repeat from * to end of row.

Row 2: P3, * [k2tog keeping stitches on needle and k into the first stitch again] three times, p3. Repeat from * to end of row.

Row 4: P3, * k1, [k2tog keeping stitches on needle and k into the first stitch again] twice, k1, p3. Repeat from * to end of row.

Repeat rows 1–4.

CHEVRON RIB

Chevron rib uses a central decrease and yarn overs that are worked through the back loop to create the appearance of bends in the rib. This stitch pattern works well with variegated yarns because it naturally pulls the knitting into zigzags that break up the variegation With its pointed cast-on edge, Chevron rib is a great cuff or edge-stitch pattern. It would also be attractive in a close-fitting garment.

level ▦ ▦ ▦

drape ▦

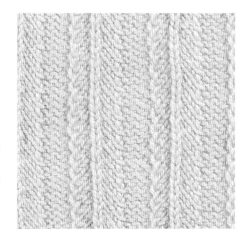

THE PATTERN

Multiple of 10 + 3

Row 1 (WS): K3, * p1 tbl, p5, p1 tbl, k3. Repeat from * to end of row.

Row 2: P3, * yo, k2, sl 2, k1, p2sso, k2, yo, p3. Repeat from * to end of row.

Repeat rows 1 and 2.

DEFINED RIB

Defined rib is a very attractive variation on the *m x n* rib. Not only does it mix 1 x 1 rib with longer spans of Reverse Stockinette stitch, but the knit stitches are twisted, giving the fabric an extra pop. Defined rib would knit into a very nice unisex sock design. It would also be a very clean edge stitch to use on most any project.

level ● ●
drape ▬

THE PATTERN

Multiple of 11 + 4

Row 1 (WS): K4, * p1, [k tbl, p1] three times, k4. Repeat from * to end of row.

Row 2: P4, * k tbl, [p1, k tbl] three times, p4. Repeat from * to end of row.

Repeat rows 1 and 2.

LACY PILLARS RIB

Lacy pillars rib has a wide repeat and some tricky stitch work, but the results are well worth it. It is not difficult to work once you get going. Lacy pillars rib would be a stunning edge stitch for any cuff or hem. It would also work well as an overall stitch pattern in a sweater or sock.

level ⊞ ⊞ ⊞
drape ⊞

THE PATTERN

Multiple of 20 + 13

Set up row (WS): K3, * p7, k3. Repeat from * to end of row. This row is only worked one time to establish the pattern.

Row 1 (RS): P3, * k3tog, yo, k1, yo, sssk, p3, k7, p3. Repeat from * to last 10 stitches, end k3tog, yo, k1, yo, sssk, p3.

Row 2: K3, * p1, yo, p3, yo, p1, k3, p7, k3. Repeat from * to last 10 stitches, end p1, yo, p3, yo, p1, k3.

Row 3: P3, * k7, p3, k7, p3. Repeat from * to end of row.

Row 4: K3, * p7, k3, p7, k3. Repeat from * to end of row.

Row 5: P3, * k3tog, yo, k1, yo, sssk, p3, k7, p3. Repeat from * to last 10 stitches, end k3tog, yo, k1, yo, sssk, p3.

Row 6: K3, * p1, yo, p3, yo, p1, k3, p7, k3. Repeat from * to last 10 stitches, end p1, yo, p3, yo, p1, k3.

Row 7: P3, * k7, p3, k7, p3. Repeat from * to end of row.

Row 8: K3, * p7, k3, p7, k3. Repeat from * to end of row.

Row 9: P3, * k3tog, yo, k1, yo, sssk, p3, k7, p3. Repeat from * to last 10 stitches, end k3tog, yo, k1, yo, sssk, p3.

Row 10: K3, * p1, yo, p3, yo, p1, k3, p7, k3. Repeat from * to last 10 stitches, end p1, yo, p3, yo, p1, k3.

Row 11: P3, * k7, p3, k3tog, yo, k1, yo, sssk, p3. Repeat from * to last 10 stitches, end k7, p3.

there's more >

LACY PILLARS RIB

more >

Row 12: K3, * p7, k3, p1, yo, p3, yo, p1, k3. Repeat from * to last 10 stitches, end p7, k3.

Row 13: P3, * k3tog, yo, k1, yo, sssk, p3, k7, p3. Repeat from * to last 10 stitches, end k3tog, yo, k1, yo, sssk, p3.

Row 14: K3, * p1, yo, p3, yo, p1, k3, p7, k3. Repeat from * to last 10 stitches, end p1, yo, p3, yo, p1, k3.

Row 15: P3, * k7, p3, k3tog, yo, k1, yo, sssk, p3. Repeat from * to last 10 stitches, end k7, p3.

Row 16: K3, * p7, k3, p1, yo, p3, yo, p1, k3. Repeat from * to last 10 stitches, end p7, k3.

Row 17: P3, * k7, p3, k7, p3. Repeat from * to end of row.

Row 18: K3, * p7, k3, p7, k3. Repeat from * to end of row.

Row 19: P3, * k7, p3, k3tog, yo, k1, yo, sssk, p3. Repeat from * to last 10 stitches, end k7, p3.

Row 20: K3, * p7, k3, p1, yo, p3, yo, p1, k3. Repeat from * to last 10 stitches, end p7, k3.

Row 21: P3, * k7, p3, k7, p3. Repeat from * to end of row.

Row 22: K3, * p7, k3, p7, k3. Repeat from * to end of row.

Row 23: P3, * k7, p3, k3tog, yo, k1, yo, sssk, p3. Repeat from * to last 10 stitches, end k7, p3.

Row 24: K3, * p7, k3, p1, yo, p3, yo, p1, k3. Repeat from * to last 10 stitches, end p7, k3.

Row 25: P3, * k3tog, yo, k1, yo, sssk, p3, k7, p3. Repeat from * to last 10 stitches, end k3tog, yo, k1, yo, sssk, p3.

Row 26: K3, * p1, yo, p3, yo, p1, k3, p7, k3. Repeat from * to last 10 stitches, end p1, yo, p3, yo, p1, k3.

Row 27: P3, * k7, p3, k3tog, yo, k1, yo, sssk, p3. Repeat from * to last 10 stitches, end k7, p3.

Row 28: K3, * p7, k3, p1, yo, p3, yo, p1, k3. Repeat from * to last 10 stitches, end p7, k3.

Repeat rows 1–28.

Note: The number of stitches is decreased by two per multiple of the pattern on rows 1, 5, 9, 11, 13, 15, 19, 23, 25, and 27.

Needle Size Chart

Metric (mm)	US	UK/CAN
2	0	14
2.25	1	13
2.5		
2.75	2	12
3		11
3.25	3	10
3.5	4	
3.75	5	9
4	6	8
4.5	7	7
5	8	6
5.5	9	5
6	10	4
6.5	10 ½	3
8	11	0
9	13	00
10	15	000
12.75	17	
15	19	
19	35	

Abbreviations and Glossary

C3 over 4: Slip 4 stitches to the cable needle and hold to the back of the work. Knit the next 3 stitches, then purl 1 stitch from the cable needle, then knit the remaining stitches from the cable needle.

C6: Slip 2 stitches onto the cable needle and hold to the front of the work, slip 2 stitches onto a second cable needle and hold to the back of the work, k2, p2 from the second cable needle, k2 from the first cable needle.

CB2: Slip 1 stitch to the cable needle and hold to the back of the work. Knit the next stitch, then knit the stitch from the cable needle.

CB3: Slip 1 stitch to the cable needle and hold to the back of the work. Knit the next 2 stitches, then knit the stitch from the cable needle.

CB4: Slip 2 stitches to the cable needle and hold to the back of the work. Knit the next 2 stitches, then knit the stitches from the cable needle.

CB5: Slip 3 stitches to the cable needle and hold to the back of the work. Knit the next 2 stitches, then knit the stitches from the cable needle.

CB6: Slip 3 stitches to the cable needle and hold to the back of the work. Knit the next 3 stitches, then knit the stitches from the cable needle.

CB8: Slip 4 stitches to the cable needle and hold to the back of the work. Knit the next 4 stitches, then knit the stitches from the cable needle.

CF2 over 3: Slip the next 3 stitches to the cable needle and hold to the back of the work. Knit the next 2 stitches, then p1, k2 from the cable needle.

CF2: Slip 1 stitch to the cable needle and hold to the front of the work. Knit the next stitch, then knit the stitch from the cable needle.

CF3: Slip 2 stitches to the cable needle and hold to the front of the work. Knit the next stitch, then knit the stitches from the cable needle.

CF4: Slip 2 stitches to the cable needle and hold to the front of the work. Knit the next 2 stitches, then knit the stitches from the cable needle.

Yarn Chart

YARN WEIGHT SYMBOL & CATEGORY NAMES	lace	super fine	fine	light	medium	bulky	super bulky
TYPE OF YARNS IN CATEGORY	Fingering, 10-count crochet thread	Sock, Fingering, Baby	Sport, Baby	DK, Light Worsted	Worsted, Afghan, Aran	Chunky, Craft, Rug	Bulky, Roving

Source: Craft Yarn Council of America's www.YarnStandards.com

CF6: Slip 3 stitches to the cable needle and hold to the front of the work. Knit the next 3 stitches, then knit the stitches from the cable needle.

CF8: Slip 4 stitches to the cable needle and hold to the front of the work. Knit the next 4 stitches, then knit the stitches from the cable needle.

Cn: Cable needle.

DI: Double increase as follows: [k1 tbl, k1] into the next stitch, then insert the left-hand needle behind the vertical strand that runs downward from between the 2 stitches just made and k1 tbl into this strand to create the third stitch.

Inc 1 pwise: Increase 1 stitch purlwise by purling into the front and the back of the next stitch.

Inc 1: Increase 1 stitch by knitting into the front and the back of the next stitch.

K: Knit.

K1b: Knit the next stitch in the row below.

K2tog: Knit 2 stitches together.

K3tog: Knit 3 stitches together.

K4tog: Knit 4 stitches together.

K tbl: Knit through the back of the loop. If the k is followed by a number, knit that many stitches through the back loop. For example, k3 tbl means knit 3 stitches (1 at a time) through the back loops.

Kwise: Knitwise.

LH: Left hand.

LT: Left twist. Knit into the back of the second stitch on the left-hand needle. Do not drop it from the left-hand needle. Knit into the front of the first stitch on the left-hand needle. Drop off both stitches from the left-hand needle. For a left twist on the wrong side of the work, simply purl the stitches instead of knitting them.

LTP: Purl through the back of the second stitch on the left-hand needle without removing it from the needle, then knit the first stitch on the left-hand needle, slipping both stitches off of the needle at the same time. If this is difficult to work, you can use a T1L1 in its place.

M1: Pick up the horizontal strand of yarn lying between the stitch just worked and the next stitch on the left-hand needle from front to back and knit into the back of it. Also referred to as M1 kwise because the new stitch is a knit stitch.

M2: Pick up the horizontal strand of yarn lying between the stitch just worked and the next stitch on the left-hand needle from front to back and knit into the back and the front of it, creating 2 new stitches.

MB (make bobble): [K1, yo, k1, yo, k1] into the next stitch on the left-hand needle. Turn work. Purl 5. Turn work. Knit 5. Turn work. P2tog, k1, p2tog. Turn work. Sl 1, k2tog, psso. Bobble is complete.

P: Purl.

P2sso: Pass 2 slipped stitches over.

P tbl: Purl through the back loop. If the p is followed by a number, purl that many stitches through the back loop. For example, p3 tbl means purl 3 stitches (1 at a time) through the back loops.

P2tog tbl: Purl 2 stitches together through the back loops. If your knitting is too tight to comfortably purl 2 stitches together through the back loops, try working an ssp in place of p2tog tbl. While it is not exactly the same decrease, it is very close.

P2tog: Purl 2 stitches together.

P3tog: Purl 3 stitches together.

Psso: Pass slipped stitch over.

Pwise: Purlwise.

RH: Right hand.

RS: Right side.

RT: Right twist. Knit into the second stitch on the left-hand needle. Do not drop it from the left-hand needle. Knit into the first stitch on the left-hand needle. Drop both stitches from the left-hand needle. For a right twist on the wrong side of the work, simply purl the stitches instead of knitting them.

RTP: Knit into the front of the second stitch on the left-hand needle without removing it from the needle, then purl the first stitch on the left-hand needle, slipping both stitches off the needle at the same time.

S5: Slip the next 5 stitches onto a cable needle (or short double-pointed needle) and hold to the front of the work. Wind the yarn counter-clockwise twice around the stitches on the cable needle, then work the stitches from the cable needle as k1, p3, k1.

Sl 1: Slip 1 stitch. When slipping stitches, it is customary to slip them purlwise unless working a decrease, when they are normally slipped knitwise. Individual instructions should indicate which direction to slip stitches.

Sl 2: Slip 2 stitches as if to k2tog.

Ssk: Working 1 stitch at a time, slip 2 stitches from the left-hand needle to the right-hand needle as if to knit. Insert the left-hand needle into the back of the 2 slipped stitches on the right-hand needle and knit the stitches together.

Ssp: Working 1 stitch at a time, slip 2 stitches from the left-hand needle to the right-hand needle as if to knit. Insert the left-hand needle into the back of the 2 slipped stitches on the right-hand needle and purl the stitches together.

Sssk: Working 1 stitch at a time, slip 3 stitches from the left-hand needle to the right-hand needle as if to knit. Insert the left-hand needle into the back of the 3 slipped stitches on the right-hand needle and knit thc stitches together.

T1L1 (travel 1 stitch to the left 1 stitch): Slip 1 stitch to the cable needle and hold to the front of the work. Purl the next stitch, then knit the stitches from the cable needle.

T1L2 (travel 1 stitch to the left 2 stitches): Slip 1 stitch to the cable needle and hold to the front of the work. Knit the next 2 stitches, then knit the stitch from the cable needle.

T1R1 (travel 1 stitch to the right 1 stitch): Slip 1 stitch to the cable needle and hold to the back of the work. Knit the next stitch, then purl the stitch from the cable needle.

T1R2 (travel 1 stitch to the right 2 stitches): Slip 2 stitches to the cable needle and hold to the back of the work. Knit the next stitch, then knit the stitches from the cable needle.

T2L1 (travel 2 stitches to the left 1 stitch): Slip 2 stitches to the cable needle and hold to the front of the work. Purl the next stitch, then knit the stitches from the cable needle.

T2L2 (travel 2 stitches to the left 2 stitches): Slip 2 stitches to the cable needle and hold to the front of the work. Purl the next 2 stitches, then knit the stitches from the cable needle.

T2R1 (travel 2 stitches to the right 1 stitch): Slip 1 stitch to the cable needle and hold to the back of the work. Knit the next 2 stitches, then purl the stitch from the cable needle.

T2R2 (travel 2 stitches to the right 2 stitches): Slip 2 stitches to the cable needle and hold to the back of the work. Knit the next 2 stitches, then purl the stitches from the cable needle.

T3L1 (travel 3 stitches to the left 1 stitch): Slip 3 stitches to the cable needle and hold to the front of the work. Purl the next stitch, then knit the stitches from the cable needle.

T3L2 (travel 3 stitches to the left 2 stitches): Slip 3 stitches to the cable needle and hold to the front of the work. Purl the next 2 stitches, then knit the stitches from the cable needle.

T3R1 (travel 3 stitches to the right 1 stitch): Slip 1 stitch to the cable needle and hold to the back of the work. Knit the next 3 stitches, then purl the stitches from the cable needle.

T3R2 (travel 3 stitches to the right 2 stitches): Slip 2 stitches to the cable needle and hold to the back of the work. Knit the next 3 stitches, then purl the stitches from the cable needle.

T4L2 (travel 4 stitches to the left 2 stitches): Slip 4 stitches to the cable needle and hold to the front of the work. Purl the next 2 stitches, then knit the stitches from the cable needle.

T4R2 (travel 4 stitches to the right 2 stitches): Slip 2 stitches to the cable needle and hold to the back of the work. Knit the next 4 stitches, then purl the stitches from the cable needle.

T8B RIB: Slip the next 4 stitches onto the cable needle and hold to back of the work, k1, p2, k1 from the left-hand needle, then k1, p2, k1 from the cable needle.

T8F RIB: Slip the next 4 stitches onto the cable needle and hold to front of the work, k1, p2, k1 from the left-hand needle, then k1, p2, k1 from the cable needle.

WS: Wrong side.

Wyib: With yarn in back of work.

Wyif: With yarn in front of work.

Yo: Yarn over.

Rib

Lace

Stitches

Welcome to The Stitch Collection—a set of handy little guides to knit stitches that are as portable as can be; pick and choose which ones to throw into your knitting bag when you're on the go, and leave the others at home in the case. By design, they are not complete guides to knitting; instead, they are mini-encyclopedias of the stitches themselves. Their purpose is to help you choose the best stitch pattern for your projects.

Like most stitch guides, these books are written in terms of knitting flat—knitting back and forth on the needles, turning after each row. The set is divided into five volumes. Book 1 covers the knit and purl stitches; Book 2 focuses on rib stitches; Book 3 contains lace stitches; Book 4 is all about cables; and Book 5 is a compilation of specialty stitches. Each booklet has some common introductory material to help you determine which pattern you want to use, followed by text that is specific to that book's category of stitch. Each individual stitch pattern is ranked according to its level of difficulty, its drape, and offers suggestions as to its best function in a project (as an overall stitch, a filler stitch, a panel stitch, or an edge stitch).

Lace

CHOOSING A STITCH PATTERN

The following sections give you suggestions on how to best use the guides in the set.

Look Before You Swatch

When choosing a stitch pattern to use for a project, be sure to look through all the books. Some patterns are included in one category, but have traits that overlap with the others. It's important to read through a pattern before starting it, too. Often an instruction can seem confusing or intimidating on paper, but will make complete sense when you have the knitting in hand and are ready to work that portion of the pattern.

fingering

Next, make a swatch. The swatches in this book are knit in varying weights of wool (worsted, sport, and fingering) provided by Lorna's Laces. In general, the patterns with small stitch multiples (less than 8 or 10) and panels are knit with Shepherd Worsted; the larger stitch multiples are done in Shepherd Sport. A few of the very large stitch repeats in Book 1 and Book 3 are worked in Shepherd Sock. The swatches have been blocked minimally for photography, and thus you may occasionally note irregularities that are inherent in hand knitting.

sport

worsted

The appearance and drape of the stitch pattern will depend on the yarn chosen--color, style of spinning, fiber content, and weight--and on the gauge used. Keep in mind that large stitch motifs can overwhelm small projects, and small stitch motifs might be lost on a large project. Scale is important. Changing the weight of yarn and gauge it is knit at can help reduce or enlarge a motif as desired. The photos on this page show an example of the Tulip lace pattern knit with three different weights of yarn at three different gauges. The appearance of the pattern changes in each case and stresses the importance of swatching.

Lace

Follow the Organization

Each book is organized from smallest stitch multiple to largest, making it easier to find the pattern that best suits the project you have in mind. A small-scale lace pattern is better for a baby sweater than a large-scale one, for instance.

Match the Pattern to the Purpose

The descriptions included with each stitch pattern also suggest the type of project for which it is best suited. Many of the descriptions also indicate whether it works well as an overall stitch, a filler stitch, a panel stitch, or an edge stitch. An overall stitch pattern is used throughout the full project rather than in just a small area. You can convert patterns presented as panels into an overall stitch pattern by simply working one or more stitches (usually Stockinette or Reverse Stockinette) between repeats of the panel.

Filler stitches are worked in small areas of a larger project to fill open space. Filler stitches appear in between panels of other stitches or as a panel themselves. Filler stitches often have a small multiple and are easier to use in sizing and shaping. When combining filler stitches with other stitches (panels or overall patterns), always check the gauge of each stitch pattern. They can vary widely, even on the same needles with the same yarn.

A panel pattern is intended to be a section of a larger project. Most often, panels are just the stitch pattern itself, and the knitter needs to add border or background stitches. Panels can be worked as either a stitch multiple, by themselves, or combined with other panels or stitch patterns. Cables are very often written as a panel, for instance.

Lastly, edge or border stitch patterns can be used as filler stitches or overall patterns, but they lie flat and look tidy along the edges, making them suitable for hems, cuffs, or edges on other patterns.

Understand the Ratings

Each stitch pattern in this collection has a skill level and a drape rating. The skill level ratings include easy (basic knitting knowledge required), advanced beginner, intermediate, and experienced. Remember what looks difficult on paper is often easier to understand with the knitting on needles in front of you.

All knitting has at least some amount of drape, so the ratings are relative and are based on using wool at the recommended gauge for the yarn. The ratings are: low (a firmer fabric), medium (reasonable amount of drape), and high (a flowing fabric). In general, the denser the fabric (e.g., more stitches per inch) is with stitches, the less drape it will have. The more open the fabric is (e.g., fewer stitches per inch), the more drape it will have. Cable patterns, for instance, will have less drape than lace patterns. However, drape also depends on the yarn chosen for a project and on the gauge used. Some fibers have more drape than others, and the finer the yarn, the more drape the fabric will have. A tighter gauge will have less drape than a looser gauge.

Understand Stitch Multiples and Balancing Stitches

Stitch patterns are presented with information about the number of stitches required to complete one pattern repeat. For panels, the information is simply how many stitches wide the panel is. For all other patterns, this information is presented as a multiple of stitches, plus any balancing stitches needed. For example, if you want to work six repeats of a pattern, and it requires four stitches and one balancing stitch (multiple of 4 + 1), you would cast on 24 stitches plus one balancing stitch, for a total of 25 stitches.

level
- easy
- advanced beginner
- intermediate
- experienced

drape
- low
- medium
- high

Lace

5

Add Selvage Stitches

The patterns in these books do not include selvage stitches, which are one or more spare stitches included at the edge of your knitting for seaming or for tidying the edge. Some knitters don't even use selvage stitches unless specifically directed to do so in a pattern. If you are a knitter who likes to use selvage stitches, you will need to add them to the edges of your projects.

Work Increases and Decreases

These guides use a variety of increases and decreases. It is important to use the correct technique for the increases and decreases called for in the pattern instructions; this insures that your stitch pattern has the proper appearance, as the various techniques create different effects, such as slants or holes. Perhaps the most common increase used in the patterns is done by knitting into the front and back of a single stitch. There are several decreases used in the patterns—some decrease one stitch at a time (single decreases), some decrease two stitches at a time (double decreases), some decrease even more! When a pattern says simply to decrease one stitch, but doesn't say which decrease to use, the assumption is that you will use a k2tog (knit two stitches together) or a p2tog (purl two stitches together), depending on whether you are on the right or wrong side of your work. Consult the Abbreviations and Glossary section (page 62) for explanations of each type of increase or decrease.

CHOOSING THE BEST YARN

How do you choose the most suitable yarn for a stitch pattern or a project? The first thing to consider is the pattern itself. The busier the stitch pattern is, the simpler the yarn should be, and vice versa. If you want to work a lace pattern or an elaborate cable pattern, choose a smooth, plain-colored yarn. A subtly variegated or kettle-dyed solid yarn might work with a fancy pattern stitch, but a yarn with extreme color changes or striping will detract from the pattern stitch.

Fiber content makes a difference, too. Plant fibers (cotton, linen, hemp, rayon) are inelastic, as is silk. When you work with plant fibers, your knitting tends to be what-you-see-is-what-you-get. Blocking will not improve it.

In contrast, animal fibers are almost magical to knit with, and a good blocking hides a multitude of sins. The fiber has memory and will retain its shape until the next time it gets wet.

Consider Yarn Requirements

Knitting a swatch before beginning a project is important, of course. But when choosing stitch patterns for a project you design, it is useful to consult a reference to see what the estimated yardage requirements are for the size and type of project you are creating at the gauge you are knitting. Yardage requirement tables are usually based on Stockinette stitch, but keep in mind that different stitch patterns require different amounts of yarn. For instance, Garter stitch has a very compressed row gauge, so it will take more yarn than Stockinette stitch. Lace is very open, so it can use less yarn than Stockinette stitch. Cables and many fancy patterns are very dense and can use *much* more yarn than Stockinette stitch.

Lace

INTRODUCTION TO LACE

Lace is composed of the standard knit and purl stitches combined with increases (almost exclusively the yarn over, which creates a nice eyelet hole) and a variety of decreases, which form distinct designs.

There are two categories of lace stitches—lace knitting and knitted lace. The essential difference between the two is that with knitted lace, the wrong side row is knit or purled. In contrast, lace knitting patterns have the "thinking rows" (yarn overs and decreases) worked on both the right and wrong side. In knitted lace, the strands of yarn between eyelets are twisted. In lace knitting, the strand of yarn is simply a strand of yarn. The easy way to remember the difference is that for knitted lace, you knit (or purl) the lace rows working back on the wrong side. For lace knitting, you are always working a lace row; it has a more open appearance than knitted lace. Both knitted lace and lace knitting will be simply referred to as lace in this book.

Lace is extremely versatile. We tend to think of lace as having a lot of drape, but more than any other category of stitch pattern, lace can be worked at just about any gauge and still look good. For instance, the same lace motif can be knit at tighter than recommended gauge in a sock pattern, at recommended gauge in a sweater pattern, and much looser than recommended gauge for a shawl pattern. The other categories of stitches don't have this latitude. Lace also works well in most any fiber type, as long as the yarn is relatively smooth, but heavily textured or variegated yarns hide lace patterns.

On the whole, lace patterns use less yarn, and weigh less, than the other categories of stitch patterns. When knitting something large and potentially heavy like a blanket, add a lacy panel and the finished project will be lighter in weight, but still plenty warm.

Lace

Also, lace borders or panels add visual interest and ventilation for a summer sweater project.

Some pattern stitches will work the increases and decreases on separate rows, so the number of stitches is changing from row to row. With these pattern motifs, you will return to the original number of stitches by the time you work through all of the rows. Sometimes, you will see lace patterns that include extra increases or decreases built into the pattern. These extra increases or decreases change the stitch count as a means of shaping the knitting.

Count your stitches at the beginning or end of a row only, to account for the increases and decreases that occur within the row. Unless noted otherwise, the patterns in this book have a consistent stitch count from row to row. Some knitters find it useful to place markers between each pattern repeat in order to more easily identify where a mistake may have occurred.

A common frustration with knitting lace is how to rip out when a mistake has been made. A lifeline—a length of smooth thin yarn or sewing thread—can be threaded intermittently through rows that are known to be correct. When a mistake is made, the knitter can then rip back only as far as the lifeline.

Lace truly benefits from the washing and block-ing process. Lace in progress frequently resembles used tissue—just strange looking! A project may come off the needles looking much smaller than you expect, but a good blocking will allow the knit-ting to expand and lie flat. Swatching is important so you get an idea of the change in size that block-ing will create. Because lace blocks out so well, it is important to cast on and bind off loosely or to use a technique that creates a more elastic edge.

PURSE STITCH

Purse stitch is one of the most basic lace knitting patterns, with one row repeated over and over again, creating a mesh-like fabric. Purse stitch is elastic and can be blocked out to be very open and airy. It is a great pattern for simple scarves or shawls because it has a lot of drape, is open, and doesn't require an edging stitch to stay flat. Purse stitch can also be used as a filler stitch in larger projects.

level ● ●
drape ▦ ▦ ▦

THE PATTERN

Multiple of 2

Row 1 (WS): P1, * yo, p2tog. Repeat from * to last stitch, end p1.

Row 2: P1, * yo, p2tog. Repeat from * to last stitch, end p1.

Repeat rows 1 and 2.

Lace

10

BASIC FAGGOTING STITCH

Faggoting patterns are traditionally found in Scottish lace work. Basic faggoting stitch is one of the simplest lace knitting patterns (where the lace is worked on both the right and wrong sides of the work). It has a mesh-like appearance that is perfect for shawls or scarves. It would also work well for a market bag.

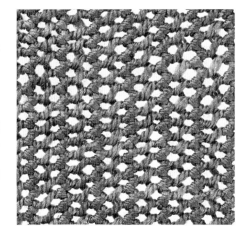

level
drape

THE PATTERN

Multiple of 2

Row 1 (WS): K1, * yo, ssk. Repeat from * to last stitch, k1.
Row 2: K1, * yo, ssk. Repeat from * to last stitch, k1.
Repeat rows 1 and 2.

Lace

11

OPENWORK STRIPES

Openwork stripes is a completely reversible lace pattern worked over an odd number of rows. Because it is based in Garter stitch, the resulting fabric lies perfectly flat, so it can either serve as an edge stitch or be used with no additional edge stitch. Openwork stripes would make a great blanket or scarf pattern. It would also be a nice accent on the border of a sweater.

level ⬤ ⬤
drape ▦ ▦

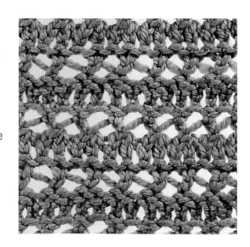

THE PATTERN

Multiple of 2

Row 1: Knit.

Row 2: K1, * yo, k1. Repeat from * to last stitch, end k1.

Row 3: K1, purl to the last stitch, end k1.

Row 4: K1, * k2tog. Repeat from * to last stitch, end k1.

Row 5: K1, * yo, k2tog. Repeat from * to last stitch, end k1.

Row 6: K1, * yo, k2tog. Repeat from * to last stitch, end k1.

Row 7: Knit.

Repeat rows 1–7.

Note: There are no right and wrong sides to this stitch pattern. Because there is an odd number of rows in the pattern, which row is worked on the right side and which row is worked on the wrong side will vary with each repeat of the seven rows. Also, notice that you will be increasing stitches on row 2 and will return to the original stitch count on row 4.

OPENWORK STRIPES VARIATION

Openwork stripes variation is not quite as reversible as Openwork stripes (page 12) because it is worked over an even number of rows. However, both sides of the fabric are attractive. Like openwork stripes, the resulting fabric lies perfectly flat, so it can either serve as an edge stitch or be used without an edge stitch. It can be used as you would Openwork stripes.

level

drape

THE PATTERN

Multiple of 2 + 1

Row 1 and all odd numbered rows (WS): Knit.

Row 2: Knit.

Row 4: K1, * yo, k2tog. Repeat from * to end of row.

Row 6: * K2tog, yo. Repeat from * to last stitch, end k1.

Row 8: K1, * yo, k2tog. Repeat from * to end of row.

Row 10: Knit.

Repeat rows 1–10.

LACY HONEYCOMB

Lacy honeycomb is a simple eyelet pattern with yarn overs worked at close, regular intervals. The end result is a knitted fabric that resembles a honeycomb. This stitch pattern does not curl along the cast-on edge, so no additional edge stitch is necessary. Lacy honeycomb would be an excellent filler stitch in a shawl or sweater. It would also work well as a simple overall pattern.

level ◐ ◐
drape ▦ ▦

THE PATTERN

Multiple of 3 + 1

Row 1 (WS): P1, * k1, p2. Repeat from * to end of row.

Row 2: K1, * yo, k1, k2tog. Repeat from * to end of row.

Row 3: P1, * p1, k1, p1. Repeat from * to end of row.

Row 4: K1, * k2tog, yo, k1. Repeat from * to end of row.

Repeat rows 1–4.

FOUNTAIN STITCH

Fountain stitch resembles little lacy sprays of water. It is a simple lace pattern with a small stitch multiple, which makes it easier to do shaping in a project and still maintain the pattern. Fountain stitch can be used effectively as a filler stitch combined with other motifs or throughout a project. It is a good pattern for sweaters, shawls, or scarves.

level

drape

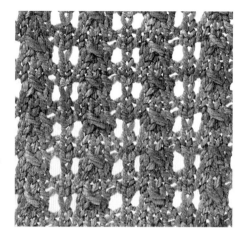

THE PATTERN

Multiple of 4 + 1

Rows 1 and 3 (WS): Purl.

Row 2: K1, * yo, k3, yo, k1. Repeat from * to end of row.

Row 4: K2, sl 1, k2tog, psso, * k3, sl 1, k2tog, psso. Repeat from * to last 2 stitches, end k2.

Repeat rows 1–4.

FAGGOTING RIB

Faggoting rib is another faggoting stitch with a more solid appearance than the Basic faggoting stitch (page 11). The rib columns make it slightly less stretchy than its basic counterpart. Faggoting rib makes an excellent edge stitch, say on a sweater or shawl, or can be used throughout a project.

level
drape

THE PATTERN

Multiple of 4 + 2

Row 1 (RS): K3, * yo, sl 1, k1, psso, k2. Repeat from * to last 3 stitches, end yo, sl 1, k1, psso, k1.

Row 2: P3, * yo, p2tog, p2. Repeat from * to last 3 stitches, end yo, p2tog, p1.

Repeat rows 1 and 2.

LACE DIAGONALS

Lace diagonals is a very clean, modern lace pattern that is quick and easy to work. This pattern is great for any project. The background of the lace is Stockinette stitch, so the edges curl; consider using a border pattern to keep the edges lying flat. Because it is such a simple lace, it is easy to make it completely reversible by changing the wrong side rows to be knit rather than purled. Lace diagonals would work up into a simple summer tank or tee.

level

drape

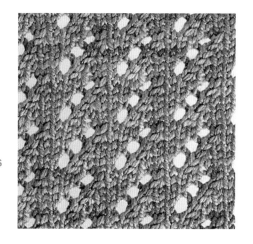

THE PATTERN

Multiple of 5 + 1

Row 1 and all odd numbered rows (WS): Purl.

Row 2: K1, * k2, k2tog, yo, k1. Repeat from * to end of row.

Row 4: K1, * k1, k2tog, yo, k2. Repeat from * to end of row.

Row 6: K1, * k2tog, yo, k3. Repeat from * to end of row.

Repeat rows 1–6.

Lace

FUCHSIA PATTERN

While the fuchsia pattern appears simple, the stitch count varies from row to row, making it slightly more difficult to work. The variation in stitch count creates a waving edge to the fabric. Fuchsia pattern works well in any project where you might normally use a rib stitch but desire a lacier appearance or more drape to the fabric, like a scarf or warm stole.

level ● ● ●
drape ▦ ▦ ▦

THE PATTERN

Multiple of 6

Row 1 (RS): * P2, k2, yo, p2. Repeat from * to end of row.
Row 2: * K2, p3, k2. Repeat from * to end of row.
Row 3: * P2, k3, yo, p2. Repeat from * to end of row.
Row 4: * K2, p4, k2. Repeat from * to end of row.
Row 5: * P2, k4, yo, p2. Repeat from * to end of row.
Row 6: * K2, p5, k2. Repeat from * to end of row.
Row 7: * P2, k3, k2tog, p2. Repeat from * to end of row.
Row 8: * K2, p4, k2. Repeat from * to end of row.
Row 9: * P2, k2, k2tog, p2. Repeat from * to end of row.
Row 10: * K2, p3, k2. Repeat from * to end of row.
Row 11: * P2, k1, k2tog, p2. Repeat from * to end of row.
Row 12: * K2, p2, k2. Repeat from * to end of row.
Repeat rows 1–12.

Note: On rows 1, 3, and 5, you will be increasing one stitch per pattern repeat. On rows 7, 9, and 11, you will be decreasing one stitch per pattern repeat.

ZIGZAG LACE

Zigzag lace is a very modern, geometric lace pattern with strong vertical lines. The bottom edge very slightly scallops because of the way the increases and decreases align in columns. The side edges curve along the lines of the zigzags. Zigzag lace would be very striking in shawls, scarves, or blankets. It would also work up into a sophisticated sweater.

level
drape

THE PATTERN

Multiple of 6 + 1

Row 1 and all odd numbered rows (WS): Purl.

Rows 2, 4, and 6: * Sl 1, k1, psso, k2, yo, k2. Repeat from * to last stitch, end k1.

Rows 8, 10, and 12: K3, * yo, k2, k2tog, k2. Repeat from * to last 4 stitches, end yo, k2, k2tog.

Repeat rows 1–12.

ENGLISH MESH LACE

English mesh lace is a nice, straightforward knitted lace pattern. Its diamond-shaped motif is over a small multiple of stitches, making it easy to fit into any size of project. The pattern is easy to visualize, so it is not difficult to work shaping and still maintain the pattern. English mesh lace is extremely versatile, being a great stitch pattern for use in shawls, stoles, sweaters, socks, baby projects, or blankets.

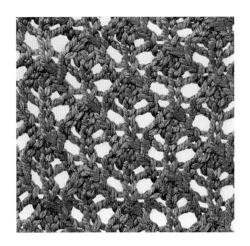

level ● ● ●
drape ▦ ▦ ▦

THE PATTERN

Multiple of 6 + 1

Row 1 and all odd numbered rows (WS): Purl.

Row 2: K1, * yo, ssk, k1, k2tog, yo, k1. Repeat from * to end of row.

Row 4: K1, * yo, k1, sl 1, k2tog, psso, k1, yo, k1. Repeat from * to end of row.

Row 6: K1, * k2tog, yo, k1, yo, ssk, k1. Repeat from * to end of row.

Row 8: K2tog, * [k1, yo] twice, k1, sl 1, k2tog, psso. Repeat from * to last 5 sts, end [k1, yo] twice, k1, ssk.

Repeat rows 1–8.

TULIP LACE

Tulip lace looks like a field of tulips in bloom. It is a knitted lace pattern over a small multiple of stitches, so it fits well into any size of project. The small stitch multiple also makes it easier to do shaping, say at an armhole or neckline, while maintaining the motif. Tulip lace is an attractive stitch pattern for use in sweaters, socks, shawls, or scarves.

level
drape

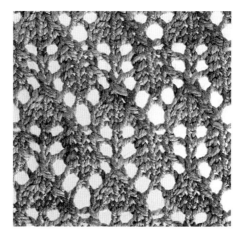

THE PATTERN

Multiple of 6 + 1

Row 1 and all odd numbered rows (WS): Purl.

Row 2: K3, * yo, k2tog tbl, k4. Repeat from * to last 4 stitches, end yo, k2tog tbl, k2.

Row 4: K1, * k2tog, yo, k1, yo, k2tog tbl, k1. Repeat from * to end of row.

Row 6: K2tog, yo, * k3, yo, sl 1, k2tog, psso, yo. Repeat from * to last 5 stitches, end k3, yo, k2tog tbl.

Row 8: K1, * yo, k2tog tbl, k1, k2tog, yo, k1. Repeat from * to end of row.

Row 10: K1, * yo, k2tog tbl, k1, k2tog, yo, k1. Repeat from * to end of row.

Repeat rows 1–10.

Lace

21

RIBBED BEEHIVE

Ribbed beehive is a traditional German stitch pattern composed of little lace beehive motifs separated by twisted stitch ribs. The motif is simple to memorize and creates a nice flat fabric. Ribbed beehive could be used as a delicate edge stitch on a sweater or mitten. It would also be attractive in a rectangular shawl or combined with the Lacy honeycomb stitch (page 14) into a larger shawl.

level ● ● ●
drape ▥ ▥ ▥

THE PATTERN

Multiple of 6 + 3

Row 1 (WS): K1, * p tbl, k1, p3, k1. Repeat from * to last 2 stitches, end p tbl, k1.

Row 2: K1, * k tbl, p1, yo, sl 1, k2tog, psso, yo, p1. Repeat from * to last 2 stitches, end k tbl, k1.

Row 3: K1, * p tbl, k1, p3, k1. Repeat from * to last 2 stitches, end p tbl, k1.

Row 4: K1, * k tbl, p1, k3, p1. Repeat from * to last 2 stitches, end k tbl, k1.

Repeat rows 1–4.

LACY WINGS

Lacy wings is a knitted lace motif resembling V's or wing shapes. It is a very simple pattern with good drape. Lacy wings is perfect for inclusion in shawls, scarves, or stoles. Because it is a simple pattern, it also works nicely in sweaters because it is not too complicated to maintain the motif and work shaping.

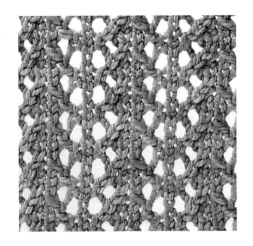

level
drape

THE PATTERN

Multiple of 7

Rows 1 and 3 (WS): Purl.

Row 2: * K1, k2tog, yo, k1, yo, sl 1, k1, psso, k1. Repeat from * to end of row.

Row 4: * K2tog, yo, k3, yo, sl 1, k1, psso. Repeat from * to end of row.

Repeat rows 1–4.

BEAD STITCH LACE

Bead stitch lace is an attractive lace knitting pattern that is not too complex to work because it is only a four-row repeat. The resulting fabric is a crossing lace work pattern. Bead stitch lace would make a nice border on a sweater or shawl. It would also be lovely as an overall pattern in any kind of wrap or top.

level ● ● ●
drape ■ ■ ■

THE PATTERN

Multiple of 7

Row 1 (RS): * K1, k2tog, yo, k1, yo, ssk, k1. Repeat from * to end of row.

Row 2: * P2tog tbl, yo, p3, yo, p2tog. Repeat from * to end of row.

Row 3: * K1, yo, ssk, k1, k2tog, yo, k1. Repeat from * to end of row.

Row 4: * P2, yo, p3tog, yo, p2.

Repeat rows 1–4.

LITTLE LACE DIAMONDS

Little lace diamonds uses the decrease stitches to strongly outline the lacy eyelets. It is a good study in seeing how different decreases slant because the appearance is so dramatic. Little lace diamonds is nice worked in heavier yarns as well as fine yarns, making it a good motif for blankets. Of course, it is appropriate for scarves, shawls, socks, or sweaters, too.

level

drape

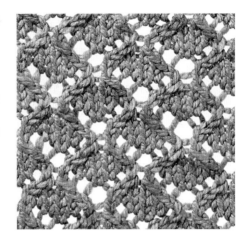

THE PATTERN

Multiple of 7 + 2

Row 1 (RS): K3, * k2tog, yo, k5. Repeat from * to end of row, ending last repeat k4.

Row 2: P2, * p2tog tbl, yo, p1, yo, p2tog, p2. Repeat from * to end of row.

Row 3: K1, * k2tog, yo, k3, yo, sl 1, k1, psso. Repeat from * to last stitch, end k1.

Row 4: Purl.

Row 5: K1, * yo, sl 1, k1, psso, k5. Repeat from * to end of row, ending last repeat k6.

Row 6: P1, * yo, p2tog, p2, p2tog tbl, yo, p1. Repeat from * to end of row, ending last repeat p2.

Row 7: K3, * yo, sl 1, k1, psso, k2tog, yo, k3. Repeat from * to end of row, ending last repeat k2.

Row 8: Purl.

Repeat rows 1–8.

Lace

SINGLE EYELET PATTERN

Single eyelet pattern is perhaps the simplest of the knitted lace patterns. The resulting fabric is primarily Stockinette, so this pattern can be used in any project for which you would normally use Stockinette stitch. It is not as open as most lace patterns, making it a good motif for tops. Single eyelet pattern is also good when you are using a yarn like cotton, where any unevenness in gauge shows. The eyelets distract the eye from any inconsistencies in gauge.

level
drape

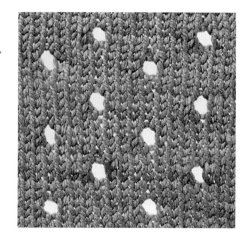

THE PATTERN

Multiple of 8

Row 1 and all odd numbered rows (WS): Purl.

Row 2: Knit.

Row 4: * K6, yo, k2tog. Repeat from * to end of row.

Row 6: Knit.

Row 8: K2, * yo, k2tog, k6. Repeat from * to end of row, ending last repeat k4.

Repeat rows 1–8.

LEAF LACE

Leaf lace is an attractive diamond pattern that resembles falling leaves. The relatively small stitch multiple and the strong diagonal lines help make this pattern easier to use as an overall motif in a project with shaping, like a triangular shawl or a sweater. Leaf lace would be a beautiful sweater border, shawl, or lacy scarf.

level
drape

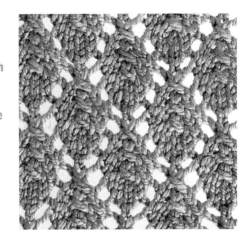

THE PATTERN

Multiple of 8 + 1

Row 1 and all odd numbered rows (WS): Purl.

Row 2: K1, * yo, k2, sl 1, k2tog, psso, k2, yo, k1. Repeat from * to end of row.

Row 4: K2, * yo, k1, sl 1, k2tog, psso, k1, yo, k3. Repeat from * to end of row, end last repeat k2.

Row 6: K3, * yo, sl 1, k2tog, psso, yo, k5. Repeat from * to end of row, end last repeat k3.

Row 8: K1, k2tog, k1, * yo, k1, yo, k2, sl 1, k2tog, psso, k2. Repeat from * to last 5 stitches, end yo, k1, yo, k1, k2tog, k1.

Row 10: K1, k2tog, * k3, yo, k1, sl 1, k2tog, psso, k1. Repeat from * to last 6 stitches, end yo, k3, yo, k2tog, k1.

Row 12: K2tog, yo, k5, yo, * sl 1, k2tog, psso, k5, yo. Repeat from * to last 2 stitches, end k2tog.

Repeat rows 1–12.

TURTLE TRACK LACE

Turtle track lace is a favorite stitch pattern. The positioning of the yarn overs and decreases gives the impression of cables. However, there are no twisted stitches, and the resulting fabric is very smooth and flat. There is a good balance of knit and purl stitches, so the cast-on edge does not curl. Turtle track lace is a wonderful overall pattern for summer sweaters. It also looks nice worked into scarves and socks.

level ● ● ●
drape ▦ ▦ ▦

THE PATTERN

Multiple of 8 + 2

Row 1 and all odd numbered rows (WS): K2, * p6, k2. Repeat from * to end of row.

Row 2: P2, *k6, p2. Repeat from * to end of row.

Row 4: P2, * yo, k2, ssk, k2, p2. Repeat from * to end of row.

Row 6: P2, * k1, yo, k2, ssk, k1, p2. Repeat from * to end of row.

Row 8: P2, * k2, yo, k2, ssk, p2. Repeat from * to end of row.

Row 10: P2, * k6, p2. Repeat from * to end of row.

Row 12: P2, * k2, k2tog, k2, yo, p2. Repeat from * to end of row.

Row 14: P2, * k1, k2tog, k2, yo, k1, p2. Repeat from * to end of row.

Row 16: P2, * k2tog, k2, yo, k2, p2. Repeat from * to end of row.

Repeat rows 1–16.

Lace

FANCY FAGGOTING STITCH

Fancy faggoting stitch is columns of diagonally placed eyelets separated by columns of faggoting stitch. It has an attractive vertically lined appearance. The fabric lies very flat, so it is appropriate for use as an edge stitch. Fancy faggoting stitch would also make up into a nice scarf, stole, or dressy pullover.

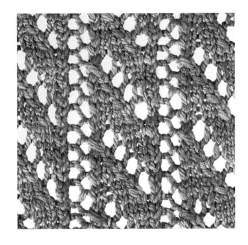

level

drape

THE PATTERN

Multiple of 8 + 4

Row 1 and all odd numbered rows (WS): P2tog, yo, p2, * p4, p2tog, yo, p2. Repeat from * to end of row.

Row 2: Ssk, yo, k2, * yo, ssk, k2, ssk, yo, k2. Repeat from * to end of row.

Row 4: Ssk, yo, k2, * k1, yo, ssk, k1, ssk, yo, k2. Repeat from * to end of row.

Row 6: Ssk, yo, k2, * k2, yo, ssk twice, yo, k2. Repeat from * to end of row.

Row 8: Ssk, yo, k2, * k3, yo, sl 1, k2tog, psso, yo, k2. Repeat from * to end of row.

Repeat rows 1–8.

TRAVELING VINE LACE

Traveling vine lace is a
French lace pattern. It is
a little more complex to
work, as the stitch count
varies between odd and
even rows, and there
are stitches that are
worked through the back
loops. However, the end
result is stunning. With
a simple border stitch to
prevent curling, traveling
vine lace is suitable for
scarves, shawls,
or blankets.

level
drape

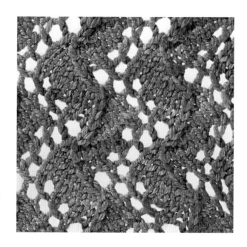

THE PATTERN

Multiple of 8 + 4

Row 1 (RS): K2, * yo, k tbl, yo, ssk, k5. Repeat from * to last
2 stitches, end k2.

Row 2: P6, * p2tog tbl, p7. Repeat from * to end of row,
end last repeat p5.

Row 3: K2, * yo, k tbl, yo, k2, ssk, k3. Repeat from * to last
2 stitches, end k2.

Row 4: P4, * p2tog tbl, p7. Repeat from * to end of row.

Row 5: K2, * k tbl, yo, k4, ssk, k1, yo. Repeat from * to last
2 stitches, end k2.

Row 6: P3, * p2tog tbl, p7. Repeat from * to last stitch,
end p1.

Row 7: K2, * k5, k2tog, yo, k tbl, yo. Repeat from * to last
2 stitches, end k2.

Row 8: P5, * p2tog, p7. Repeat from * to last 6 stitches,
end p6.

Row 9: K2, * k3, k2tog, k2, yo, k tbl, yo. Repeat from * to last
2 stitches, end k2.

Row 10: * P7, p2tog. Repeat from * to last 4 stitches, end p4.

Lace

there's more >

TRAVELING VINE LACE

more > Row 11: K2, * yo, k1, k2tog, k4, yo, k tbl. Repeat from * to last
2 stitches, end k2.

Row 12: P1, * p7, p2tog. Repeat from * to last 3 stitches,
end p3.

Repeat rows 1–12.

Note: On all odd-numbered (RS) rows, you will be adding one
extra stitch per repeat. You will return to the original number of
stitches on all even-numbered (WS) rows.

Lace

ROSEBUD LACE

Rosebud lace gets its name from the budding roses it resembles. The alignment of the decreases and increases creates gently curving edges to the fabric with a naturally scalloping cast-on edge. Rosebud lace is very elegant in shawls and scarf designs. It would also work well in sweaters, especially for little girls.

level ● ● ●
drape ▦ ▦ ▦

THE PATTERN

Multiple of 8 + 5

Row 1: Purl.

Row 2: K3, * yo, k2, p3tog, k2, yo, k1. Repeat from * to last 2 stitches, end k2.

Row 3: Purl.

Row 4: K3, * yo, k2, p3tog, k2, yo, k1. Repeat from * to last 2 stitches, end k2.

Row 5: Purl.

Row 6: K3, * yo, k2, p3tog, k2, yo, k1. Repeat from * to last 2 stitches, end k2.

Row 7: Purl.

Row 8: K2, p2tog, * k2, yo, k1, yo, k2, p3tog. Repeat from * to last 9 stitches, end k2, yo, k1, yo, k2, p2tog, k2.

Row 9: Purl.

Row 10: K2, p2tog, * k2, yo, k1, yo, k2, p3tog. Repeat from * to last 9 stitches, end k2, yo, k1, yo, k2, p2tog, k2.

Row 11: Purl.

Row 12: K2, p2tog, * k2, yo, k1, yo, k2, p3tog. Repeat from * to last 9 stitches, end k2, yo, k1, yo, k2, p2tog, k2.

Repeat rows 1–12.

SNOWDROP LACE

Snowdrop lace is made up of columns of cute little snowdrop flower motifs. It has a clean, linear look that is still delicate and feminine. Snowdrop lace would be an excellent border stitch for a summer top or little girl's dress. It would also be a nice overall motif for a cardigan or shoulder shawl.

level
drape

THE PATTERN

Multiple of 8 + 5

Row 1 and all odd numbered rows (WS): Purl.

Row 2: K1, * yo, sl 1, k2tog, psso, yo, k5. Repeat from * to last 4 stitches, end yo, sl l, k2tog, psso, yo, k1.

Row 4: K1, * yo, sl 1, k2tog, psso, yo, k5. Repeat from * to last 4 stitches, end yo, sl l, k2tog, psso, yo, k1.

Row 6: K1, * k3, yo, sl1, k1, psso, k1, k2tog, yo. Repeat from * to last 4 stitches, end k4.

Row 8: K1, * yo, sl 1, k2tog, psso, yo, k1. Repeat from * to last 4 stitches, end yo, sl l, k2tog, psso, yo, k1.

Repeat rows 1–8.

GRAPEVINE LATTICE LACE

Grapevine lattice lace is a more geometric lace with the appearance of a garden trellis. It works up into a nice afghan pattern. It would also make an attractive cardigan pattern when knit at the recommended gauge for the yarn. By using a looser gauge in a finer yarn, grapevine lattice would create an elegant shawl or wrap.

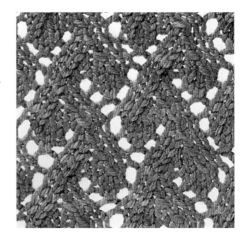

level ● ● ●
drape ▥ ▥ ▥

THE PATTERN

Multiple of 8 + 6

Row 1 and all odd numbered rows (WS): Purl.

Row 2: K2, * k2tog, k1, yo, k1, ssk, k2. Repeat from * to last 4 stitches, end k4.

Row 4: K1, k2tog, k1, yo, * k1, yo, k1, ssk, k2tog, k1, yo. Repeat from * to last 2 stitches, end k2.

Row 6: K3, yo, * k3, yo, k1, ssk, k1, yo. Repeat from * to last 3 stitches, end k3.

Row 8: K5, * k2tog, k1, yo, k1, ssk, k2. Repeat from * to last 2 stitches, end k2.

Row 10: K4, * k2tog, k1, [yo, k1] twice, ssk. Repeat from * to last 3 stitches, end k3.

Row 12: K3, k2tog, * k1, yo, k3, yo, k1, k2tog. Repeat from * to last 2 stitches, end k2.

Repeat rows 1–12.

Note: On rows 2 and 8, you will be decreasing one stitch per pattern repeat. On rows 6 and 12, you will return to the initial number of stitches.

TRIPLE EYELET LACE

Triple eyelet lace is a very simple and attractive lace motif. Because it is so simple, it works well in projects that have shaping, as it is easier to keep the motif consistent than with many lace patterns. This characteristic, along with the fact that is a bit more solid than most lace patterns, makes it appealing for sweaters. Triple eyelet lace is also good for use as a filler pattern.

level

drape

THE PATTERN

Multiple of 8 + 7

Row 1 and all odd numbered rows (WS): Purl.

Row 2: Knit.

Row 4: K2, yo, sl 1, k2tog, psso, yo, * k5, yo, sl 1, k2tog, psso, yo. Repeat from * to last 2 stitches, end k2.

Row 6: K3, yo, ssk, * k6, yo, ssk. Repeat from * to last 2 stitches, end k2.

Row 8: Knit.

Row 10: K1, * k5, yo, sl 1, k2tog, psso, yo. Repeat from * to last 6 stitches, end k6.

Row 12: K7, * yo, ssk, k6. Repeat from * to end of row.

Repeat rows 1-12.

CORN STALKS

Corn stalks is remi-
niscent of ears of corn
snug in their husks
on the stalks. It is a
Stockinette-stitch based
pattern that isn't too
lacy. The decreases cre-
ate pleasing alternating
diagonals. Corn stalks
would be a nice pattern
stitch for a knit top or
for a pair of socks. With
a simple edge stitch, it
would work up into a
good afghan pattern, too.

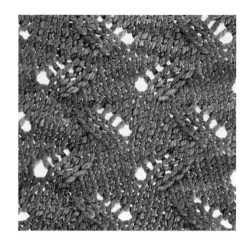

level ● ● ●
drape ▦ ▦

THE PATTERN

Multiple of 9 + 3

Row 1 (WS): Purl.

Row 2: K3, * k2tog, k1, yo, k6. Repeat from * to end of row.

Row 3: P1, * p6, yo, p1, p2tog. Repeat from * to last 2 stitches, end p2.

Row 4: K1, * k2tog, k1, yo, k6. Repeat from * to last 2 stitches, end k2.

Row 5: P3, * p6, yo, p1, p2tog. Repeat from * to end of row.

Row 6: Knit.

Row 7: Purl.

Row 8: * K6, yo, k1, ssk. Repeat from * to last 3 stitches, end k3.

Row 9: P2, * p2tog tbl, p1, yo, p6. Repeat from * to last stitch, end p1.

Row 10: K2, * k6, yo, k1, ssk. Repeat from * to last stitch, end k1.

Row 11: * P2tog tbl, p1, yo, p6. Repeat from * to last 3 stitches, end p3.

Row 12: Knit.

Repeat rows 1–12.

VINE LACE

Vine lace is an easy pattern to memorize since it is only four rows long. The alignment of yarn overs and decreases naturally create attractive scallops along the bottom edge of the knitting, so no additional edging is required. It is important to cast on loosely, though, to help prevent the scallops from curling. The pattern has excellent drape, but can be knit more firmly for uses like the cuff of a sock. It also works well in just about any fiber type and yarn weight.

level
drape

THE PATTERN

Multiple of 9 + 4

Row 1 (WS): Purl.

Row 2: K3, * yo, k2, ssk, k2tog, k2, yo, k1. Repeat from * to last stitch, end k1.

Row 3: Purl.

Row 4: K2, * yo, k2, ssk, k2tog, k2, yo, k1. Repeat from * to last 2 stitches, end k2.

Repeat rows 1–4.

LITTLE PINWHEELS

Little pinwheels is far from the traditional lace pattern. The little pinwheels are created by small areas of Stockinette and Garter stitches separated by lacy eyelets. This playful motif is perfect for use in projects for children, like sweaters or blankets, but also works up into a fun sock.

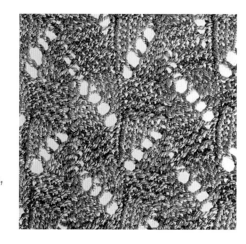

level ◉ ◉

drape ▥ ▥

THE PATTERN

Multiple of 10 + 1

Row 1 (WS): K1, * k4, p5, k1. Repeat from * to end of row.

Row 2: P1, * k4, k2tog, k3, yo, p1. Repeat from * to end of row.

Row 3: K1, * p5, k5. Repeat from * to end of row.

Row 4: P1, * k4, k2tog, k2, yo, k1, p1. Repeat from * to end of row.

Row 5: K1, * p5, k5. Repeat from * to end of row.

Row 6: P1, * k4, k2tog, k1, yo, k2, p1. Repeat from * to end of row.

Row 7: K1, * p5, k5. Repeat from * to end of row.

Row 8: P1, * k4, k2tog, yo, k3, p1. Repeat from * to end of row.

Row 9: K1, * p5, k5. Repeat from * to end of row.

Row 10: P1, * yo, k3, k2tog, k4, p1. Repeat from * to end of row.

Row 11: K1, * k4, p5, k1. Repeat from * to end of row.

Row 12: P1, * k1, yo, k2, k2tog, k4, p1. Repeat from * to end of row.

Row 13: K1, * k4, p5, k1. Repeat from * to end of row.

there's more >

LITTLE PINWHEELS

more >   Row 14: P1, * k2, yo, k1, k2tog, k4, p1. Repeat from * to end of row.

Row 15: K1, * k4, p5, k1. Repeat from * to end of row.

Row 16: P1, * k3, yo, k2tog, k4, p1. Repeat from * to end of row.

Repeat rows 1–16.

EYELET BUTTERFLIES

Eyelet butterflies is a cute little knitted lace pattern where the yarn overs form wings and a slipped stitch makes the body. It is a very feminine motif. Eyelet butterflies would be a perfect addition to garments for girls or a women's summer sweater. Combined with a floral motif, eyelet butterflies would be pretty in a shawl.

level ● ● ●
drape ▥ ▥

THE PATTERN

Multiple of 10

Row 1 (WS): Purl.

Row 2: * K2tog, yo, k1, yo, sl 1, k1, psso, k5. Repeat from * to end of row.

Row 3: * P7, sl 1 pwise, p2. Repeat from * to end of row.

Row 4: * K2tog, yo, k1, yo, sl 1, k1, psso, k5. Repeat from * to end of row.

Row 5: * P7, sl 1 pwise, p2. Repeat from * to end of row.

Row 6: Knit.

Row 7: Purl.

Row 8: * K5, k2tog, yo, k1, yo, sl 1, k1, psso. Repeat from * to end of row.

Row 9: * P2, sl 1 pwise, p7. Repeat from * to end of row.

Row 10: * K5, k2tog, yo, k1, yo, sl 1, k1, psso. Repeat from * to end of row.

Row 11: * P2, sl 1 pwise, p7. Repeat from * to end of row.

Row 12: Knit.

Repeat rows 1–12.

FERN LACE

Fern lace is a diamond-shaped lace motif where the decreases form a lattice-like outline around the yarn overs. It is a nice motif worked in any weight of yarn. Fern lace is perfectly shaped for triangular shawls, but is also lovely for sweaters, stoles, scarves, and blankets.

level

drape

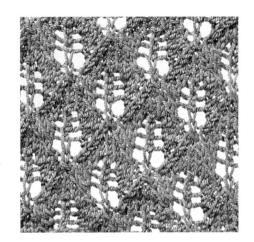

THE PATTERN

Multiple of 10 + 1

Row 1 and all odd numbered rows (WS): Purl.

Row 2: K3, * k2tog, yo, k1, yo, ssk, k5. Repeat from * to end of row, ending last repeat k3.

Row 4: K2, * k2tog, [k1, yo] twice, k1, ssk, k3. Repeat from * to end of row, ending last repeat k2.

Row 6: K1, * k2tog, k2, yo, k1, yo, k2, ssk, k1. Repeat from * to end of row.

Row 8: K2tog, * k3, yo, k1, yo, k3, sl 1, k2tog, psso. Repeat from * to last 9 stitches, ending k3, yo, k1, yo, k3, ssk.

Row 10: K1, * yo, ssk, k5, k2tog, yo, k1. Repeat from * to end of row.

Row 12: K1, * yo, k1, ssk, k3, k2tog, k1, yo, k1. Repeat from * to end of row.

Row 14: K1, * yo, k2, ssk, k1, k2tog, k2, yo, k1. Repeat from * to end of row.

Row 16: K1, * yo, k3, sl 1, k2tog, psso, k3, yo, k1. Repeat from * to end of row.

Repeat rows 1–16.

Lace

LOTUS BLOSSOM

Lotus blossom is a Japanese lace motif. It is very delicate in appearance, with open-work on both the right and wrong side rows. The cast-on edge forms a gentle scallop, and the amount of Garter stitch that is worked on the initial rows of the pattern repeat eliminates the necessity for an edge stitch. Lotus blossom lace is perfect for scarves, stoles, shawls, and blankets. It is also ideal for a fancy sweater border.

level ● ● ● ●
drape ▦ ▦ ▦

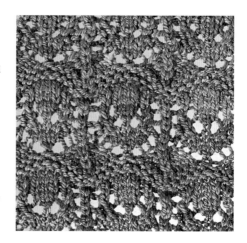

THE PATTERN

Multiple of 10 + 1 stitches

Rows 1, 2, 3, 4, and 5: Knit.

Row 6 (WS): P1, * yo, p3, sl2, p1, p2sso, p3, yo, p1. Repeat from * to end of row.

Row 7: K2, * yo, k2, sl2, k1, p2sso, k2, yo, k3. Repeat from * to end of row, end last repeat k2.

Row 8: P3, * yo, p1, sl2, p1, p2sso, p1, yo, p5. Repeat from * to end of row, end last repeat p3.

Row 9: K4, * yo, sl2, k1, p2sso, yo, k7. Repeat from * to end of row, end last repeat k4.

Row 10: P2, * k2, p3. Repeat from * to end of row, end last repeat p2.

Row 11: K1, * yo, ssk, p1, yo, sl2, k1, p2sso, yo, p1, k2tog, yo, k1. Repeat from * to end of row.

Row 12: P3, * k1, p3, k1, p5. Repeat from * to end of row, end last repeat p3.

Row 13: K2, * yo, ssk, yo, sl2, k1, p2sso, yo, k2tog, yo, k3. Repeat from * to end of row, end last repeat k2.

Row 14: P2, * k1, p5, k1, p3. Repeat from * to end of row, end last repeat p2.

there's more >

Lace

LOTUS BLOSSOM

more > Row 15: K2, * p1, k1, yo, sl2, k1, p2sso, yo, k1, p1, k3. Repeat from * to end of row, end last repeat k2.

Row 16: P2, * k1, p5, k1, p3. Repeat from * to end of row, end last repeat p2.

Repeat rows 1–16.

HORSESHOE LACE

Horseshoe lace is a Bavarian lace pattern that automatically forms a scallop along the cast-on edge. This pattern is easily modified by adding additional purl stitches to the column between horseshoe motifs. With the addition of more purl stitches, the motif acts almost like a ribbing, making a fancy edging for a sweater or other project.

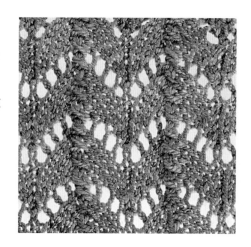

level
drape

THE PATTERN

Multiple of 10 + 1

Row 1 (WS): Purl.

Row 2: K1, * yo, k3, sl 1, k2tog, psso, k3, yo, k1. Repeat from * to end of row.

Row 3: Purl.

Row 4: P1, * k1, yo, k2, sl 1, k2tog, psso, k2, yo, k1, p1. Repeat from * to end of row.

Row 5: K1, * p9, k1. Repeat from * to end of row.

Row 6: P1, * k2, yo, k1, sl 1, k2tog, psso, k1, yo, k2, p1. Repeat from * to end of row.

Row 7: K1, * p9, k1. Repeat from * to end of row.

Row 8: P1, * k3, yo, sl 1, k2tog, psso, yo, k3, p1. Repeat from * to end of row.

Repeat rows 1–8.

Lace

CAT'S PAW

Cat's paw is a traditional Shetland lace pattern that also surfaces in Russian and Estonian lace work. It is a knitted lace, meaning the wrong side rows are purled rather than having openwork. Cat's paw makes an excellent filler stitch for the center of a shawl, scarf, or blanket. It would also work in a sweater. Because is it a simple motif, the wrong side purl rows can be changed to knits to create a Garter stitch background.

level
drape

THE PATTERN

Multiple of 11

Row 1 and all odd numbered rows (WS): Purl.

Row 2: * K3, k2tog, yo, k1, yo, k2tog tbl, k3. Repeat from * to end of row.

Row 4: * K2, k2tog, yo, k3, yo, k2tog tbl, k2. Repeat from * to end of row.

Row 6: * K4, yo, sl 1, k2tog, psso, yo, k4. Repeat from * to end of row.

Repeat rows 1-6.

Lace

45

LACE ARCS

Lace arcs is a lace pattern, reminiscent of French rococo architecture, with arcing lacy columns. The motif forms delicate vertical lines with a naturally scalloped cast-on edge. Lace arcs is an elegant pattern for sweaters because it is not too open. It would also look nice in scarf or stole patterns.

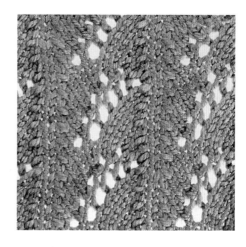

level ● ● ●
drape ▦ ▦ ▦

THE PATTERN

Multiple of 11 + 1

Row 1 and all odd numbered rows (WS): Purl.

Row 2: * K1, k2tog, k4, [yo, k1] twice, ssk. Repeat from * to last stitch, end k1.

Row 4: * K1, k2tog, k3, yo, k1, yo, k2, ssk. Repeat from * to last stitch, end k1.

Row 6: * K1, k2tog, k2, yo, k1, yo, k3, ssk. Repeat from * to last stitch, end k1.

Row 8: * K1, k2tog, [k1, yo] twice, k4, ssk. Repeat from * to last stitch, end k1.

Row 10: * K1, k2tog, yo, k1, yo, k5, ssk. Repeat from * to last stitch, end k1.

Repeat rows 1–10.

CLIMBING VINE

Climbing vine is a knit-
ted lace pattern with a
strong central zigzag
vine scattered with eyelet
leaves. The pattern is
very linear in appear-
ance, making it well
suited for rectangular or
square-shaped projects
like stoles, scarves, or
blankets. Climbing vine
would also create an
elegant summer shell or
lightweight cardigan.

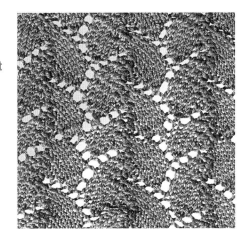

level

drape

THE PATTERN

Multiple of 11 + 1

Row 1 and all odd numbered rows (WS): Purl.

Row 2: K2tog, * k5, yo, k1, yo, k2, sl 1, k2tog, psso. Repeat
from * to end of row, end last repeat ssk.

Row 4: K2tog, * k4, yo, k3, yo, k1, sl 1, k2tog, psso. Repeat
from * to end of row, end last repeat ssk.

Row 6: K2tog, * k3, yo, k5, yo, sl 1, k2tog, psso. Repeat from *
to end of row, end last repeat ssk.

Row 8: K2tog, * k2, yo, k1, yo, k5, sl 1, k2tog, psso. Repeat
from * to end of row, end last repeat ssk.

Row 10: K2tog, * k1, yo, k3, yo, k4, sl 1, k2tog, psso. Repeat
from * to end of row, end last repeat ssk.

Row 12: K2tog, * yo, k5, yo, k3, sl 1, k2tog, psso. Repeat from
* to end of row, end last repeat ssk.

Repeat rows 1–12.

FALLING LEAVES LACE

Falling leaves lace is reminiscent of leaves drifting down from a tree. It makes liberal use of some less common double decreases (k3tog and sssk). This beautiful stitch pattern would be nice incorporated into a sweater or shawl. Falling leaves lace would also work well into a scarf or stole design.

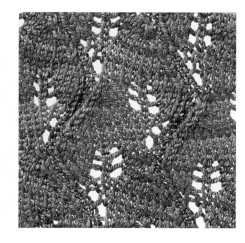

level ● ● ●
drape ▓ ▓ ▓

THE PATTERN

Multiple of 12

Row 1 (RS): * P1, k2, yo, k1, yo, k4, k3tog, p1. Repeat from * to end of row.

Rows 2, 4, 6, 14, 16, and 18: * K1, p10, k1. Repeat from * to end of row.

Row 3: * P1, k3, yo, k1, yo, k3, k3tog, p1. Repeat from * to end of row.

Row 5: * P1, k4, yo, k1, yo, k2, k3tog, p1. Repeat from * to end of row.

Rows 7, 9, and 11: * P1, ssk, k8, yo, p1. Repeat from * to end of row.

Rows 8, 10, and 12: * K1, p9, p tbl, k1. Repeat from * to end of row.

Row 13: * P1, sssk, k4, yo, k1, yo, k2, p1. Repeat from * to end of row.

Row 15: * P1, sssk, k3, yo, k1, yo, k3, p1. Repeat from * to end of row.

Row 17: * P1, sssk, k2, yo, k1, yo, k4, p1. Repeat from * to end of row.

Rows 19, 21, and 23: * P1, yo, k8, k2tog, p1. Repeat from * to end of row.

Rows 20, 22, and 24: * K1, p tbl, p9, k1. Repeat from * to end of row.

Repeat rows 1–24.

CREST OF THE WAVE

Crest of the wave is a traditional Shetland lace pattern. The columns of yarn overs and decreases make the Garter stitch ridges resemble ocean waves, and the cast-on edge scallops. There is just enough Garter stitch in this pattern to prevent the side edges from curling, so no additional edge stitch is necessary. Crest of the wave is perfect for scarves or stoles. It would also be striking to use in a sweater design.

level

drape

THE PATTERN

Multiple of 12 + 1

Rows 1 and 3 (RS): Knit.

Rows 2 and 4: Knit.

Row 5: K1 * k2tog twice, [yo, k1] 3 times, yo, ssk twice, k1. Repeat from * to end of row.

Row 6: Purl.

Row 7: K1 * k2tog twice, [yo, k1] 3 times, yo, ssk twice, k1. Repeat from * to end of row.

Row 8: Purl.

Row 9: K1 * k2tog twice, [yo, k1] 3 times, yo, ssk twice, k1. Repeat from * to end of row.

Row 10: Purl.

Row 11: K1 * k2tog twice, [yo, k1] 3 times, yo, ssk twice, k1. Repeat from * to end of row.

Row 12: Purl.

Repeat rows 1–12.

MADEIRA LEAF PATTERN

Madeira leaf pattern is a traditional Spanish lace pattern. It is a lace knitting pattern—the openwork is worked on every row. The structure causes the edges to scallop dramatically. Madeira leaf pattern would be perfect for shawls or stoles. It would also make an elegant edge to a fine-gauge sweater.

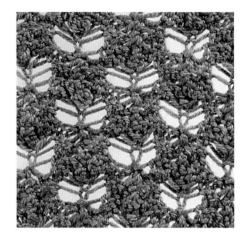

level ● ● ●
drape ▥ ▥ ▥

THE PATTERN

Multiple of 12 + 5

Rows 1-6: K2, * k1, yo, k4, p3tog, k4, yo. Repeat from * to last 3 sts, end k3.

Rows 7-12: K2, p2tog, * k4, yo, k1, yo, k4, p3tog. Repeat from * to last 13 sts, end k4, yo, k1, yo, k4, p2tog, k2.

Repeat rows 1–12.

BLOCK LACE

Block lace is a nice interweaving, geometric knitted-lace motif. The finished project resembles fancy tile work. This is a nice pattern for rectangular projects—scarves, stoles, or blankets—that mirror the lace motif. It would also be attractive used in a cardigan design.

level ● ● ●

drape ● ● ●

THE PATTERN

Multiple of 14 + 3

Row 1 and all odd numbered rows (WS): Purl.

Row 2: K2, * k2tog, yo, k1, yo, ssk, k3, k2tog, yo, k4. Repeat from * to last stitch, end k1.

Row 4: K1, * k2tog, yo, k3, yo, ssk, k1, k2tog, yo, k4. Repeat from * to last 2 stitches, end k2.

Row 6: K2tog, yo, * k5, yo, sl 1, k2tog, psso, yo, k4, k2tog, yo. Repeat from * to last stitch, end k1.

Row 8: K2, * yo, ssk, k4, yo, ssk, k3, k2tog, yo, k1. Repeat from * to last stitch, end k1.

Row 10: K3, * yo, ssk, k4, yo, ssk, k1, k2tog, yo, k3. Repeat from * to end of row.

Row 12: K4, * yo, ssk, k4, yo, k3tog, yo, k5. Repeat from * to end of row, end last repeat k4.

Repeat rows 1-12.

PEACOCK FEATHERS

Peacock feathers is a Shetland lace pattern in the Old shale lace (page 61) family. The groupings of increases and decreases pull the knitted fabric into gentle curves. Peacock feathers is lovely for shawls or scarves. It is also quite nice in heavier yarns, so it works well for sweaters or mitten cuffs. Because the knitting scallops, this pattern can work with variegated yarns.

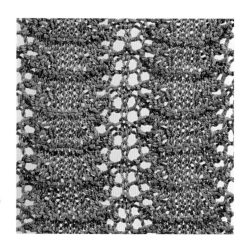

level ● ●
drape ▥ ▥ ▥

THE PATTERN

Multiple of 15

Row 1 (WS): Knit.

Row 2: * K1, ssk twice, [k1, yo] 4 times, k1, k2tog twice, k1. Repeat from * to end of row.

Row 3: Purl.

Row 4: * K1, ssk twice, [k1, yo] 4 times, k1, k2tog twice, k1. Repeat from * to end of row.

Row 5: Purl.

Row 6: Knit.

Repeat rows 1–6.

FLOWING ARROWS

Flowing arrows is a knitted lace pattern where the increases and decreases shape the knitting into a gently undulating arrow motif. Because of the shaping, this pattern can work well with variegated yarns. Flowing arrows is a good pattern stitch for sweaters, socks, and other accessories. It would also work nicely in a rectangular stole or scarf pattern with the addition of a fancy edge stitch.

level

drape

THE PATTERN

Multiple of 15 +1

Row 1 and all odd numbered rows (WS): Purl.

Row 2: K1, * yo, k2, ssk, k6, k2tog, k2, yo, k1. Repeat from * to end of row.

Row 4: K1, * k1, yo, k2, ssk, k4, k2tog, k2, yo, k2. Repeat from * to end of row.

Row 6: K1, * k2, yo, k2, ssk, k2, k2tog, k2, yo, k3. Repeat from * to end of row.

Row 8: K1, * k3, yo, k2, ssk, k2tog, k2, yo, k4. Repeat from * to end of row.

Repeat rows 1–8.

GENTLE CURVES

Gentle curves is a knitted lace pattern filled with columns of paired decreases that swirl the knitting ever so slightly. This pattern is actually a lace pattern that can work well with variegated yarns. Gentle curves is more solid than many of the openwork patterns. It works quite well in projects like sweaters or socks.

level ● ● ●
drape ▥ ▥

THE PATTERN

Multiple of 15 + 2

Row 1 (RS): K1, * yo, k1, yo, k4, k2tog twice, k6. Repeat from * to last stitch, end k1.

Row 2 and other even numbered rows: Purl.

Row 3: K1, * k1, yo, k1, yo, k3, k2tog twice, k6. Repeat from * to last stitch, end k1.

Row 5: K1, * k2, yo, k1, yo, k2, k2tog twice, k6. Repeat from * to last stitch, end k1.

Row 7: K1, * k3, yo, k1, yo, k1, k2tog twice, k6. Repeat from * to last stitch, end k1.

Row 9: K1, * k4, yo, k1, yo, k2tog twice, k6. Repeat from * to last stitch, end k1.

Row 11: K1, * k5, yo, k1, k2tog, k7. Repeat from * to last stitch, end k1.

Row 13: K1, * k6, yo, k2tog, k7. Repeat from * to last stitch, end k1.

Row 15: K1, * k6, yo, k2tog, k7. Repeat from * to last stitch, end k1.

Row 17: Knit.

Row 19: K1, * k6, ssk twice, k4, yo, k1, yo. Repeat from * to last stitch, end k1.

Lace

there's more >

GENTLE CURVES

more >   Row 21: K1, * k6, ssk twice, k3, yo, k1, yo, k1. Repeat from * to last stitch, end k1.

Row 23: K1, * k6, ssk twice, k2, yo, k1, yo, k2. Repeat from * to last stitch, end k1.

Row 25: K1, * k6, ssk twice, k1, yo, k1, yo, k3. Repeat from * to last stitch, end k1.

Row 27: K1, * k6, ssk twice, yo, k1, yo, k4. Repeat from * to last stitch, end k1.

Row 29: K1, * k7, ssk, k1, yo, k5. Repeat from * to last stitch, end k1.

Row 31: K1,* k7, ssk, yo, k6. Repeat from * to last stitch, end k1.

Row 33: K1, * k7, ssk, yo, k6. Repeat from * to last stitch, end k1.

Row 35: Knit.

Repeat rows 1–36.

FEATHER AND FAN PLUMES

Feather and fan plumes
is another variation
on the Old shale lace
pattern (page 61). It is
a Shetland lace pattern
in which the motif is
offset every 16 rows,
completely changing the
appearance of the knitted
fabric. This is a beautiful
stitch pattern for
shawls, stoles, or
scarves. It would also
make up into a stunning
dressy sweater.

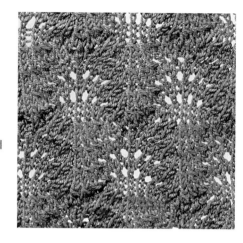

level ● ● ●
drape ▥ ▥ ▥

THE PATTERN

Multiple of 16 + 1

Row 1 and all odd numbered rows (WS): Purl.

Row 2: Knit.

Row 4: [K1, yo] 3 times, * ssk twice, sl 2, k1, p2sso, k2tog twice, [yo, k1] 5 times, yo. Repeat from * to last 14 stitches, end ssk twice, sl 2, k1, p2sso, k2tog twice, [yo, k1] 3 times.

Row 6: Knit.

Row 8: [K1, yo] 3 times, * ssk twice, sl 2, k1, p2sso, k2tog twice, [yo, k1] 5 times, yo. Repeat from * to last 14 stitches, end ssk twice, sl 2, k1, p2sso, k2tog twice, [yo, k1] 3 times.

Row 10: Knit.

Row 12: [K1, yo] 3 times, * ssk twice, sl 2, k1, p2sso, k2tog twice, [yo, k1] 5 times, yo. Repeat from * to last 14 stitches, end ssk twice, sl 2, k1, p2sso, k2tog twice, [yo, k1] 3 times.

Row 14: Knit.

Row 16: [K1, yo] 3 times, * ssk twice, sl 2, k1, p2sso, k2tog twice, [yo, k1] 5 times, yo. Repeat from * to last 14 stitches, end ssk twice, sl 2, k1, p2sso, k2tog twice, [yo, k1] 3 times.

Row 18: Knit.

Row 20: K2tog 3 times, * [yo, k1] 5 times, yo, ssk twice, sl 2, k1, p2sso, k2tog twice. Repeat from * to last 11 stitches, end [yo, k1] 5 times, yo, ssk 3 times.

there's more >

Lace

FEATHER AND FAN PLUMES

more >

Row 22: Knit.

Row 24: K2tog 3 times, * [yo, k1] 5 times, yo, ssk twice, sl 2, k1, p2sso, k2tog twice. Repeat from * to last 11 stitches, end [yo, k1] 5 times, yo, ssk 3 times.

Row 26: Knit.

Row 28: K2tog 3 times, * [yo, k1] 5 times, yo, ssk twice, sl 2, k1, p2sso, k2tog twice. Repeat from * to last 11 stitches, end [yo, k1] 5 times, yo, ssk 3 times.

Row 30: Knit.

Row 32: K2tog 3 times, * [yo, k1] 5 times, yo, ssk twice, sl 2, k1, p2sso, k2tog twice. Repeat from * to last 11 stitches, end [yo, k1] 5 times, yo, ssk 3 times.

Repeat rows 1–32.

Lace

ART DECO ARCHES

Art deco arches is a very ornate lace pattern. The combination of twisted stitches and lace creates a refined and elegant pattern. It would make a stunning sweater or pair of socks. Art deco arches would also be a magnificent addition to a shawl design.

level ◉ ◉ ◉ ◉
drape ▦ ▦

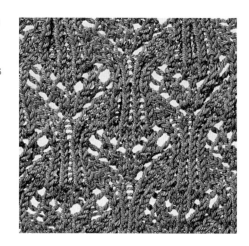

THE PATTERN

Multiple of 16 + 1

Row 1 (WS): K1, * p1 tbl, k1, p11, k1, p1 tbl, k1. Repeat from * to end of row.

Row 2: K1, * yo, k3, k2tog, p1, k1 tbl, p1, k1 tbl, p1, ssk, k3, yo, k1. Repeat from * to end of row.

Row 3: P1, * p5, k1, p1 tbl, k1, p1 tbl, k1, p6. Repeat from * to end of row.

Row 4: K1, * k1, yo, k2, k2tog, p1, k1 tbl, p1, k1 tbl, p1, ssk, k2, yo, k2. Repeat from * to end of row.

Row 5: P1, * p5, k1, p1 tbl, k1, p1 tbl, k1, p6. Repeat from * to end of row.

Row 6: K1, * k2, yo, k1, k2tog, p1, k1 tbl, p1, k1 tbl, p1, ssk, k1, yo, k3. Repeat from * to end of row.

Row 7: P1, * p5, k1, p1 tbl, k1, p1 tbl, k1, p6. Repeat from * to end of row.

Row 8: K1, * yo, ssk, k1, yo, k2tog, p1, k1 tbl, p1, k1 tbl, p1, ssk, yo, k1, k2tog, yo, k1. Repeat from * to end of row.

Row 9: P1, * p5, k1, p1 tbl, k1, p1 tbl, k1, p6. Repeat from * to end of row.

Row 10: K1, * k1, yo, ssk, yo, k2tog, p1, k1 tbl, p1, k1 tbl, p1, ssk, yo, k2tog, yo, k2. Repeat from * to end of row.

there's more >

ART DECO ARCHES

more >

Row 11: P1, * p5, k1, p1 tbl, k1, p1 tbl, k1, p6. Repeat from * to end of row.

Row 12: K1, * k3, yo, k2tog, p1, k1 tbl, p1, k1 tbl, p1, ssk, yo, k4. Repeat from * to end of row.

Row 13: P1, * p5, k1, p1 tbl, k1, p1 tbl, k1, p6. Repeat from * to end of row.

Row 14: P1, * k1 tbl, p1, ssk, k3, yo, k1, yo, k3, k2tog, p1, k1 tbl, p1. Repeat from * to end of row.

Row 15: K1, * p1 tbl, k1, p11, k1, p1 tbl, k1. Repeat from * to end of row.

Row 16: P1, * k1 tbl, p1, ssk, k2, yo, k3, yo, k2, k2tog, p1, k1 tbl, p1. Repeat from * to end of row.

Row 17: K1, * p1 tbl, k1, p11, k1, p1 tbl, k1. Repeat from * to end of row.

Row 18: P1, * k1 tbl, p1, ssk, k1, yo, k5, yo, k1, k2tog, p1, k1 tbl, p1. Repeat from * to end of row.

Row 19: K1, * p1 tbl, k1, p11, k1, p1 tbl, k1. Repeat from * to end of row.

Row 20: P1, * k1 tbl, p1, ssk, yo, k1, k2tog, yo, k1, yo, ssk, k1, yo, k2tog, p1, k1 tbl, p1. Repeat from * to end of row.

Row 21: K1, * p1 tbl, k1, p11, k1, p1 tbl, k1. Repeat from * to end of row.

Row 22: P1, * k1 tbl, p1, ssk, yo, k2tog, yo, k3, yo, ssk, yo, k2tog, p1, k1 tbl, p1. Repeat from * to end of row.

Row 23: K1, * p1 tbl, k1, p11, k1, p1 tbl, k1. Repeat from * to end of row.

Row 24: P1, * k1 tbl, p1, ssk, yo, k7, yo, k2tog, p1, k1 tbl, p1. Repeat from * to end of row.

Repeat rows 1–24.

FLYING V'S

Flying V's is a basic lace chevron pattern. The strong lace V's are separated by a small faggoting stitch panel. Flying V's would make a striking addition to any shawl, stole, or blanket design. It would also be an attractive pattern worked into the border of a sweater.

level ◉ ◉ ◉
drape ▩ ▩ ▩

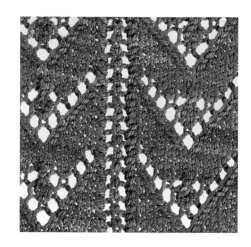

THE PATTERN

Multiple of 17 + 1

Row 1 (WS): Purl.

Row 2: K1, * [yo, ssk, k4, k2tog] twice, yo, k1. Repeat from * to end of row.

Row 3: Purl.

Row 4: K1, * [yo, ssk, k3, k2tog, yo, k1] twice. Repeat from * to end of row.

Row 5: Purl.

Row 6: K1, * yo, ssk, k2, k2tog, yo, k3, yo, ssk, k2, k2tog, yo, k1. Repeat from * to end of row.

Row 7: Purl.

Row 8: K1, * yo, ssk, k1, k2tog, yo, k1, yo, k3tog, yo, k1, yo, ssk, k1, k2tog, yo, k1. Repeat from * to end of row.

Row 9: P8, * inc 1, p15. Repeat from * to end of row, ending the last repeat p8.

Row 10: K1, * yo, ssk, k2tog, yo, k8, yo, ssk, k2tog, yo, k1. Repeat from * to end of row.

Row 11: Purl.

Row 12: K1, * yo, sl 1, k2tog, psso, yo, k10, yo, k3tog, yo, k1. Repeat from * to end of row.

Repeat rows 1–12.

Note: On row 2, you will be decreasing one stitch per pattern repeat. On row 9, you will return to the original stitch count.

OLD SHALE LACE

Old shale lace, also known as Feather and fan lace, is a classic Shetland lace pattern that is seen in several variations. The cast-on edge scallops gently because of the way the increases and decreases align vertically. There is just enough Garter stitch built into the pattern so that it works as an edge stitch, say for the border of a sweater. It also makes excellent scarves, shawls, or blankets. Old shale lace works well knitted at the recommended gauge for the yarn or more loosely as desired.

level

drape

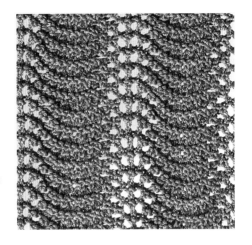

THE PATTERN

Multiple of 18 + 1

Row 1 (RS): Knit.

Row 2: Purl.

Row 3: K1, * k2tog 3 times, [yo, k1] 5 times, yo, k2tog 3 times, k1. Repeat from * to end of row.

Row 4: Knit.

Repeat rows 1–4.

Needle Size Chart

Metric (mm)	US	UK/CAN
2	0	14
2.25	1	13
2.5		
2.75	2	12
3		11
3.25	3	10
3.5	4	
3.75	5	9
4	6	8
4.5	7	7
5	8	6
5.5	9	5
6	10	4
6.5	10 ½	3
8	11	0
9	13	00
10	15	000
12.75	17	
15	19	
19	35	

Abbreviations and Glossary

C3 over 4: Slip 4 stitches to the cable needle and hold to the back of the work. Knit the next 3 stitches, then purl 1 stitch from the cable needle, then knit the remaining stitches from the cable needle.

C6: Slip 2 stitches onto the cable needle and hold to the front of the work, slip 2 stitches onto a second cable needle and hold to the back of the work, k2, p2 from the second cable needle, k2 from the first cable needle.

CB2: Slip 1 stitch to the cable needle and hold to the back of the work. Knit the next stitch, then knit the stitch from the cable needle.

CB3: Slip 1 stitch to the cable needle and hold to the back of the work. Knit the next 2 stitches, then knit the stitch from the cable needle.

CB4: Slip 2 stitchcs to thc cablc nccdle and hold to the back of the work. Knit the next 2 stitches, then knit the stitches from the cable needle.

CB5: Slip 3 stitches to the cable needle and hold to the back of the work. Knit the next 2 stitches, then knit the stitches from the cable needle.

CB6: Slip 3 stitches to the cable needle and hold to the back of the work. Knit the next 3 stitches, then knit the stitches from the cable needle.

CB8: Slip 4 stitches to the cable needle and hold to the back of the work. Knit the next 4 stitches, then knit the stitches from the cable needle.

CF2 over 3: Slip the next 3 stitches to the cable needle and hold to the back of the work. Knit the next 2 stitches, then p1, k2 from the cable needle.

CF2: Slip 1 stitch to the cable needle and hold to the front of the work. Knit the next stitch, then knit the stitch from the cable needle.

CF3: Slip 2 stitches to the cable needle and hold to the front of the work. Knit the next stitch, then knit the stitches from the cable needle.

CF4: Slip 2 stitches to the cable needle and hold to the front of the work. Knit the next 2 stitches, then knit the stitches from the cable needle.

Yarn Chart

YARN WEIGHT SYMBOL & CATEGORY NAMES	0 lace	1 super fine	2 fine	3 light	4 medium	5 bulky	6 super bulky
TYPE OF YARNS IN CATEGORY	Fingering, 10-count crochet thread	Sock, Fingering, Baby	Sport, Baby	DK, Light Worsted	Worsted, Afghan, Aran	Chunky, Craft, Rug	Bulky, Roving

Source: Craft Yarn Council of America's www.YarnStandards.com

Lace

CF6: Slip 3 stitches to the cable needle and hold to the front of the work. Knit the next 3 stitches, then knit the stitches from the cable needle.

CF8: Slip 4 stitches to the cable needle and hold to the front of the work. Knit the next 4 stitches, then knit the stitches from the cable needle.

Cn: Cable needle.

DI: Double increase as follows: [k1 tbl, k1] into the next stitch, then insert the left-hand needle behind the vertical strand that runs downward from between the 2 stitches just made and k1 tbl into this strand to create the third stitch.

Inc 1 pwise: Increase 1 stitch purlwise by purling into the front and the back of the next stitch.

Inc 1: Increase 1 stitch by knitting into the front and the back of the next stitch.

K: Knit.

K1b: Knit the next stitch in the row below.

K2tog: Knit 2 stitches together.

K3tog: Knit 3 stitches together.

K4tog: Knit 4 stitches together.

K tbl: Knit through the back of the loop. If the k is followed by a number, knit that many stitches through the back loop. For example, k3 tbl means knit 3 stitches (1 at a time) through the back loops.

Kwise: Knitwise.

LH: Left hand.

LT: Left twist. Knit into the back of the second stitch on the left-hand needle. Do not drop it from the left-hand needle. Knit into the front of the first stitch on the left-hand needle. Drop off both stitches from the left-hand needle. For a left twist on the wrong side of the work, simply purl the stitches instead of knitting them.

LTP: Purl through the back of the second stitch on the left-hand needle without removing it from the needle, then knit the first stitch on the left-hand needle, slipping both stitches off of the needle at the same time. If this is difficult to work, you can use a T1L1 in its place.

M1: Pick up the horizontal strand of yarn lying between the stitch just worked and the next stitch on the left-hand needle from front to back and knit into the back of it. Also referred to as M1 kwise because the new stitch is a knit stitch.

M2: Pick up the horizontal strand of yarn lying between the stitch just worked and the next stitch on the left-hand needle from front to back and knit into the back and the front of it, creating 2 new stitches.

MB (make bobble): [K1, yo, k1, yo, k1] into the next stitch on the left-hand needle. Turn work. Purl 5. Turn work. Knit 5. Turn work. P2tog, k1, p2tog. Turn work. Sl 1, k2tog, psso. Bobble is complete.

P: Purl.

P2sso: Pass 2 slipped stitches over.

P tbl: Purl through the back loop. If the p is followed by a number, purl that many stitches through the back loop. For example, p3 tbl means purl 3 stitches (1 at a time) through the back loops.

P2tog tbl: Purl 2 stitches together through the back loops. If your knitting is too tight to comfortably purl 2 stitches together through the back loops, try working an ssp in place of p2tog tbl. While it is not exactly the same decrease, it is very close.

P2tog: Purl 2 stitches together.

P3tog: Purl 3 stitches together.

Psso: Pass slipped stitch over.

Pwise: Purlwise.

RH: Right hand.

RS: Right side.

RT: Right twist. Knit into the second stitch on the left-hand needle. Do not drop it from the left-hand needle. Knit into the first stitch on the left-hand needle. Drop both stitches from the left-hand needle. For a right twist on the wrong side of the work, simply purl the stitches instead of knitting them.

RTP: Knit into the front of the second stitch on the left-hand needle without removing it from the needle, then purl the first stitch on the left-hand needle, slipping both stitches off the needle at the same time.

S5: Slip the next 5 stitches onto a cable needle (or short double-pointed needle) and hold to the front of the work. Wind the yarn counter-clockwise twice around the stitches on the cable needle, then work the stitches from the cable needle as k1, p3, k1.

Lace

Sl 1: Slip 1 stitch. When slipping stitches, it is customary to slip them purlwise unless working a decrease, when they are normally slipped knitwise. Individual instructions should indicate which direction to slip stitches.

Sl 2: Slip 2 stitches as if to k2tog.

Ssk: Working 1 stitch at a time, slip 2 stitches from the left-hand needle to the right-hand needle as if to knit. Insert the left-hand needle into the back of the 2 slipped stitches on the right-hand needle and knit the stitches together.

Ssp: Working 1 stitch at a time, slip 2 stitches from the left-hand needle to the right-hand needle as if to knit. Insert the left-hand needle into the back of the 2 slipped stitches on the right-hand needle and purl the stitches together.

Sssk: Working 1 stitch at a time, slip 3 stitches from the left-hand needle to the right-hand needle as if to knit. Insert the left-hand needle into the back of the 3 slipped stitches on the right-hand needle and knit the stitches together.

T1L1 (travel 1 stitch to the left 1 stitch): Slip 1 stitch to the cable needle and hold to the front of the work. Purl the next stitch, then knit the stitches from the cable needle.

T1L2 (travel 1 stitch to the left 2 stitches): Slip 1 stitch to the cable needle and hold to the front of the work. Knit the next 2 stitches, then knit the stitch from the cable needle.

T1R1 (travel 1 stitch to the right 1 stitch): Slip 1 stitch to the cable needle and hold to the back of the work. Knit the next 1 stitch, then purl the stitch from the cable needle.

T1R2 (travel 1 stitch to the right 2 stitch-es): Slip 2 stitches to the cable needle and hold to the back of the work. Knit the next stitch, then knit the stitches from the cable needle.

T2L1 (travel 2 stitches to the left 1 stitch): Slip 2 stitches to the cable needle and hold to the front of the work. Purl the next stitch, then knit the stitches from the cable needle.

T2L2 (travel 2 stitches to the left 2 stitch-es): Slip 2 stitches to the cable needle and hold to the front of the work. Purl the next 2 stitches, then knit the stitches from the cable needle.

T2R1 (travel 2 stitches to the right 1 stitch): Slip 1 stitch to the cable needle and hold to the back of the work. Knit the next 2 stitches, then purl the stitch from the cable needle.

T2R2 (travel 2 stitches to the right 2 stitch-es): Slip 2 stitches to the cable needle and hold to the back of the work. Knit the next 2 stitches, then purl the stitches from the cable needle.

T3L1 (travel 3 stitches to the left 1 stitch): Slip 3 stitches to the cable needle and hold to the front of the work. Purl the next stitch, then knit the stitches from the cable needle.

T3L2 (travel 3 stitches to the left 2 stitches): Slip 3 stitches to the cable needle and hold to the front of the work. Purl the next 2 stitches, then knit the stitches from the cable needle.

T3R1 (travel 3 stitches to the right 1 stitch): Slip 1 stitch to the cable needle and hold to the back of the work. Knit the next 3 stitches, then purl the stitches from the cable needle.

T3R2 (travel 3 stitches to the right 2 stitch-es): Slip 2 stitches to the cable needle and hold to the back of the work. Knit the next 3 stitches, then purl the stitches from the cable needle.

T4L2 (travel 4 stitches to the left 2 stitches): Slip 4 stitches to the cable needle and hold to the front of the work. Purl the next 2 stitches, then knit the stitches from the cable needle.

T4R2 (travel 4 stitches to the right 2 stitch-es): Slip 2 stitches to the cable needle and hold to the back of the work. Knit the next 4 stitches, then purl the stitches from the cable needle.

T8B RIB: Slip the next 4 stitches onto the cable needle and hold to back of the work, k1, p2, k1 from the left-hand needle, then k1, p2, k1 from the cable needle.

T8F RIB: Slip the next 4 stitches onto the cable needle and hold to front of the work, k1, p2, k1 from the left-hand needle, then k1, p2, k1 from the cable needle.

WS: Wrong side.

Wyib: With yarn in back of work.

Wyif: With yarn in front of work.

Yo: Yarn over.

Cables

Welcome to The Stitch Collection—a set of handy little guides to knit stitches that are as portable as can be; pick and choose which ones to throw into your knitting bag when you're on the go, and leave the others at home in the case. By design, they are not complete guides to knitting; instead, they are mini-encyclopedias of the stitches themselves. Their purpose is to help you choose the best stitch pattern for your projects.

Like most stitch guides, these books are written in terms of knitting flat—knitting back and forth on the needles, turning after each row. The set is divided into five volumes. Book 1 covers the knit and purl stitches; Book 2 focuses on rib stitches; Book 3 contains lace stitches; Book 4 is all about cables; and Book 5 is a compilation of specialty stitches. Each booklet has some common introductory material to help you determine which pattern you want to use, followed by text that is specific to that book's category of stitch. Each individual stitch pattern is ranked according to its level of difficulty, its drape, and offers suggestions as to its best function in a project (as an overall stitch, a filler stitch, a panel stitch, or an edge stitch).

Cables

2

CHOOSING A STITCH PATTERN

The following sections give you suggestions on how to best use the guides in the set.

Look Before You Swatch

When choosing a stitch pattern to use for a project, be sure to look through all the books. Some patterns are included in one category, but have traits that overlap with the others. It's important to read through a pattern before starting it, too. Often an instruction can seem confusing or intimidating on paper, but will make complete sense when you have the knitting in hand and are ready to work that portion of the pattern.

fingering

Next, make a swatch. The swatches in this book are knit in varying weights of wool (worsted, sport, and fingering) provided by Lorna's Laces. In general, the patterns with small stitch multiples (less than 8 or 10) and panels are knit with Shepherd Worsted; the larger stitch multiples are done in Shepherd Sport. A few of the very large stitch repeats in Book 1 and Book 3 are worked in Shepherd Sock. The swatches have been blocked minimally for photography, and thus you may occasionally note irregularities that are inherent in hand knitting.

sport

worsted

The appearance and drape of the stitch pattern will depend on the yarn chosen—color, style of spinning, fiber content, and weight—and on the gauge used. Keep in mind that large stitch motifs can overwhelm small projects, and small stitch motifs might be lost on a large project. Scale is important. Changing the weight of yarn and gauge it is knit at can help reduce or enlarge a motif as desired. The photos on this page show an example of the Tulip lace pattern knit with three different weights of yarn at three different gauges. The appearance of the pattern changes in each case and stresses the importance of swatching.

Cables

Follow the Organization

Each book is organized from smallest stitch multiple to largest, making it easier to find the pattern that best suits the project you have in mind. A small-scale lace pattern is better for a baby sweater than a large-scale one, for instance.

Match the Pattern to the Purpose

The descriptions included with each stitch pattern also suggest the type of project for which it is best suited. Many of the descriptions also indicate whether it works well as an overall stitch, a filler stitch, a panel stitch, or an edge stitch. An overall stitch pattern is used throughout the full project rather than in just a small area. You can convert patterns presented as panels into an overall stitch pattern by simply working one or more stitches (usually Stockinette or Reverse Stockinette) between repeats of the panel.

Filler stitches are worked in small areas of a larger project to fill open space. Filler stitches appear in between panels of other stitches or as a panel themselves. Filler stitches often have a small multiple and are easier to use in sizing and shaping. When combining filler stitches with other stitches (panels or overall patterns), always check the gauge of each stitch pattern. They can vary widely, even on the same needles with the same yarn.

A panel pattern is intended to be a section of a larger project. Most often, panels are just the stitch pattern itself, and the knitter needs to add border or background stitches. Panels can be worked as either a stitch multiple, by themselves, or combined with other panels or stitch patterns. Cables are very often written as a panel, for instance.

Lastly, edge or border stitch patterns can be used as filler stitches or overall patterns, but they lie flat and look tidy along the edges, making them suitable for hems, cuffs, or edges on other patterns.

Cables

4

Understand the Ratings

Each stitch pattern in this collection has a skill level and a drape rating. The skill level ratings include easy (basic knitting knowledge required), advanced beginner, intermediate, and experienced. Remember what looks difficult on paper is often easier to understand with the knitting on needles in front of you.

All knitting has at least some amount of drape, so the ratings are relative and are based on using wool at the recommended gauge for the yarn. The ratings are: low (a firmer fabric), medium (reasonable amount of drape), and high (a flowing fabric). In general, the denser the fabric (e.g., more stitches per inch) is with stitches, the less drape it will have. The more open the fabric is (e.g., fewer stitches per inch), the more drape it will have. Cable patterns, for instance, will have less drape than lace patterns. However, drape also depends on the yarn chosen for a project and on the gauge used. Some fibers have more drape than others, and the finer the yarn, the more drape the fabric will have. A tighter gauge will have less drape than a looser gauge.

Understand Stitch Multiples and Balancing Stitches

Stitch patterns are presented with information about the number of stitches required to complete one pattern repeat. For panels, the information is simply how many stitches wide the panel is. For all other patterns, this information is presented as a multiple of stitches, plus any balancing stitches needed. For example, if you want to work six repeats of a pattern, and it requires four stitches and one balancing stitch (multiple of 4 + 1), you would cast on 24 stitches plus one balancing stitch, for a total of 25 stitches.

level
- easy
- advanced beginner
- intermediate
- experienced

drape
- low
- medium
- high

Cables

5

Add Selvage Stitches

The patterns in these books do not include selvage stitches, which are one or more spare stitches included at the edge of your knitting for seaming or for tidying the edge. Some knitters don't even use selvage stitches unless specifically directed to do so in a pattern. If you are a knitter who likes to use selvage stitches, you will need to add them to the edges of your projects.

Work Increases and Decreases

These guides use a variety of increases and decreases. It is important to use the correct technique for the increases and decreases called for in the pattern instructions; this insures that your stitch pattern has the proper appearance, as the various techniques create different effects, such as slants or holes. Perhaps the most common increase used in the patterns is done by knitting into the front and back of a single stitch. There are several decreases used in the patterns—some decrease one stitch at a time (single decreases), some decrease two stitches at a time (double decreases), some decrease even more! When a pattern says simply to decrease one stitch, but doesn't say which decrease to use, the assumption is that you will use a k2tog (knit two stitches together) or a p2tog (purl two stitches together), depending on whether you are on the right or wrong side of your work. Consult the Abbreviations and Glossary section (page 62) for explanations of each type of increase or decrease.

CHOOSING
THE BEST YARN

How do you choose the most suitable yarn for a stitch pattern or a project? The first thing to consider is the pattern itself. The busier the stitch pattern is, the simpler the yarn should be, and vice versa. If you want to work a lace pattern or an elaborate cable pattern, choose a smooth, plain-colored yarn. A subtly variegated or kettle-dyed solid yarn might work with a fancy pattern stitch, but a yarn with extreme color changes or striping will detract from the pattern stitch.

Fiber content makes a difference, too. Plant fibers (cotton, linen, hemp, rayon) are inelastic, as is silk. When you work with plant fibers, your knitting tends to be what-you-see-is-what-you-get. Blocking will not improve it.

In contrast, animal fibers are almost magical to knit with, and a good blocking hides a multitude of sins. The fiber has memory and will retain its shape until the next time it gets wet.

Consider Yarn Requirements

Knitting a swatch before beginning a project is important, of course. But when choosing stitch patterns for a project you design, it is useful to consult a reference to see what the estimated yardage requirements are for the size and type of project you are creating at the gauge you are knitting. Yardage requirement tables are usually based on Stockinette stitch, but keep in mind that different stitch patterns require different amounts of yarn. For instance, Garter stitch has a very compressed row gauge, so it will take more yarn than Stockinette stitch. Lace is very open, so it can use less yarn than Stockinette stitch. Cables and many fancy patterns are very dense and can use *much* more yarn than Stockinette stitch.

Cables

7

INTRODUCTION TO CABLES

Cable knitting is most often associated with the traditional knitting of the Aran Isles, where cable patterns, influenced by Celtic culture, were the basis of the warm fishermen's sweaters. Traditional Aran sweaters are composed of panels of cables, hence the reason many cable patterns are written as panels rather than in multiples. The elaborate cables were combined with simpler cables and filler stitches, such as Seed stitch (Book 1, page 15), Moss stitch (Book 1, page 16), and Trinity stitch (Book 5, page 27). This chapter presents a variety of cable stitches, from the traditional to the more modern, from panels to overall stitch patterns.

Cables are formed by twisting sets of stitches over each other, knitting them out of order. Stitches are slipped to a cable needle and held to the front or the back of the knitting, then one or more stitches are worked from the left-hand needle. Finally, the stitches are worked from the cable needle. Holding the cable needle to the back of the work forms a twist to the right, while holding the cable needle to the front of the work forms a twist to the left.

Cable needles usually come in three diameters–small, medium, and large. They are also available in a few different shapes, such as a short double-pointed needle, short double-pointed needle with a bend in the middle, and a fishhook shape. If you don't have a cable needle readily available, a short double-pointed needle can work in its place. Which shape of cable needle to use is simply a matter of preference. All three shapes allow you to work off of both ends, as does a double-pointed needle, which is the underlying purpose. When selecting the cable

Cables

needle size, you will want to use a cable needle that is the same size or smaller than the knitting needles you are using. Cables stretch the stitches just by the process of working them, so a smaller cable needle is better.

Working in all knit stitches forms twists or braids, while combining knit and purl stitches "travels" the cable across the knitting. Cable patterns may be written to start with a wrong-side row. This first row also serves the purpose of being a set-up row—it does the initial placement of the knit and purl stitches before the cabling starts.

In reality, knitting a cable is simple. The trickier part is following the pattern, which can be long and involved. Cable stitches are almost always worked on the right-side rows, with the wrong-side rows be-ing knit the knit stitches and purl the purl stitches. Thus, it is easier to work cable patterns back and forth flat than in the round because the wrong-side rows are readily identifiable and simple to work.

Generally speaking, cable patterns should be knit at the recommended gauge or more firmly. This helps prevent holes where stitches are stretched and helps the cables stand out from the back-ground fabric. It is typically easier to manipulate cables with more elastic fibers, like wool, because the stitches do undergo so much stretching. Cable stitch definition is crisper with a tightly spun or plied yarn. The fabrics created by cable patterns (with the possible exception of those patterns that are combined with lace) are dense and have little drape, and they are also typically not reversible.

There are a couple of important considerations when using cable patterns. Firstly, because of the way cables are constructed, the knitted fabric pulls in much more than it does with other stitch patterns. This means that cable stitch patterns will have a significantly tighter stitch gauge than other patterns, and because of this, they tend to use up more yarn than other pattern stitches. To get the same width of knitting, more stitches are required and more yarn is used.

A second consideration is cable splay, which is caused by the difference between the gauge for the cable stitch pattern and for the edge pattern above or below it. Make gauge swatches for each pattern and compare; increase stitches on the first row (set-up row) of the cable section to make up for the gauge difference, and decrease to remove them at the end of the cable portion.

There are three general categories of cable patterns—twists, braids, and traveling cables. Typically all styles are worked on a background of Reverse Stockinette stitch, which really allows the cables to shine. Examples of each style are included in this book. The most basic cable is the rope cable, which is a simple cable twist to the left or the right. Rope cables are almost always written up over an even number of stitches, where one half of the stitches are twisted over the other half of the stitches. The patterns can be as small as one stitch over one stitch, though a more typical number is crossing two to four stitches over. Braids use the same twisting technique as rope cables, but the direction of the twists is combined and the twists occur more frequently. Traveling cables are simply cables that move across the knitted fabric. The technique to travel a cable is not all that different than to twist it. The key difference is that, usually, some of the stitches are purled.

Rope cables are extremely versatile. They can be used overall as a pattern stitch, or as panels or accents in any pattern—sweaters, blankets, or accessories. By varying the number of rows between twists, you can compress (fewer rows) or elongate (more rows) the appearance of the cable. If you choose to turn your rope cables into an overall pattern, it is fun to vary the number of rows between twists, either randomly or according to some plan.

By varying the number of stitches in the rope cable pattern, you can also change the width of the cable. The more stitches the cable is worked over, the chunkier the cable will appear and the more the fabric will draw in. Also, the more stitches that are crossed over each other, the more difficult the cable is to work, simply because the stitches are stretching so much. A rope cable probably should not be any wider than 16 to 20 stitches, meaning that 8 to 10 stitches would be crossed over each other. The wider the cable is, the more rows you may wish to work in between twists, in order to maintain the proper proportions.

Note that the rope cable patterns that begin this book are written as panels, meaning that the patterns are only for the cables themselves. The swatches show the cables separated by Reverse Stockinette stitch, which is not included in the pattern text itself.

Cables

2 OVER 2 ROPE CABLE RIGHT TWIST

2 over 2 rope cable right twist is an example of the most basic cabling technique. A column of four knit stitches is twisted by crossing the first two of the stitches behind the second two. By cabling to the back of the work, a right twist is created. The swatch shows what happens if you vary the number of rows between cable twists to create short, medium, and elongated rope cables. Working a 2 over 2 rope cable right twist over eight rows is standard and gives the medium-height cable appearance. 2 over 2 rope cables are nice narrow panels in a more complex pattern. They can also be used as an overall pattern or as a rib-like edge stitch for a project.

Over 12 rows, left; over 6 rows, center; over 8 rows, right

level ● ●
drape ▪

THE PATTERN

Panel of 4
Over 8 rows
Row 1 and all odd numbered rows (WS): Purl.
Row 2: Knit.
Row 4: CB4.
Row 6: Knit.
Row 8: Knit.
Repeat rows 1–8.

Over 6 rows
Row 1 and all odd numbered rows (WS): Purl.
Row 2: Knit.
Row 4: CB4.
Row 6: Knit.
Repeat rows 1–6.

there's more >

2 OVER 2 ROPE CABLE RIGHT TWIST

more > *Over 12 rows*

Row 1 and all odd numbered rows (WS): Purl.

Row 2: Knit.

Row 4: CB4.

Row 6: Knit.

Row 8: Knit.

Row 10: Knit.

Row 12: Knit.

Repeat rows 1–12.

2 OVER 2 ROPE CABLE LEFT TWIST

2 over 2 rope cable left twist is the opposite of 2 over 2 rope cable right twist (page 12); a column of four knit stitches is twisted by crossing the first two of the stitches in front of the second two. By cabling to the front of the work, a left twist is created. Short, medium, and elongated rope cables are also created here by varying the number of rows between cable twists. Eight rows is the standard and creates a medium-height cable.

level ● ●
drape ▣

Over 12 rows, left; over 6 rows, center; over 8 rows, right

THE PATTERN

Panel of 4
Over 8 rows
Row 1 and all odd numbered rows (WS): Purl.
Row 2: Knit.
Row 4: CF4.
Row 6: Knit.
Row 8: Knit.
Repeat rows 1–8.

Over 6 rows
Row 1 and all odd numbered rows (WS): Purl.
Row 2: Knit.
Row 4: CF4.
Row 6: Knit.
Repeat rows 1–6.

Cables

14

there's more >

2 OVER 2 ROPE CABLE LEFT TWIST

more > *Over 12 rows*

Row 1 and all odd numbered rows (WS): Purl.

Row 2: Knit.

Row 4: CF4.

Row 6: Knit.

Row 8: Knit.

Row 10: Knit.

Row 12: Knit.

Repeat rows 1–12.

Cables

15

3 OVER 3 ROPE CABLE RIGHT TWIST

3 over 3 rope cable right twist is another example of the most basic cabling technique. A column of six knit stitches is twisted by crossing the first three of the stitches behind the second three. By cabling to the back of the work, a right twist is created. 3 over 3 rope cables are nice narrow panels in a more complex pattern. They can also be used as an overall pattern or as a ribbing-like edge stitch for a project. Try varying the number of rows worked between twists to alter the appearance.

level ● ●
drape ■

Over 12 rows, left; over 6 rows, center; over 8 rows, right

THE PATTERN

Panel of 4
Over 8 rows
Row 1 and all odd numbered rows (WS): Purl.
Row 2: Knit.
Row 4: CB6.
Row 6: Knit.
Row 8: Knit.
Repeat rows 1–8.

Over 6 rows
Row 1 and all odd numbered rows (WS): Purl.
Row 2: Knit.
Row 4: CB6.
Row 6: Knit.
Repeat rows 1–6.

there's more >

Cables

16

more > *Over 12 rows*

Row 1 and all odd numbered rows (WS): Purl.

Row 2: Knit.

Row 4: CB6.

Row 6: Knit.

Row 8: Knit.

Row 10: Knit.

Row 12: Knit.

Repeat rows 1–12.

3 OVER 3 ROPE CABLE LEFT TWIST

3 over 3 rope cable left twist is the opposite of 3 over 3 rope cable right twist (page 16); a column of six knit stitches is twisted by crossing the first three of the stitches in front of the second three. By cabling to the front of the work, a left twist is created. 3 over 3 rope cables are used like the 3 over 3 rope cable right twist pattern.

Over 12 rows, left; over 6 rows, center; over 8 rows, right

level ● ●
drape

THE PATTERN

Panel of 6

Over 8 rows

Row 1 and all odd numbered rows (WS): Purl.

Row 2: Knit.

Row 4: CF6.

Row 6: Knit.

Row 8: Knit.

Repeat rows 1–8.

Over 6 rows

Row 1 and all odd numbered rows (WS): Purl.

Row 2: Knit.

Row 4: CF6.

Row 6: Knit.

Repeat rows 1–6.

Cables

there's more >

3 OVER 3 ROPE CABLE LEFT TWIST

more >   *Over 12 rows*

Row 1 and all odd numbered rows (WS): Purl.

Row 2: Knit.

Row 4: CF6.

Row 6: Knit.

Row 8: Knit.

Row 10: Knit.

Row 12: Knit.

Repeat rows 1–12.

4 OVER 4 ROPE CABLE RIGHT TWIST

4 over 4 rope cable right twist is a column of eight knit stitches twisted by crossing the first four of the stitches behind the second four. By cabling to the back of the work, a right twist is created. The number of rows worked between twists is larger in this pattern because this cable is wider. Like 2 over 2 and 3 over 3 rope cables, this pattern makes nice narrow panels in a more complex project, can be used as an overall pattern, or as an edge stitch. Vary the number of rows worked between twists to alter the appearance.

level ● ●
drape ●

THE PATTERN

Panel of 8

Row 1 and all odd numbered rows (WS): Purl.

Row 2: Knit.

Row 4: CB8.

Row 6: Knit.

Row 8: Knit.

Row 10: Knit.

Repeat rows 1-10.

4 OVER 4 ROPE CABLE LEFT TWIST

4 over 4 rope cable left twist is the opposite of 4 over 4 rope cable right twist (page 20). A column of eight knit stitches is twisted by crossing the first four of the stitches in front of the second four. By cabling to the front of the work, a left twist is created. The number of rows worked between twists is larger in this pattern because this cable is wider. Use this pattern as you would 4 over 4 rope cable right twist.

level
drape

THE PATTERN

Panel of 8

Row 1 and all odd numbered rows (WS): Purl.

Row 2: Knit.

Row 4: CF8.

Row 6: Knit.

Row 8: Knit.

Row 10: Knit.

Repeat rows 1–10.

SNAKING ROPE CABLE

Snaking rope cable is basically a rope cable, but instead of twisting the same direction every time, the twists alternate between right and left. By doing so, the cable appears to snake rather than twist. Snaking rope cable can be substituted anywhere a 3 over 3 rope cable appears. It should be worked on a Reverse Stockinette stitch background.

level ● ● ●
drape ▧

THE PATTERN

Panel of 6

Row 1 and all odd numbered rows (WS): Purl.

Row 2: Knit.

Row 4: CB6.

Row 6: Knit.

Row 8: Knit.

Row 10: Knit.

Row 12: CF6.

Row 14: Knit.

Row 16: Knit.

Repeat rows 1–16.

X-O CABLE

X-O cable is a traditional Aran pattern. The cable crosses form a series of nested X's and O's. The cable is best worked on a background of Reverse Stockinette stitch. X-O cable is the perfect addition to any Aran project. It is also attractive on its own for a simple sweater motif, for instance.

level
drape

THE PATTERN

Panel of 8

Row 1 and all odd numbered rows (WS): Purl.
Row 2: Knit.
Row 4: C4F, C4B.
Row 6: Knit.
Row 8: C4B, C4F.
Row 10: Knit.
Row 12: C4B, C4F.
Row 14: Knit.
Row 16: C4F, C4B.
Repeat rows 1–16.

Cables

OPEN ROPE CABLE

Open rope cable is
another variation on the
basic rope cable. In this
case, branches of the
cable travel outward,
then in again to create a
rope cable that sur-
rounds a small bit of
Reverse Stockinette
stitch. This pattern can
be substituted for a rope
cable in any project.

level ● ● ●
drape ▫

THE PATTERN

Panel of 8

Row 1 (WS): K2, p4, k2.

Row 2: P2, CB4, p2.

Row 3: K2, p4, k2.

Row 4: P1, T2R1, T2L1, p1.

Row 5: K1, p2, k2, p2, k1.

Row 6: T2R1, p2, T2L1.

Row 7: P2, k4, p2.

Row 8: K2, p4, k2.

Row 9: P2, k4, p2.

Row 10: T2L1, p2, T2R1.

Row 11: K1, p2, k2, p2, k1.

Row 12: P1, T2L1, T2R1, p1.

Repeat rows 1–12.

Cables

LACE DIAMONDS AND CABLE WAVES

Lace diamonds and cable waves is a zigzag cable pattern with little eyelet diamonds nested in each bend. This pattern is best worked on a Stockinette stitch background. It makes an excellent panel in projects like an Aran afghan, because the lace adds more airiness to a heavier pattern. The lace also gives the motif a bit more drape than is usually associated with cable patterns.

level
drape

THE PATTERN

Panel of 12

Row 1 and all odd numbered rows (WS): Purl.
Row 2: [K2tog, yo] 3 times, k6.
Row 4: K1, [k2tog, yo] twice, k1, CB3, k3.
Row 6: K2, k2tog, yo, k1, CB3, k4.
Row 8: K4, CB3, k1, yo, ssk, k2.
Row 10: K3, CB3, k1, [yo, ssk] twice, k1.
Row 12: K6, [yo, ssk] 3 times.
Row 14: K3, CF3, k1, [yo, ssk] twice, k1.
Row 16: K4, CF3, k1, yo, ssk, k2.
Row 18: K2, k2tog, yo, k1, CF3, k4.
Row 20: K1, [k2tog, yo] twice, k1, CF3, k3.
Repeat rows 1–20.

Cables

ARAN DIAMONDS

Aran diamonds is a classic stitch motif in Aran sweaters. In this particular version of the motif, the diamonds are simply filled with Reverse Stockinette stitch.

This pattern is a good central panel in a smaller project, like a child's sweater, or an accent panel in a larger project, like an adult's sweater or a blanket.

level ● ● ●
drape ■

THE PATTERN

Panel of 12

Row 1 (WS): K4, p4, k4.

Row 2: P3, T2R1, T2L1, p3.

Row 3: K3, p2, k2, p2, k3.

Row 4: P2, T2R1, p2, T2L1, p2.

Row 5: K2, p2, k4, p2, k2.

Row 6: P1, T2R1, p4, T2L1, p1.

Row 7: K1, p2, k6, p2, k1.

Row 8: T2R1, p6, T2L1.

Row 9: P2, k8, p2.

Row 10: T2L1, p6, T2R1.

Row 11: K1, p2, k6, p2, k1.

Row 12: P1, T2L1, p4, T2R1, p1.

Row 13: K2, p2, k4, p2, k2.

Row 14: P2, T2L1, p2, T2R1, p2.

Row 15: K3, p2, k2, p2, k3.

Row 16: P3, T2L1, T2R1, p3.

Row 17: K4, p4, k4.

Row 18: P4, CB4, p4.

Repeat rows 1–18.

HORSESHOE CABLE

Horseshoe cable derives its name from the fact that it is shaped very much like a horseshoe. Its rounded appearance is a nice complement to some of the other cable motifs. Horseshoe cable is a suitable accent panel in any Aran project. It is a little narrow to serve as the central panel, except in baby sweaters.

level
drape

THE PATTERN

Panel of 12
Row 1 (WS): K2, p8, k2.
Row 2: P2, CB4, CF4, p2.
Row 3: K2, p8, k2.
Row 4: P2, k8, p2.
Row 5: K2, p8, k2.
Row 6: P2, k8, p2.
Row 7: K2, p8, k2.
Row 8: P2, k8, p2.
Repeat rows 1–8.

ARAN BRAID

Aran braid is a very dense cable pattern, as the cabling occurs every other row. The strong graphic appearance makes a striking addition to a complex Aran sweater. However, Aran braid is also pleasing as the sole cable in a simple Stockinette stitch pullover or cardigan.

level
drape

THE PATTERN

Panel of 12

Rows 1 and 3 (WS): K2, p8, k2.
Row 2: P2, CB4 twice, p2.
Row 4: P2, k2, CF4, k2, p2.
Repeat rows 1–4.

ARAN DIAMONDS WITH MOSS STITCH

Aran diamonds with Moss stitch is another traditional Aran pattern. The Moss stitch (Book 1, page 16) adds a textural variation to the insides of the diamonds formed by the cables. Aran diamonds with moss stitch is a good central panel for a traditional Aran sweater or blanket.

level
drape

THE PATTERN

Panel of 13

Row 1 (WS): K4, p5, k4.
Row 2: P3, CB3, p1, CF3, p3.
Row 3: K3, p3, k1, p3, k3.
Row 4: P2, CB3, p1, k1, p1, CF3, p2.
Row 5: K2, p3, k1, p1, k1, p3, k2.
Row 6: P1, CB3, p1, [k1, p1] twice, CF3, p1.
Row 7: K1, p3, k1, [p1, k1] twice, p3, k1.
Row 8: CB3, p1, [k1, p1] 3 times, CF3.
Row 9: P3, k1, [p1, k1] 3 times, p3.
Row 10: K2, p1, [k1, p1] 4 times, k2.
Row 11: P2, k1, [p1, k1] 4 times, p2.
Row 12: T2L1, p1, [k1, p1] 3 times, T2R1.
Row 13: K1, p2, k1, [p1, k1] 3 times, p2, k1.
Row 14: P1, T2L1, p1, [k1, p1] twice, T2R1, p1.
Row 15: K2, p2, k1, [p1, k1] twice, p2, k2.
Row 16: P2, T2L1, p1, k1, p1, T2R1, p2.
Row 17: K3, p2, k1, p1, k1, p2, k3.
Row 18: P3, T2L1, p1, T2R1, p3.
Row 19: K4, p2, k1, p2, k4.
Row 20: P4, CB5, p4.
Repeat rows 1–20.

TREE OF LIFE

Tree of life is a very basic pine tree shape created by effectively twisted stitches and is yet another traditional Aran pattern. It will show best when worked in a smooth, tightly twisted yarn on a Reverse Stockinette stitch background.

level ● ● ●
drape ■

THE PATTERN

Panel of 15

Row 1 (RS): P2, k1, p4, sl 1 wyib, p4, k1, p2.
Row 2: K2, sl 1 wyif, k4, p1, k4, sl 1 wyif, k2.
Row 3: P2, CF2, p3, sl 1 wyib, p3, CB2, p2.
Row 4: K3, sl 1 wyif, k3, p1, k3, sl 1 wyif, k3.
Row 5: P3, CF2, p2, sl 1 wyib, p2, CB2, p3.
Row 6: K4, sl 1 wyif, k2, p1, k2, sl 1 wyif, k4.
Row 7: P4, CF2, p1, sl 1 wyib, p1, CB2, p4.
Row 8: K5, sl 1 wyif, k1, p1, k1, sl 1 wyif, k5.
Row 9: P2, k1, p2, CF2, sl 1 wyib, CB2, p2, k1, p2.
Row 10: K2, sl 1 wyif, k4, p1, k4, sl 1 wyif, k2.
Repeat rows 3–10. (Rows 1 and 2 are set-up rows.)

Cables

RIBBED DOUBLE CABLE

Ribbed double cable is interesting because the cable itself is worked in a ribbing pattern rather than plain Stockinette stitch. The unique appearance makes it an interesting addition to a mix of cables. Plus, the wrong side looks as good as the right side. Ribbed double cable panels can be repeated to create a nice overall pattern, too.

level
drape

THE PATTERN

Panel of 16

Row 1 and all odd numbered rows (WS): P1, k2, [p2, k2] 3 times, p1.

Row 2: K1, p2, [k2, p2] 3 times, k1.

Row 4: T8B RIB, T8F RIB.

Row 6: K1, p2, [k2, p2] 3 times, k1.

Row 8: K1, p2, [k2, p2] 3 times, k1.

Row 10: K1, p2, [k2, p2] 3 times, k1.

Row 12: K1, p2, [k2, p2] 3 times, k1.

Repeat rows 1–12.

CLUSTERED CABLE BRAID

Clustered cable braid
is a fancy cable panel
that combines traveling
cables and rope cables.
Additionally, the cable
is wrapped with yarn to
add a smocked effect.
Clustered cable braid is
a beautiful center motif
or it can also be used
by itself to enhance a
plain Stockinette stitch
sweater.

level ● ● ●
drape ■

THE PATTERN

Panel of 16

Row 1 (WS): K2, p4, k4, p4, k2.
Row 2: P2, CB4, p4, CF4, p2.
Row 3: K2, p4, k4, p4, k2.
Row 4: P1, T2R1, T2L1, p2, T2R1, T2L1, p1.
Row 5: K1, [p2, k2] 3 times, p2, k1.
Row 6: [T2R1, p2, T2L1] twice.
Row 7: P2, k4, p4, k4, p2.
Row 8: K2, p4, CB4, p4, k2.
Row 9: P2, k4, p4, k4, p2.
Row 10: K2, p4, k4, p4, k2.
Row 11: P2, k4, p4, k4, p2.
Row 12: K2, p4, CB4, p4, k2.
Row 13: P2, k4, p4, k4, p2.
Row 14: [T2L1, p2, T2R1] twice.
Row 15: K1, [p2, k2] 3 times, p2, k1.
Row 16: P1, T2L1, T2R1, p2, T2L1, T2R1, p1.
Row 17: K2, p4, k4, p4, k2.
Row 18: P2, CB4, p4, CF4, p2.
Row 19: K2, p4, k4, p4, k2.

Cables

there's more >

more > Row 20: P1, T2R1, T2L1, p2, T2R1, T2L1, p1.

Row 21: K1, [p2, k2] 3 times, p2, k1.

Row 22: P1, [k2, p2] twice, k2, slip last 6 stitches worked onto cn and wrap yarn 4 times counterclockwise around these stitches, then slip them back to RH needle, p2, k2, p1.

Row 23: K1, [p2, k2] 3 times, p2, k1.

Row 24: P1, T2L1, T2R1, p2, T2L1, T2R1, p1.

Repeat rows 1–24.

Cables

BOBBLE BOUQUETS

Bobble bouquets creates delicate little nosegays with traveling stitch stems and bobble flowers. It is most effective worked in a smooth, tightly spun yarn. Bobble bouquets is a feminine addition to Aran sweater designs, but it would also be a nice pattern on its own, perhaps along the openings of a cardigan.

level ● ● ● ●
drape ▪

THE PATTERN

Panel of 16

Row 1 (WS): K7, p2, k7.
Row 2: P6, CB2, CF2, p6.
Row 3: K5, T1L1, p2, T1R1, k5.
Row 4: P4, T1R1, CB2, CF2, T1L1, p4.
Row 5: K3, T1L1, k1, p4, k1, T1R1, k3.
Row 6: P2, T1R1, p1, T1R1, k2, T1L1, p1, T1L1, p2.
Row 7: [K2, p1] twice, k1, p2, k1, [p1, k2] twice.
Row 8: P2, MB, p1, T1R1, p1, k2, p1, T1L1, p1, MB, p2.
Row 9: K4, p1, k2, p2, k2, p1, k4.
Row 10: P4, MB, p2, k2, p2, MB, p4.
Repeat rows 1–10.

LADDER OF LIFE

Ladder of life is very easy
to work. It is composed
of a simple knit-purl ladder surrounded by mir-
rored rope cables. Ladder
of life is a nice side panel
in an Aran sweater or
blanket, or as the central
panel in an Aran designed
for a baby or toddler.

level
drape

THE PATTERN

Panel of 17

Row 1 (WS): P4, k2, p5, k2, p4.

Row 2: CF4, p2, k5, p2, CB4.

Row 3: P4, k2, p5, k2, p4.

Row 4: K4, p2, k5, p2, k4.

Row 5: P4, k2, p5, k2, p4.

Row 6: K4, p9, k4.

Repeat rows 1–6.

Cables

DOWNWARD STAGHORN CABLE

Downward staghorn cable appears much more complex than it is. This cable is basically paired, mirrored rope cables. To show best, this cable should be worked on a Reverse Stockinette stitch background. It works well as a central sweater panel and is also attractive repeated or alternated with Upward staghorn cable (page 37).

level ● ● ●
drape ■

THE PATTERN

Panel of 20

Row 1 (WS): K2, p16, k2.
Row 2: P2, k4, CB4, CF4, k4, p2.
Row 3: K2, p16, k2.
Row 4: P2, k2, CB4, k4, CF4, k2, p2.
Row 5: K2, p16, k2.
Row 6: P2, CB4, k8, CF4, p2.
Repeat rows 1–6.

UPWARD STAGHORN CABLE

Upward staghorn cable isn't as complex as it appears. This cable is essentially mirrored rope cables. Upward staghorn cable works well as a central cable panel in an Aran sweater and would be attractive repeated or alternated with Downward staghorn cable (page 36).

level
drape

THE PATTERN

Panel of 20

Row 1 (WS): K2, p16, k2.

Row 2: P2, CF4, k8, CB4, p2.

Row 3: K2, p16, k2.

Row 4: P2, k2, CF4, k4, CB4, k2, p2.

Row 5: K2, p16, k2.

Row 6: P2, k4, CF4, CB4, k4, p2.

Repeat rows 1-6.

Cables

37

SAXONY BRAID CABLE

Saxony braid cable is a
classic central cable in
Aran sweater patterns.
It mixes traveling cables,
twists, and braids into
one beautiful cable.
Saxony braid cable is
perfect when combined
with other cable patterns
into a complex project,
but it is elaborate
enough to hold its own
in a pattern, too.

level ● ● ● ●
drape ■

THE PATTERN

Panel of 24

Row 1 (WS): K2, p4, k4, p4, k4, p4, k2.
Row 2: P2, CB4, p4, CB4, p4, CB4, p2.
Row 3: K2, p4, k4, p4, k4, p4, k2.
Row 4: P1, T2R1, [T2L2, T2R2] twice, T2L1, p1.
Row 5: K1, p2, k3, p4, k4, p4, k3, p2, k1.
Row 6: T2R1, p3, CF4, p4, CF4, p3, T2L1.
Row 7: P2, k4, p4, k4, p4, k4, p2.
Row 8: K2, p2, [T2R2, T2L2] twice, p2, k2.
Row 9: P2, k2, p2, k4, p4, k4, p2, k2, p2.
Row 10: [K2, p2] twice, p2, CB4, p2, [p2, k2] twice.
Row 11: P2, k2, p2, k4, p4, k4, p2, k2, p2.
Row 12: K2, p2, [T2L2, T2R2] twice, p2, k2.
Row 13: P2, k4, p4, k4, p4, k4, p2.
Row 14: T2L1, p3, CF4, p4, CF4, p3, T2R1.
Row 15: K1, p2, k3, p4, k4, p4, k3, p2, k1.
Row 16: P1, T2L1, [T2R2, T2L2] twice, T2R1, p1.
Repeat rows 1–16.

Cables

ALL-OVER CABLE WEAVE

All-over cable weave is a pretty little pattern that forms columns of waving cables. This stitch pattern can be used as a small panel or accent in a more elaborate cabled project. It is a nice overall stitch for warm sweaters, hats, or mittens. Knit at a finer gauge, it would make a sophisticated top.

level
drape

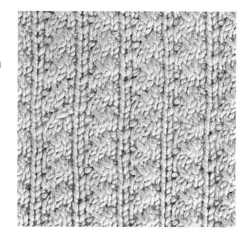

THE PATTERN

Multiple of 5 + 1

Rows 1 and 3 (WS): Purl.
Row 2: K1, * T2L1, k2. Repeat from * to end of row.
Row 4: * K2, T2R1. Repeat from * to last stitch, end k1.
Repeat rows 1–4.

LIGHTNING CABLES

Lightning cables are dramatic cabled zigzags across a background of Reverse Stockinette stitch. Worked in a multiple of one or two, this pattern would be a nice accent panel in a larger project. Worked as an overall pattern, Lightning cables would make a nice sweater in any size or a fun blanket with a simple edging.

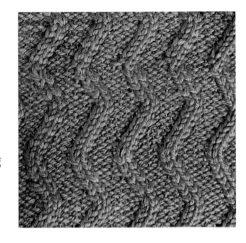

level ● ● ●
drape ■

THE PATTERN

Multiple of 6 + 2

Row 1 (WS): K1, * p2, k4. Repeat from * to the last stitch, end k1.

Row 2: P4, T2R1, * p3, T2R1. Repeat from * to the last stitch, end p1.

Row 3: K2, * p2, k4. Repeat from * to end of row.

Row 4: * P3, T2R1. Repeat from * to the last 2 stitches, end p2.

Row 5: K3, p2, * k4, p2. Repeat from * to the last 3 stitches, end k3.

Row 6: P2, * T2R1, p3. Repeat from * to end of row.

Row 7: * K4, p2. Repeat from * to the last 2 stitches, end k2.

Row 8: P1, * T2R1, p3. Repeat from * to the last stitch, end p1.

Row 9: K5, p2, * k4, p2. Repeat from * to the last stitch, end k1.

Row 10: P1, * T2L1, p3. Repeat from * to the last stitch, end p1.

Row 11: * K4, p2. Repeat from * to the last 2 stitches, end k2.

Row 12: P2, * T2L1, p3. Repeat from * to end of row.

there's more >

Cables

more > Row 13: K3, p2, * k4, p2. Repeat from * to the last 3 stitches, end k3.

Row 14: * P3, T2L1. Repeat from * to the last 2 stitches, end p2.

Row 15: K2, * p2, k4. Repeat from * to end of row.

Row 16: P4, T2L1, * p3, T2L1. Repeat from * to the last stitch, end p1.

Repeat rows 1–16.

LITTLE O CABLE

Little O cable is columns of small round cables on a Reverse Stockinette stitch background. The cables are created with a twist stitch, so no cable needle is necessary. Little O cable works well as an edge stitch for Aran projects. When worked as a single column, it also is a very good dividing stitch between other cable patterns and can be used as an overall stitch in a close-fitting top, too.

level ● ● ●
drape ▪

THE PATTERN

Multiple of 6 + 2

Row 1 (WS): K2, * p4, k2. Repeat from * to end of row.
Row 2: P2, * RT, LT, p2. Repeat from * to end of row.
Row 3: K2, * p4, k2. Repeat form * to end of row.
Row 4: P2, * LT, RT, p2. Repeat from * to end of row.
Repeat rows 1–4.

SCOTTISH FAGGOTING CABLE

Scottish faggoting cable is a lovely mix of cables and lace knitting. It adds airiness to heavily textured patterns and is very simple to work. While it is a nice accent stitch, it would also be elegant as an overall stitch in a sweater design.

level
drape

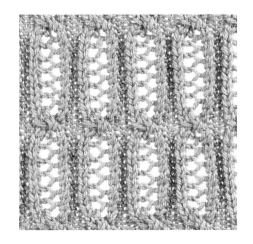

THE PATTERN

Multiple of 6 + 2

Row 1 (RS): P2, * k2, yo, k2tog, p2. Repeat from * to end of row.

Row 2: K2, * p2, yo, p2tog, k2. Repeat from * to end of row.

Row 3: P2, * k2, yo, k2tog, p2. Repeat from * to end of row.

Row 4: K2, * p2, yo, p2tog, k2. Repeat from * to end of row.

Row 5: P2, * k2, yo, k2tog, p2. Repeat from * to end of row.

Row 6: K2, * p2, yo, p2tog, k2. Repeat from * to end of row.

Row 7: P2, * CF4, p2. Repeat from * to end of row.

Row 8: K2, * p2, yo, p2tog, k2. Repeat from * to end of row.

Row 9: P2, * k2, yo, k2tog, p2. Repeat from * to end of row.

Row 10: K2, * p2, yo, p2tog, k2. Repeat from * to end of row.

Row 11: P2, * k2, yo, k2tog, p2. Repeat from * to end of row.

Row 12: K2, * p2, yo, p2tog, k2. Repeat from * to end of row.

Row 13: P2, * k2, yo, k2tog, p2. Repeat from * to end of row.

Row 14: K2, * p2, yo, p2tog, k2. Repeat from * to end of row.

Row 15: P2, * k2, yo, k2tog, p2. Repeat from * to end of row.

Row 16: K2, * p2, yo, p2tog, k2. Repeat from * to end of row.

Repeat rows 1–16.

Cables

HONEYCOMB CABLE

Honeycomb cable is a rather dense overall cable pattern that resembles a bee's honeycomb. It looks intricate, but is straightforward to work. While it is an overall pattern, honeycomb is at its most effective when used as a panel in a more complex Aran sweater or blanket project. The small stitch multiple and geometric repeat make it a nice foil to more complex cables.

level ● ● ●
drape

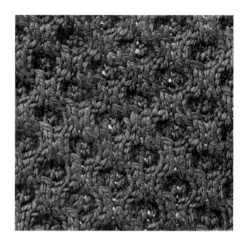

THE PATTERN

Multiple of 8

Row 1 and all odd numbered rows (WS): Purl.

Row 2: * CB4, CF4. Repeat from * to end of row.

Row 4: Knit.

Row 6: * CF4, CB4. Repeat from * to end of row.

Row 8: Knit.

Repeat rows 1–8.

Cables

BASKETWEAVE CABLE

Basketweave cable has an elaborate appearance, but is not difficult to work. Cables are twisted over and under each other into a beautiful woven pattern. Basketweave cable is written as an overall pattern, but it is equally effective knit up as a panel. It is very striking to use as the central panel to a pullover, either alone or combined with other stitch patterns.

level
drape

THE PATTERN

Multiple of 8 + 4

Row 1 and all odd numbered rows (WS): K2, purl to last 2 stitches, end k2.

Row 2: P2, knit to last 2 stitches, end p2.

Row 4: P2, knit to last 2 stitches, end p2.

Row 6: P2, * CB8. Repeat from * to last 2 stitches, end p2.

Row 8: P2, knit to last 2 stitches, end p2.

Row 10: P2, knit to last 2 stitches, end p2.

Row 12: P2, k4, * CF8. Repeat from * to last 6 stitches, end k4, p2.

Repeat rows 1–12.

GULL STITCH

Gull stitch is a rather flat cable that forms a bird-like motif. Because the stitches to be cabled are slipped, it is possible to drop them off the needle and twist them without the use of a cable needle. Gull stitch can be used as a panel in socks or between larger motifs in a sweater, but it can also be worked as an overall pattern to make an interesting cabled sweater.

level
drape

THE PATTERN

Multiple of 8 + 2

Row 1 (WS): K2, * p6, k2. Repeat from * to end of row.

Row 2: P2, * k2, sl 2 pwise, k2, p2. Repeat from * to end of row.

Row 3: K2, * p2, sl 2 wyif, p2, k2. Repeat from * to end of row.

Row 4: P2, * T1R2, T1L2, p2. Repeat from * to end of row.

Repeat rows 1–4.

TIGHTLY TWISTED CABLE

In Tightly twisted cable, the cable twists are worked on every right side row. Doing so creates a very dense, yet beautiful, cable. Tightly twisted cable is equally appropriate for use as an overall stitch pattern or as a panel in a project. It is like a rope cable, so could be used similarly.

level
drape

THE PATTERN

Multiple of 10 + 2

Rows 1 and 3 (WS): K2, * p8, k2. Repeat from * to end of row.
Row 2: P2, * CB4 twice, p2. Repeat from * to end of row.
Row 4: P2, * k2, CB4, k2, p2. Repeat from * to end of row.
Repeat rows 1–4.

CABLES AND LACE

Cables and lace is a nice pattern because the lace adds lightness and drape to the denseness of the cables. It is most effectively used as an overall pattern. Cables and lace would make a lovely summer sweater. Since the cables are simple rope cables, this pattern would work just fine in an inelastic yarn like cotton.

level ● ● ●
drape ▩ ▩

THE PATTERN

Multiple of 11 + 7

Row 1 and all odd numbered rows (WS): Purl.

Row 2: K1, * yo, ssk, k1, k2tog, yo, k6. Repeat from * to last 6 stitches, end yo, ssk, k1, k2tog, yo, k1.

Row 4: K2, * yo, sl 1, k2tog, psso, yo, k1, CB6, k1. Repeat from * to last 5 stitches, end yo, sl 1, k2tog, psso, yo, k2.

Row 6: K1, * yo, ssk, k1, k2tog, yo, k6. Repeat from * to last 6 stitches, end yo, ssk, k1, k2tog, yo, k1.

Row 8: K2, * yo, sl 1, k2tog, psso, yo, k8. Repeat from * to last 5 stitches, end yo, sl 1, k2tog, psso, yo, k2.

Repeat rows 1–8.

CABLE COLUMNS

Cable columns is a simple cable pattern that alternates rope cables with columns of twisted stitches, and the results are rather striking. For the pattern to show best, work it in a smooth, tightly spun yarn. Cable columns can be used as an edge stitch, or it can be worked as an overall pattern in an attractive vest or sweater.

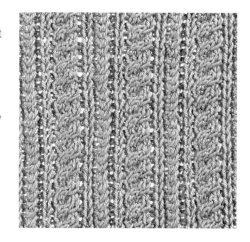

level
drape

THE PATTERN

Multiple of 12 + 8

Rows 1 and 3: K1, p1, k1, p2, k1, p1, k1, * p4, k1, p1, k1, p2, k1, p1, k1. Repeat from * to end of row.

Row 2: P1, sl 1, p1, RT, p1, sl 1, p1, * k4, p1, sl 1, p1, RT, p1, sl 1, p1. Repeat from * to end of row.

Row 4: P1, sl 1, p1, RT, p1, sl 1, p1, * CB4, p1, sl 1, p1, RT, p1, sl 1, p1. Repeat from * to end of row.

Repeat rows 1–4.

DRUNKEN CABLES

Drunken cables tilt this way and that. The slanting of the cables happens because of the shifting of the lace pattern. Drunken cables is most effective as an overall pattern. It is a good motif for lightweight sweaters, scarves, or blankets, as the lace makes the fabric lighter and more open.

level
drape ▨ ▨

THE PATTERN

Multiple of 13 + 2

Row 1 (WS): K2, * p5, k1, p5, k2. Repeat from * to end of row.

Row 2: P2, * k1, [yo, k2tog] twice, p1, k5, p2. Repeat from * to end of row.

Row 3: K2, * p4, k2, p5, k2. Repeat from * to end of row.

Row 4: P2, * k1, [yo, k2tog] twice, p2, k4, p2. Repeat from * to end of row.

Row 5: K2, * p4, k2, p5, k2. Repeat from * to end of row.

Row 6: P2, * k1, [yo, k2tog] twice, p2, CB4, p2. Repeat from * to end of row.

Row 7: K2, * p4, k2, p5, k2. Repeat from * to end of row.

Row 8: P2, * k1, [yo, k2tog] twice, p2, k4, p2. Repeat from * to end of row.

Row 9: K2, * p4, k2, p5, k2. Repeat from * to end of row.

Row 10: P2, * k1, [yo, k2tog] twice, p2, CB4, p2. Repeat from * to end of row.

Row 11: K2, * p4, k2, p5, k2. Repeat from * to end of row.

Row 12: P2, * k1, [yo, k2tog] twice, p2, k4, p2. Repeat from * to end of row.

Cables

there's more >

more > Row 13: K2, * p5, k1, p5, k2. Repeat from * to end of row.

Row 14: P2, * k5, p1, [ssk, yo] twice, k1, p2. Repeat from * to end of row.

Row 15: K2, * p5, k2, p4, k2. Repeat from * to end of row.

Row 16: P2, * k4, p2, [ssk, yo] twice, k1, p2. Repeat from * to end of row.

Row 17: K2, * p5, k2, p4, k2. Repeat from * to end of row.

Row 18: P2, * CF4, p2, [ssk, yo] twice, k1, p2. Repeat from * to end of row.

Row 19: K2, * p5, k2, p4, k2. Repeat from * to end of row.

Row 20: P2, * k4, p2, [ssk, yo] twice, k1, p2. Repeat from * to end of row.

Row 21: K2, * p5, k2, p4, k2. Repeat from * to end of row.

Row 22: P2, * CF4, p2, [ssk, yo] twice, k1, p2. Repeat from * to end of row.

Row 23: K2, * p5, k2, p4, k2. Repeat from * to end of row.

Row 24: P2, * k4, p2, [ssk, yo] twice, k1, p2. Repeat from * to end of row.

Repeat rows 1–24.

Cables

SCROLLING CABLE WITH BOBBLES

Scrolling cable with bobbles is a nice pattern to use as a panel as well as an overall stitch. In fact, it works well to knit the cable as a hatband or sweater hem—knit a single panel the desired length, then pick up stitches along the side to knit the main body. Scrolling cable with bobbles is a whimsical addition to children's garments as well.

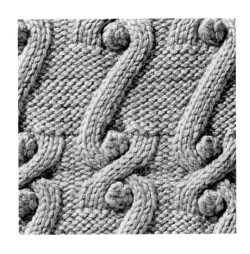

level
drape ▪

THE PATTERN

Multiple of 13 + 2

Row 1 (WS): K2, *k2, p3, k1, p3, k4. Repeat from * to end of row.

Row 2: P2, * p2, C3 over 4, p4. Repeat from * to end of row.

Row 3: K2, * k2, p3, k1, p3, k4. Repeat from * to end of row.

Row 4: P2, * T3R2, p1, T3L2, p2. Repeat from * to end of row.

Row 5: K2, * p3, k5, p3, k2. Repeat from * to end of row.

Row 6: P2, * k3, p2, MB, p2, k3, p2. Repeat from * to end of row.

Row 7: K2, * p3, k5, p3, k2. Repeat from * to end of row.

Row 8: P2, * p7, T3R1, p2. Repeat from * to end of row.

Row 9: K2, * k1, p3, k9. Repeat from * to end of row.

Row 10: P2, * p6, T3R1, p3. Repeat from * to end of row.

Row 11: K2, * k2, p3, k8. Repeat from * to end of row.

Row 12: P2, * p5, T3R1, p4. Repeat from * to end of row.

Row 13: K2, * k3, p3, k7. Repeat from * to end of row.

Row 14: P2, * p4, T3R1, p5. Repeat from * to end of row.

Row 15: K2, * k4, p3, k6. Repeat from * to end of row.

Row 16: P2, * p3, T3R1, p6. Repeat from * to end of row.

Row 17: K2, * k5, p3, k5. Repeat from * to end of row.

Row 18: P2, * p2, T3R1, p7. Repeat from * to end of row.

there's more >

Cables

SCROLLING CABLE WITH BOBBLES

more > Row 19: K2, * k6, p3, k4. Repeat from * to end of row.

Row 20: P2, * p1, T3R1, p8. Repeat from * to end of row.

Row 21: K2, * p3, k4, p3, k3. Repeat from * to end of row.

Row 22: P2, * T3R1, p4, k3, p2. Repeat from * to end of row.

Row 23: K2, * p3, k5, p3, k2. Repeat from * to end of row.

Row 24: P2, * k3, p2, MB, p2, k3, p2. Repeat from * to end of row.

Row 25: K2, * p3, k5, p3, k2. Repeat from * to end of row.

Row 26: P2, * T3L2, p1, T3R2, p2. Repeat from * to end of row.

Repeat rows 1–26.

CABLES IN CABLES

Cables in cables is a motif in which paired rope cables diverge to surround other simple rope cables. The pattern is not terribly difficult, yet looks elaborate. Cables in cables would be a great overall stitch pattern for a blanket or a sweater. Worked as a single repeat, the pattern is an appealing panel, too.

level ● ● ●
drape ▪

THE PATTERN

Multiple of 14 + 2

Row 1 (WS): K2, * k2, p8, k4. Repeat from * to end of row.

Row 2: P2, * p2, CB4 twice, p4. Repeat from * to end of row.

Row 3: K2, * k2, p8, k4. Repeat from * to end of row.

Row 4: P2, * T2R2, CB4, T2L2, p2. Repeat from * to end of row.

Row 5: K2, * p2, k2, p4, k2, p2, k2. Repeat from * to end of row.

Row 6: P2, * k2, p2, k4, p2, k2, p2. Repeat from * to end of row.

Row 7: K2, * p2, k2, p4, k2, p2, k2. Repeat from * to end of row.

Row 8: P2, * k2, p2, CB4, p2, k2, p2. Repeat from * to end of row.

Row 9: K2, * p2, k2, p4, k2, p2, k2. Repeat from * to end of row.

Row 10: P2, * k2, p2, k4, p2, k2, p2. Repeat from * to end of row.

Row 11: K2, * p2, k2, p4, k2, p2, k2. Repeat from * to end of row.

Row 12: P2, * k2, p2, CB4, p2, k2, p2. Repeat from * to end of row.

there's more >

Cables

CABLES IN CABLES

more >   Row 13: K2, * p2, k2, p4, k2, p2, k2. Repeat from * to end of row.

Row 14: P2, * k2, p2, k4, p2, k2, p2. Repeat from * to end of row.

Row 15: K2, * p2, k2, p4, k2, p2, k2. Repeat from * to end of row.

Row 16: P2, * k2, p2, CB4, p2, k2, p2. Repeat from * to end of row.

Row 17: K2, * p2, k2, p4, k2, p2, k2. Repeat from * to end of row.

Row 18: P2, * k2, p2, k4, p2, k2, p2. Repeat from * to end of row.

Row 19: K2, * p2, k2, p4, k2, p2, k2. Repeat from * to end of row.

Row 20: P2, * k2, p2, CB4, p2, k2, p2. Repeat from * to end of row.

Row 21: K2, * p2, k2, p4, k2, p2, k2. Repeat from * to end of row.

Row 22: P2, * k2, p2, k4, p2, k2, p2. Repeat from * to end of row.

Row 23: K2, * p2, k2, p4, k2, p2, k2. Repeat from * to end of row.

Row 24: P2, * T2L2, CB4, T2R2, p2. Repeat from * to end of row.

Repeat rows 1–24.

CANDY CABLES

Candy cables is a series of cables that resembles wrapped bonbons. The characteristics of the resulting fabric are very similar to that of rope cables. This motif is an overall cable pattern that can be worked as a panel if desired. Candy cables would be a great pattern for children's sweaters or baby blankets.

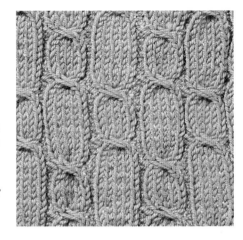

level ● ● ●
drape ▪

THE PATTERN

Multiple of 14 + 9

Row 1 and all odd numbered rows (WS): K2, p5, k2, * p5, k2, p5, k2. Repeat from * to end of row.

Row 2: P2, k5, p2, * k5, p2, k5, p2. Repeat from * to end of row.

Row 4: P2, k5, p2, * k5, p2, k5, p2. Repeat from * to end of row.

Row 6: P2, C5 (Sl 1 st onto cn and hold to front of work, sl 3 sts onto 2nd cn and hold to back of work, k1, k3 from 2nd cn, k1 from 1st cn), p2, * k5, p2, C5, p2. Repeat from * to end of row.

Row 8: P2, k5, p2, * k5, p2, k5, p2. Repeat from * to end of row.

Row 10: P2, k5, p2, * C5, p2, k5, p2. Repeat from * to end of row.

Row 12: P2, k5, p2, * k5, p2, k5, p2. Repeat from * to end of row.

Row 14: P2, k5, p2, * k5, p2, k5, p2. Repeat from * to end of row.

Row 16: P2, k5, p2, * k5, p2, k5, p2. Repeat from * to end of row.

there's more >

Cables

CANDY CABLES

more > Row 18: P2, k5, p2, * C5, p2, k5, p2. Repeat from * to end of row.

Row 20: P2, k5, p2, * k5, p2, k5, p2. Repeat from * to end of row.

Row 22: P2, C5, p2, * k5, p2, C5, p2. Repeat from * to end of row.

Row 24: P2, k5, p2, * k5, p2, k5, p2. Repeat from * to end of row.

Repeat rows 1–24.

CABLED CHECKERBOARD

Cabled checkerboard is a pattern of rope cables alternating with Reverse Stockinette stitch, which creates a checkerboard pattern. Because of the amount of cabling, the knitted fabric is fairly dense. Cabled checkerboard makes an excellent blanket pattern with a simple border. It would also work well in sweaters for men or children.

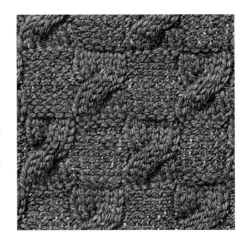

level ● ● ●
drape ■

THE PATTERN

Multiple of 12 + 6

Rows 1, 3, 5, 7, and 9 (WS): K6, * p6, k6. Repeat from * to end of row.

Rows 2 and 4: P6, * k6, p6. Repeat from * to end of row.

Row 6: P6, * CB6, p6. Repeat from * to end of row.

Rows 8 and 10: P6, * k6, p6. Repeat from * to end of row.

Rows 11, 13, 15, 17, and 19: P6, * k6, p6. Repeat from * to end of row.

Rows 12 and 14: K6, * p6, k6. Repeat from * to end of row.

Row 16: CB6, * p6, CB6. Repeat from * to end of row.

Rows 18 and 20: K6, * p6, k6. Repeat from * to end of row.

Repeat rows 1–20.

LACE PANELS WITH CABLES

The combination of lace with cables gives the fabric more drape than a typical cable pattern. It is also more lightweight, making it excellent for projects like blankets that get heavy when knit in a dense pattern stitch. Lace panels with cables would make a very pretty sweater pattern.

level
drape

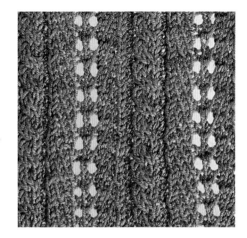

THE PATTERN

Multiple of 17 + 8

Rows 1 and 3 (WS): K2, p4, k2, * p9, k2, p4, k2. Repeat from * to end of row.

Row 2: P2, k4, p2, * k9, p2, k4, p2. Repeat from * to end of row.

Row 4: P2, CF4, p2, * ssk, k2, yo, k1, yo, k2, k2tog, p2, CF4, p2. Repeat from * to end of row.

Repeat rows 1–4.

SMOCKING CABLES

This basic traveling cable forms diamonds that resemble smocked fabric. The pattern can be used as an overall pattern or as a panel. Because the cables only travel or twist over one stitch, the fabric does not pull in much compared to other cable patterns and has more drape, making it suitable for afghans, wraps, and scarves In addition to projects like sweaters. The bottom edge does not curl, so this stitch pattern can be used without an edging.

level ● ● ●
drape ◼ ◼

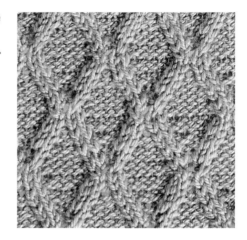

THE PATTERN

Multiple of 20 + 2

Row 1 (WS): K1 * p2, k6, p4, k6, p2. Repeat from * to last stitch, end k1.

Row 2: P1, * LT, p6, RT, LT, p6, RT. Repeat from * to last stitch, end p1.

Row 3: K1, * p2, k6, p4, k6, p2. Repeat from * to last stitch, end k1.

Row 4: P1, * T2L1, p4, T2R1, T2L1, p4, T2R1. Repeat from * to last stitch, end k1.

Row 5: K1, * k1, p2, k4, p2, k2, p2, k4, p2, k1. Repeat from * to last stitch, end k1.

Row 6: P1, * p1, T2L1, p2, T2R1, p2, T2L1, p2, T2R1, p1. Repeat from * to last stitch, end p1.

Row 7: K1, * k2, p2, k2, p2, k4, p2, k2, p2, k2. Repeat from * to last stitch, end k1.

Row 8: P1, * p2, T2L1, T2R1, p4, T2L1, T2R1, p2. Repeat from * to last stitch, end p1.

Row 9: K1, * k3, p4, k6, p4, k3. Repeat from * to last stitch, end k1.

Row 10: P1, * p3, RT, LT, p6, RT, LT, p3. Repeat from * to last stitch, end p1.

there's more >

Cables

SMOCKING CABLES

more >

Row 11: K1, * k3, p4, k6, p4, k3. Repeat from * to last stitch, end k1.

Row 12: P1, * p2, T2R1, T2L1, p4, T2R1, T2L1, p2. Repeat from * to last stitch, end p1.

Row 13: K1, * k2, p2, k2, p2, k4, p2, k2, p2, k2. Repeat from * to last stitch, end k1.

Row 14: P1, * p1, T2R1, p2, T2L1, p2, T2R1, p2, T2L1, p1. Repeat from * to last stitch, end p1.

Row 15: K1, * k1, p2, k4, p2, k2, p2, k4, p2, k1. Repeat from * to last stitch, end k1.

Row 16: P1, * T2R1, p4, T2L1, T2R1, p4, T2L1. Repeat from * to last stitch, end p1.

Repeat rows 1–16.

Needle Size Chart

Metric (mm)	US	UK/CAN
2	0	14
2.25	1	13
2.5		
2.75	2	12
3		11
3.25	3	10
3.5	4	
3.75	5	9
4	6	8
4.5	7	7
5	8	6
5.5	9	5
6	10	4
6.5	10 ½	3
8	11	0
9	13	00
10	15	000
12.75	17	
15	19	
19	35	

Abbreviations and Glossary

C3 over 4: Slip 4 stitches to the cable needle and hold to the back of the work. Knit the next 3 stitches, then purl 1 stitch from the cable needle, then knit the remaining stitches from the cable needle.

C6: Slip 2 stitches onto the cable needle and hold to the front of the work, slip 2 stitches onto a second cable needle and hold to the back of the work, k2, p2 from the second cable needle, k2 from the first cable needle.

CB2: Slip 1 stitch to the cable needle and hold to the back of the work. Knit the next stitch, then knit the stitch from the cable needle.

CB3: Slip 1 stitch to the cable needle and hold to the back of the work. Knit the next 2 stitches, then knit the stitch from the cable needle.

CB4: Slip 2 stitches to the cable needle and hold to the back of the work. Knit the next 2 stitches, then knit the stitches from the cable needle.

CB5: Slip 3 stitches to the cable needle and hold to the back of the work. Knit the next 2 stitches, then knit the stitches from the cable needle.

CB6: Slip 3 stitches to the cable needle and hold to the back of the work. Knit the next 3 stitches, then knit the stitches from the cable needle.

CB8: Slip 4 stitches to the cable needle and hold to the back of the work. Knit the next 4 stitches, then knit the stitches from the cable needle.

CF2 over 3: Slip the next 3 stitches to the cable needle and hold to the back of the work. Knit the next 2 stitches, then p1, k2 from the cable needle.

CF2: Slip 1 stitch to the cable needle and hold to the front of the work. Knit the next stitch, then knit the stitch from the cable needle.

CF3: Slip 2 stitches to the cable needle and hold to the front of the work. Knit the next stitch, then knit the stitches from the cable needle.

CF4: Slip 2 stitches to the cable needle and hold to the front of the work. Knit the next 2 stitches, then knit the stitches from the cable needle.

Yarn Chart

YARN WEIGHT SYMBOL & CATEGORY NAMES	lace	super fine	fine	light	medium	bulky	super bulky
TYPE OF YARNS IN CATEGORY	Fingering, 10-count crochet thread	Sock, Fingering, Baby	Sport, Baby	DK, Light Worsted	Worsted, Afghan, Aran	Chunky, Craft, Rug	Bulky, Roving

Source: Craft Yarn Council of America's www.YarnStandards.com

Cables

CF6: Slip 3 stitches to the cable needle and hold to the front of the work. Knit the next 3 stitches, then knit the stitches from the cable needle.

CF8: Slip 4 stitches to the cable needle and hold to the front of the work. Knit the next 4 stitches, then knit the stitches from the cable needle.

Cn: Cable needle.

DI: Double increase as follows: [k1 tbl, k1] into the next stitch, then insert the left-hand needle behind the vertical strand that runs downward from between the 2 stitches just made and k1 tbl into this strand to create the third stitch.

Inc 1 pwise: Increase 1 stitch purlwise by purling into the front and the back of the next stitch.

Inc 1: Increase 1 stitch by knitting into the front and the back of the next stitch.

K: Knit.

K1b: Knit the next stitch in the row below.

K2tog: Knit 2 stitches together.

K3tog: Knit 3 stitches together.

K4tog: Knit 4 stitches together.

K tbl: Knit through the back of the loop. If the k is followed by a number, knit that many stitches through the back loop. For example, k3 tbl means knit 3 stitches (1 at a time) through the back loops.

Kwise: Knitwise.

LH: Left hand.

LT: Left twist. Knit into the back of the second stitch on the left-hand needle. Do not drop it from the left-hand needle. Knit into the front of the first stitch on the left-hand needle. Drop off both stitches from the left-hand needle. For a left twist on the wrong side of the work, simply purl the stitches instead of knitting them.

LTP: Purl through the back of the second stitch on the left-hand needle without removing it from the needle, then knit the first stitch on the left-hand needle, slipping both stitches off of the needle at the same time. If this is difficult to work, you can use a T1L1 in its place.

M1: Pick up the horizontal strand of yarn lying between the stitch just worked and the next stitch on the left-hand needle from front to back and knit into the back of it. Also referred to as M1 kwise because the new stitch is a knit stitch.

M2: Pick up the horizontal strand of yarn lying between the stitch just worked and the next stitch on the left-hand needle from front to back and knit into the back and the front of it, creating 2 new stitches.

MB (make bobble): [K1, yo, k1, yo, k1] into the next stitch on the left-hand needle. Turn work. Purl 5. Turn work. Knit 5. Turn work. P2tog, k1, p2tog. Turn work. Sl 1, k2tog, psso. Bobble is complete.

P: Purl.

P2sso: Pass 2 slipped stitches over.

P tbl: Purl through the back loop. If the p is followed by a number, purl that many stitches through the back loop. For example, p3 tbl means purl 3 stitches (1 at a time) through the back loops.

P2tog tbl: Purl 2 stitches together through the back loops. If your knitting is too tight to comfortably purl 2 stitches together through the back loops, try working an ssp in place of p2tog tbl. While it is not exactly the same decrease, it is very close.

P2tog: Purl 2 stitches together.

P3tog: Purl 3 stitches together.

Psso: Pass slipped stitch over.

Pwise: Purlwise.

RH: Right hand.

RS: Right side.

RT: Right twist. Knit into the second stitch on the left-hand needle. Do not drop it from the left-hand needle. Knit into the first stitch on the left-hand needle. Drop both stitches from the left-hand needle. For a right twist on the wrong side of the work, simply purl the stitches instead of knitting them.

RTP: Knit into the front of the second stitch on the left-hand needle without removing it from the needle, then purl the first stitch on the left-hand needle, slipping both stitches off the needle at the same time.

S5: Slip the next 5 stitches onto a cable needle (or short double-pointed needle) and hold to the front of the work. Wind the yarn counterclockwise twice around the stitches on the cable needle, then work the stitches from the cable needle as k1, p3, k1.

Cables

Sl 1: Slip 1 stitch. When slipping stitches, it is customary to slip them purlwise unless working a decrease, when they are normally slipped knitwise. Individual instructions should indicate which direction to slip stitches.

Sl 2: Slip 2 stitches as if to k2tog.

Ssk: Working 1 stitch at a time, slip 2 stitches from the left-hand needle to the right-hand needle as if to knit. Insert the left-hand needle into the back of the 2 slipped stitches on the right-hand needle and knit the stitches together.

Ssp: Working 1 stitch at a time, slip 2 stitches from the left-hand needle to the right-hand needle as if to knit. Insert the left-hand needle into the back of the 2 slipped stitches on the right-hand needle and purl the stitches together.

Sssk: Working 1 stitch at a time, slip 3 stitches from the left-hand needle to the right-hand needle as if to knit. Insert the left-hand needle into the back of the 3 slipped stitches on the right-hand needle and knit the stitches together.

T1L1 (travel 1 stitch to the left 1 stitch): Slip 1 stitch to the cable needle and hold to the front of the work. Purl the next stitch, then knit the stitches from the cable needle.

T1L2 (travel 1 stitch to the left 2 stitches): Slip 1 stitch to the cable needle and hold to the front of the work. Knit the next 2 stitches, then knit the stitch from the cable needle.

T1R1 (travel 1 stitch to the right 1 stitch): Slip 1 stitch to the cable needle and hold to the back of the work. Knit the next stitch, then purl the stitch from the cable needle.

T1R2 (travel 1 stitch to the right 2 stitches): Slip 2 stitches to the cable needle and hold to the back of the work. Knit the next stitch, then knit the stitches from the cable needle.

T2L1 (travel 2 stitches to the left 1 stitch): Slip 2 stitches to the cable needle and hold to the front of the work. Purl the next stitch, then knit the stitches from the cable needle.

T2L2 (travel 2 stitches to the left 2 stitches): Slip 2 stitches to the cable needle and hold to the front of the work. Purl the next 2 stitches, then knit the stitches from the cable needle.

T2R1 (travel 2 stitches to the right 1 stitch): Slip 1 stitch to the cable needle and hold to the back of the work. Knit the next 2 stitches, then purl the stitch from the cable needle.

T2R2 (travel 2 stitches to the right 2 stitches): Slip 2 stitches to the cable needle and hold to the back of the work. Knit the next 2 stitches, then purl the stitches from the cable needle.

T3L1 (travel 3 stitches to the left 1 stitch): Slip 3 stitches to the cable needle and hold to the front of the work. Purl the next stitch, then knit the stitches from the cable needle.

T3L2 (travel 3 stitches to the left 2 stitches): Slip 3 stitches to the cable needle and hold to the front of the work. Purl the next 2 stitches, then knit the stitches from the cable needle.

T3R1 (travel 3 stitches to the right 1 stitch): Slip 1 stitch to the cable needle and hold to the back of the work. Knit the next 3 stitches, then purl the stitches from the cable needle.

T3R2 (travel 3 stitches to the right 2 stitches): Slip 2 stitches to the cable needle and hold to the back of the work. Knit the next 3 stitches, then purl the stitches from the cable needle.

T4L2 (travel 4 stitches to the left 2 stitches): Slip 4 stitches to the cable needle and hold to the front of the work. Purl the next 2 stitches, then knit the stitches from the cable needle.

T4R2 (travel 4 stitches to the right 2 stitches): Slip 2 stitches to the cable needle and hold to the back of the work. Knit the next 4 stitches, then purl the stitches from the cable needle.

T8B RIB: Slip the next 4 stitches onto the cable needle and hold to back of the work, k1, p2, k1 from the left-hand needle, then k1, p2, k1 from the cable needle.

T8F RIB: Slip the next 4 stitches onto the cable needle and hold to front of the work, k1, p2, k1 from the left-hand needle, then k1, p2, k1 from the cable needle.

WS: Wrong side.

Wyib: With yarn in back of work.

Wyif: With yarn in front of work.

Yo: Yarn over.

Specialty

Welcome to The Stitch Collection—a set of handy little guides to knit stitches that are as portable as can be; pick and choose which ones to throw into your knitting bag when you're on the go, and leave the others at home in the case. By design, they are not complete guides to knitting; instead, they are mini-encyclopedias of the stitches themselves. Their purpose is to help you choose the best stitch pattern for your projects.

Like most stitch guides, these books are written in terms of knitting flat—knitting back and forth on the needles, turning after each row. The set is divided into five volumes. Book 1 covers the knit and purl stitches; Book 2 focuses on rib stitches; Book 3 contains lace stitches; Book 4 is all about cables; and Book 5 is a compilation of specialty stitches. Each booklet has some common introductory material to help you determine which pattern you want to use, followed by text that is specific to that book's category of stitch. Each individual stitch pattern is ranked according to its level of difficulty, its drape, and offers suggestions as to its best function in a project (as an overall stitch, a filler stitch, a panel stitch, or an edge stitch).

Specialty

CHOOSING A STITCH PATTERN

The following sections give you suggestions on how to best use the guides in the set.

Look Before You Swatch

When choosing a stitch pattern to use for a project, be sure to look through all the books. Some patterns are included in one category, but have traits that overlap with the others. It's important to read through a pattern before starting it, too. Often an instruction can seem confusing or intimidating on paper, but will make complete sense when you have the knitting in hand and are ready to work that portion of the pattern.

Next, make a swatch. The swatches in this book are knit in varying weights of wool (worsted, sport, and fingering) provided by Lorna's Laces. In general, the patterns with small stitch multiples (less than 8 or 10) and panels are knit with Shepherd Worsted; the larger stitch multiples are done in Shepherd Sport. A few of the very large stitch repeats in Book 1 and Book 3 are worked in Shepherd Sock. The swatches have been blocked minimally for photography, and thus you may occasionally note irregularities that are inherent in hand knitting.

The appearance and drape of the stitch pattern will depend on the yarn chosen—color, style of spinning, fiber content, and weight—and on the gauge used. Keep in mind that large stitch motifs can overwhelm small projects, and small stitch motifs might be lost on a large project. Scale is important. Changing the weight of yarn and gauge it is knit at can help reduce or enlarge a motif as desired. The photos on this page show an example of the Tulip lace pattern knit with three different weights of yarn at three different gauges. The appearance of the pattern changes in each case and stresses the importance of swatching.

fingering

sport

worsted

Specialty

3

Follow the Organization

Each book is organized from smallest stitch multiple to largest, making it easier to find the pattern that best suits the project you have in mind. A small-scale lace pattern is better for a baby sweater than a large-scale one, for instance.

Match the Pattern to the Purpose

The descriptions included with each stitch pattern also suggest the type of project for which it is best suited. Many of the descriptions also indicate whether it works well as an overall stitch, a filler stitch, a panel stitch, or an edge stitch. An overall stitch pattern is used throughout the full project rather than in just a small area. You can convert patterns presented as panels into an overall stitch pattern by simply working one or more stitches (usually Stockinette or Reverse Stockinette) between repeats of the panel.

Filler stitches are worked in small areas of a larger project to fill open space. Filler stitches appear in between panels of other stitches or as a panel themselves. Filler stitches often have a small multiple and are easier to use in sizing and shaping. When combining filler stitches with other stitches (panels or overall patterns), always check the gauge of each stitch pattern. They can vary widely, even on the same needles with the same yarn.

A panel pattern is intended to be a section of a larger project. Most often, panels are just the stitch pattern itself, and the knitter needs to add border or background stitches. Panels can be worked as either a stitch multiple, by themselves, or combined with other panels or stitch patterns. Cables are very often written as a panel, for instance.

Lastly, edge or border stitch patterns can be used as filler stitches or overall patterns, but they lie flat and look tidy along the edges, making them suitable for hems, cuffs, or edges on other patterns.

Specialty

Understand the Ratings

Each stitch pattern in this collection has a skill level and a drape rating. The skill level ratings include easy (basic knitting knowledge required), advanced beginner, intermediate, and experienced. Remember what looks difficult on paper is often easier to understand with the knitting on needles in front of you.

All knitting has at least some amount of drape, so the ratings are relative and are based on using wool at the recommended gauge for the yarn. The ratings are: low (a firmer fabric), medium (reasonable amount of drape), and high (a flowing fabric). In general, the denser the fabric (e.g., more stitches per inch) is with stitches, the less drape it will have. The more open the fabric is (e.g., fewer stitches per inch), the more drape it will have. Cable patterns, for instance, will have less drape than lace patterns. However, drape also depends on the yarn chosen for a project and on the gauge used. Some fibers have more drape than others, and the finer the yarn, the more drape the fabric will have. A tighter gauge will have less drape than a looser gauge.

Understand Stitch Multiples and Balancing Stitches

Stitch patterns are presented with information about the number of stitches required to complete one pattern repeat. For panels, the information is simply how many stitches wide the panel is. For all other patterns, this information is presented as a multiple of stitches, plus any balancing stitches needed. For example, if you want to work six repeats of a pattern, and it requires four stitches and one balancing stitch (multiple of 4 + 1), you would cast on 24 stitches plus one balancing stitch, for a total of 25 stitches.

level

- easy
- advanced beginner
- intermediate
- experienced

drape

- low
- medium
- high

Specialty

5

Add Selvage Stitches

The patterns in these books do not include selvage stitches, which are one or more spare stitches included at the edge of your knitting for seaming or for tidying the edge. Some knitters don't even use selvage stitches unless specifically directed to do so in a pattern. If you are a knitter who likes to use selvage stitches, you will need to add them to the edges of your projects.

Work Increases and Decreases

These guides use a variety of increases and decreases. It is important to use the correct technique for the increases and decreases called for in the pattern instructions; this insures that your stitch pattern has the proper appearance, as the various techniques create different effects, such as slants or holes. Perhaps the most common increase used in the patterns is done by knitting into the front and back of a single stitch. There are several decreases used in the patterns—some decrease one stitch at a time (single decreases), some decrease two stitches at a time (double decreases), some decrease even more! When a pattern says simply to decrease one stitch, but doesn't say which decrease to use, the assumption is that you will use a k2tog (knit two stitches together) or a p2tog (purl two stitches together), depending on whether you are on the right or wrong side of your work. Consult the Abbreviations and Glossary section (page 61) for explanations of each type of increase or decrease.

CHOOSING THE BEST YARN

How do you choose the most suitable yarn for a stitch pattern or a project? The first thing to consider is the pattern itself. The busier the stitch pattern is, the simpler the yarn should be, and vice versa. If you want to work a lace pattern or an elaborate cable pattern, choose a smooth, plain-colored yarn. A subtly variegated or kettle-dyed solid yarn might work with a fancy pattern stitch, but a yarn with extreme color changes or striping will detract from the pattern stitch.

Fiber content makes a difference, too. Plant fibers (cotton, linen, hemp, rayon) are inelastic, as is silk. When you work with plant fibers, your knitting tends to be what-you-see-is-what-you-get. Blocking will not improve it.

In contrast, animal fibers are almost magical to knit with, and a good blocking hides a multitude of sins. The fiber has memory and will retain its shape until the next time it gets wet.

Consider Yarn Requirements

Knitting a swatch before beginning a project is important, of course. But when choosing stitch patterns for a project you design, it is useful to consult a reference to see what the estimated yardage requirements are for the size and type of project you are creating at the gauge you are knitting. Yardage requirement tables are usually based on Stockinette stitch, but keep in mind that different stitch patterns require different amounts of yarn. For instance, Garter stitch has a very compressed row gauge, so it will take more yarn than Stockinette stitch. Lace is very open, so it can use less yarn than Stockinette stitch. Cables and many fancy patterns are very dense and can use *much* more yarn than Stockinette stitch.

Specialty

INTRODUCTION TO SPECIALTY STITCHES

This book contains patterns that don't quite fit into the other categories. What the patterns have in common is some special manipulation of stitches—slipped stitches, twisted stitches, traveling stitches, decreases, or increases—and a striking appearance. Read the instructions carefully. Some of the stitch motifs are created with unusual techniques. While many of these patterns are a little slower to work, the efforts are worth it, because the finished results are remarkable.

Because of the manipulation that happens with the specialty stitch patterns, they generally will require more yarn than, say, Stockinette stitch. Most will look best knit at the recommended gauge for the yarn used, because their appeal is in the elaborate texture of the pattern. Many of these stitches create a dense fabric. More than other categories of stitches, specialty stitches can work well with variegated yarns because of the stitch manipulations, especially the slip-stitch motifs.

The twisted stitch and traveling stitch patterns will show up best when used with a tightly spun, solid (or nearly solid) colored yarn knit at a firm gauge—the recommended gauge or tighter. They also tend to look nicest in lighter-weight yarns, but feel free to experiment, as that is part of the joy of knitting.

Specialty stitch patterns vary greatly in their characteristics, so it is particularly important to swatch before starting a project. You will want to insure that the appearance and feel are what you are looking for. As you'll see, there are specialty stitches suitable for any imaginable project.

HEEL STITCH

Because every other stitch is slipped on the right-side rows, Heel stitch forms a very dense and somewhat elastic fabric. It is called Heel stitch because it is most often seen in the heel flap of socks. The floats behind the slipped stitches help the fabric last longer in a high-wear area. However, this stitch pattern would also work well for any project in which you want a knitted fabric that behaves more like a woven fabric, such as a jacket.

level
drape

THE PATTERN

Multiple of 2 + 1
Row 1 (WS): Purl.
Row 2: K1, * sl 1 wyib, k1. Repeat from * to end of row.
Repeat rows 1 and 2.

Multiple of 2
Set up row (WS): Purl.
Row 1 (RS): * Sl 1 wyib, k1. Repeat from * to end of row.
Row 2: Sl 1 wyif, purl to end of row.
Repeat rows 1 and 2.

Specialty

EYE OF PARTRIDGE STITCH

Eye of partridge stitch is essentially an offset Heel stitch (page 9). Because every other stitch is slipped on the right-side rows, Eye of partridge stitch forms a very dense and somewhat elastic fabric. It can be used similarly to Heel stitch.

level
drape ▥

THE PATTERN

Multiple of 2 + 1

Row 1 and all odd numbered rows (WS): Purl.

Row 2: K1, * sl 1 wyib, k1. Repeat from * to end of row.

Row 4: K2, * sl 1 wyib, k1. Repeat from * to last stitch, end k1.

Repeat rows 1–4.

LITTLE FLOWERS

Little flowers is a highly textured stitch created by working two stitches together, then working into the first stitch again. The end effect is something like little floral blooms. This stitch pattern is nice because it lies very flat and is tidy at the edges, so it can be used without an additional edge stitch. The small stitch multiple makes it appropriate for use as a filler stitch. Little flowers would be a good pattern for knitted jackets or small projects like hats and mittens.

level
drape

THE PATTERN

Multiple of 2

Rows 1 and 3 (WS): Purl.

Row 2: * K2tog, without slipping the stitches from the LH needle. Insert the RH needle between the two stitches and knit into the first stitch again, slipping both stitches off of the LH needle. Repeat from * to end of row.

Row 4: K1, * k2tog, without slipping the stitches from the LH needle. Insert the RH needle between the two stitches and knit into the first stitch again, slipping both stitches off of the LH needle. Repeat from * to last stitch, end k1.

Repeat rows 1–4.

GRANITE STITCH

Granite stitch is a firm, not terribly elastic stitch. Its combination of knits and purls make it lie flat, so it is an attractive edge stitch option. This stitch pattern comes off the needles looking slanted, and a good blocking evens it out nicely. However, you may want to avoid using it across large areas because the larger the area, the harder it is to block out the slant. Granite stitch is an appropriate filler stitch or motif for smaller projects.

level ◉ ◉
drape ▦

THE PATTERN

Multiple of 2

Row 1 (WS): Purl.

Row 2: Knit.

Row 3: * K2tog. Repeat from * to end of row.

Row 4: * [K1, p1] into each st. Repeat from * to end of row.

Repeat rows 1–4.

TWEEDY STITCH

Tweedy stitch is a dense stitch pattern with a surprising amount of drape. The tweed effect is created by passing a slipped stitch over other stitches. Tweedy stitch has a small stitch multiple and nice texture, so it makes a very good filler stitch. It is also an attractive overall pattern for projects like knitted jackets or tops.

level
drape

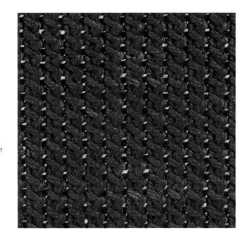

THE PATTERN

Multiple of 2 + 2

Row 1 (WS): Purl.

Row 2: K1, * sl 1 pwise, k1, yo, psso over both the k1 and yo stitches. Repeat from * to last stitch, end k1.

Repeat rows 1 and 2.

TILTED STITCH

Tilted stitch is created by working stitches together on the wrong side of the work to make it appear that the knit stitches on the right side of the work are slanting. The small stitch multiple and nice texture make this pattern a good filler stitch. Tilted stitch is also a pleasing overall pattern for knitted cardigans or jackets and would be pretty in hats and mittens.

level ⬤ ⬤ ⬤
drape ▥

THE PATTERN

Multiple of 2 + 2

Rows 1 and 3 (RS): Knit.

Row 2: * P2tog without removing the stitches from LH needle, k2tog through the same two stitches. Repeat from * to end of row.

Row 4: P1, * p2tog without removing the stitches from LH needle, k2tog through the same 2 stitches. Repeat from * to last stitch, end p1.

Repeat rows 1–4.

Specialty

14

WRAPPED STITCH

Wrapped stitch has the look of horizontal bars running across the fabric because of the yarn over that is passed over other stitches. This horizontal bar breaks up the knitted fabric in such a way that the pattern stitch would work well in variegated yarns. Wrapped stitch is a pretty overall pattern for sweaters, especially summer sweaters, and small projects like socks. It can also be used as a filler stitch.

level ⊕ ⊕ ⊕
drape ⊕ ⊕

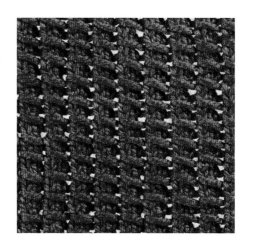

THE PATTERN

Multiple of 2 + 2

Row 1 (WS): Purl.

Row 2: K1, * yo, k2, pass yo over the 2 knit stitches. Repeat from * to last st, end k1.

Repeat rows 1 and 2.

RIDGES

The Ridges pattern is worked similarly to Granite stitch (page 12), but the appearance is much flatter. This pattern is relatively dense when knit at the recommended gauge. The fabric slants from all of the decreases, so it is not recommended for large areas. However, it could be used as an interesting design element, as in a scarf or the fronts of a cardigan.

level ● ● ●
drape ▬

THE PATTERN

Multiple of 2 + 2

Row 1 (WS): Purl.

Row 2: K1, *k2tog. Repeat from * to last stitch, end k1.

Row 3: K1, * M1, k1. Repeat from * to last stitch, end k1.

Row 4: Knit.

Repeat rows 1–4.

BRIOCHE STITCH

Although Brioche stitch looks like a rib, it is not constructed like one. It is warm and thick like a dense stitch pattern, but feels airy and light to the touch, and is perfect for projects like scarves because it is reversible and doesn't curl. It would also work well as an edging for a sweater, hat, or mittens. When Brioche stitch is knit at a looser gauge or with a finer yarn, it will have more of a lacy appearance because of the yarn overs.

level

drape

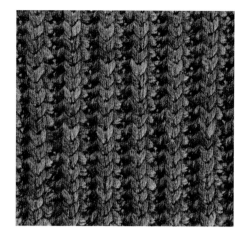

THE PATTERN

Multiple of 2 + 2

Row 1: K1, * yo, sl 1, k1. Repeat from * to last stitch, end k1. [This row is worked once.]

Row 2: K1, * yo, sl 1, k2tog. Repeat from * to last stitch, end k1.

Repeat row 2.

Last row: K1, * p1, k2tog. Repeat from * to last stitch, end k1. [This row is worked once.]

Note: You will be adding one extra stitch per pattern repeat on row 1. You will return to the original number of stitches on the very last row.

Specialty

17

LITTLE WAVES

Little waves has right and left twists that create a wave-like texture on a background of Stockinette stitch. The small stitch multiple and good texture are appropriate for use as a filler stitch. Little waves can be worked in sweaters, blankets, or just about any small accessory project. It would be a very good pattern for baby sweaters and blankets.

level
drape

THE PATTERN

Multiple of 3 + 1

Row 1 (WS): Purl.

Row 2: P1, * LT, p1. Repeat from * to end of row.

Row 3: K1, * RT, k1. Repeat from * to end of row.

Row 4: Knit.

Repeat rows 1–4.

PORTCULLIS STITCH

Portcullis stitch has strong vertical lines that almost look like crochet. It lies flat, so is suitable to use as an edge stitch. It is not a terribly elastic stitch pattern, so is best used as a border or in projects that require more drape than elasticity, such as scarves, shawls, or blankets. Try working this stitch in stripes of two or more colors for a bit of added interest.

level
drape

THE PATTERN

Multiple of 4 + 1

Row 1 (WS): Purl.

Row 2: K2tog, * (k1, yo, k1) into the next stitch, sl 1, k2tog, psso. Repeat from * to the last 3 stitches, end (k1, yo, k1) into the next stitch, ssk.

Repeat rows 1 and 2.

FANCY PILLARS

Fancy pillars is a dense pattern made up of tightly paired twists. The net effect is the appearance of cables without the effort of using a cable needle. Because the fabric is so thick, it will lie flat, making it suitable to use at the edge of a project. Fancy pillars would be a nice pattern for socks and other accessories. It would also be a good motif for a dressy sweater in a fine yarn.

level ◉ ◉ ◉
drape ▦

THE PATTERN

Multiple of 4
Row 1 (WS): Purl.
Row 2: * RT, LT. Repeat from * to end of row.
Repeat rows 1 and 2.

ELEGANT RIB

Elegant rib is a 2 x 2 rib that travels together, crosses, then diverges. The knitted fabric lies flat and pulls in a fair amount, but is very elastic. Elegant rib is perfect for a fancy edge stitch, like a sweater hem or sock cuff, or for an elegant overall stitch pattern in a fitted top.

level
drape

THE PATTERN

Multiple of 4

Rows 1, 3, 5, 11, and 13 (WS): * P1, k2, p1. Repeat from * to end of row.

Rows 2, 4, 12, and 14: *K1, p2, k1. Repeat from * to end of row.

Row 6: * LT, RT. Repeat from * to end of row.

Rows 7 and 9: * K1, p2, k1. Repeat from * to end of row.

Row 8: * P1, RT, p1. Repeat from * to end of row.

Row 10: * RT, LT. Repeat from * to end of row.

Repeat rows 1–14.

Specialty

21

TWISTED CHECKERBOARD

Twisted checkerboard is a traditional Irish pattern. At first glance it looks like a knit-purl pattern with some cables. In actuality, the "cables" come from working a simple right twist, and the plain rows are worked by knitting or purling through the back loop. The result is a more deeply textured pattern. Twisted checkerboard is perfect anywhere you would use a small stitch motif, such as in sweaters or accessories.

level ● ● ●
drape ▦ ▦

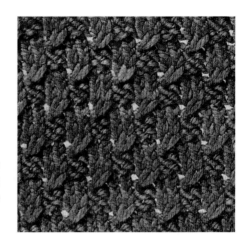

THE PATTERN

Multiple of 4 + 2

Row 1 (WS): P tbl.

Row 2: P2, * RT, p2. Repeat from * to end of row.

Row 3: K2, * p2, k2. Repeat from * to end of row.

Row 4: K tbl.

Row 5: P tbl.

Row 6: RT, * p2, RT. Repeat from * to end of row.

Row 7: P2, * k2, p2. Repeat from * to end of row.

Row 8: K tbl.

Repeat rows 1–8.

THIS WAY AND THAT

This way and that is essentially a rib pattern with fancy stitch work in the knit columns. Because of the balance of knit and purl stitches, the stitch pattern will pull in as it is being knit, but it blocks out nicely. Unlike most rib stitches, This way and that is not reversible because the fancy stitch work only happens on the right side. This pattern is suitable for use as an edge stitch or an overall pattern. It is perfect for socks and would look great in a sweater.

level ▥ ▥ ▥
drape ▥

THE PATTERN

Multiple of 4 + 1

Row 1 and all odd numbered rows (WS): K1, * p3, k1. Repeat from * to end of row.
Row 2: P1, * k1, RT, p1. Repeat from * to end of row.
Row 4: P1, * RT, k1, p1. Repeat from * to end of row.
Row 6: P1, * k1, RT, p1. Repeat from * to end of row.
Row 8: P1, * RT, k1, p1. Repeat from * to end of row.
Row 10: P1, * k3, p1. Repeat from * to end of row.
Row 12: P1, * LT, k1, p1. Repeat from * to end of row.
Row 14: P1, * k1, LT, p1. Repeat from * to end of row.
Row 16: P1, * LT, k1, p1. Repeat from * to end of row.
Row 18: P1.* k1, LT, p1. Repeat from * to end of row.
Row 20: P1 * k3, p1. Repeat from * to end of row.
Repeat rows 1–20.

BALLOONS

Balloons is a pattern stitch that is very similar to a bobble, but the balloon is worked over multiple rows. The resulting texture is flatter than the traditional bobble. Balloons would be a very effective stitch to use in a panel amongst other stitch patterns. It would also be a cute pattern for hats, mittens, or children's sweaters.

level ◉ ◉ ◉
drape ▥ ▥

THE PATTERN

Multiple of 4 + 3

Row 1 (WS): Knit.

Row 2: * P3, (k1, yo, k1) in the next stitch. Repeat from * to last 3 sts, end p3.

Row 3: K3, * p3, k3. Repeat from * to end of row.

Row 4: * P3, k3. Repeat from * to last 3 stitches, end p3.

Row 5: K3, * p3tog, k3. Repeat from * to end of row.

Row 6: Purl.

Row 7: Knit.

Row 8: * P1, (k1, yo, k1) in the next stitch, p2. Repeat from * to end of row, ending last repeat p1.

Row 9: K1, * p3, k3. Repeat from * to last 4 stitches, end p3, k1.

Row 10: P1, * k3, p3. Repeat from * to last 5 stitches, end k3, p1.

Row 11: K1, * p3tog, k3. Repeat from * to last 4 stitches, end p3tog, k1.

Row 12: Purl.

Repeat rows 1–12.

Note: You will be increasing two stitches per repeat on rows 2 and 8. You will return to the original number of stitches on rows 5 and 11.

FILIGREE

Filigree is a nice little pattern where the combining of stitches creates a lovely texture that resembles ornate metal work. The motif combines knits and purls in proportions that make the fabric lie very flat. While it can be used as a filler stitch, filigree is a pretty overall pattern for sweaters, hats, mittens, or blankets.

level

drape

THE PATTERN

Multiple of 4 + 1

Row 1 (WS): K1, * [p1, k1] twice. Repeat from * to end of row.

Row 2: P1, * [k1, p1] twice. Repeat from * to end of row.

Row 3: K1, * (p3tog, yo, p3tog) into next 3 stitches, k1.
Repeat from * to end of row.

Row 4: Knit.

Row 5: K1, * [p1, k1] twice. Repeat from * to end of row.

Row 6: P1, * [k1, p1] twice. Repeat from * to end of row.

Row 7: K1, p1, * k1, (p3tog, yo, p3tog) into next 3 stitches.
Repeat from * to last 3 stitches, end k1, p1, k1.

Row 8: Knit.

Repeat rows 1–8.

STAR STITCH

Star stitch produces a very spongy, thick fabric, but it is not terribly dense because of the yarn overs. Although the p3tog may be a bit tedious, the results are worth the effort. Choosing a more elastic fiber (like wool) will make the knitting easier. Star stitch makes a nice blanket or border on a sweater. Try alternating colors every four rows for a striped effect.

level ◐ ◐ ◐
drape ▦ ▦

THE PATTERN

Multiple of 4 + 1

Row 1 (RS): Knit.

Row 2: P1, * (p3tog, yo, p3tog) into the next 3 stitches, p1. Repeat from * to end of row.

Row 3: Knit.

Row 4: P3, (p3tog, yo, p3tog) into the next 3 stitches, * p1, (p3tog, yo, p3tog) into the next 3 stitches. Repeat from * to the last 3 stitches, end p3.

Repeat rows 1–4.

Specialty

TRINITY STITCH

This stitch's name is an allusion to the Holy Trinity, with its working of three stitches together. It is a common filler pattern for Aran sweaters because of its small stitch repeat and dramatic texture. Trinity stitch can be used as an overall pattern, too. There is some openness to it, so when it is knit with finer yarn on a relatively large needle, it takes on a lacy appearance. It is also referred to as Bramble stitch.

level ⬤ ⬤ ⬤
drape ⬤ ⬤

THE PATTERN

Multiple of 4 + 2

Row 1 (RS): Purl.

Row 2: K1, * (k1, p1, k1) into the next stitch, p3tog. Repeat from * to last stitch, end k1.

Row 3: Purl.

Row 4: K1, * p3tog, (k1, p1, k1) into the next stitch. Repeat from * to last stitch, end k1.

Repeat rows 1–4.

Specialty

27

DOUBLE CROSSED RIB

Double crossed rib is similar to the Elegant rib pattern (page 21). However, Double crossed rib twists the knit stitches to make the knit ribs more pronounced, and works an additional twist when the knit ribs travel together. The knitted fabric lies flat and pulls in a fair amount, but is very elastic. Double crossed rib is perfect for a fancy edge stitch, such as a sweater hem or sock cuff, or for an elegant overall stitch pattern in a fitted top.

level ◉ ◉ ◉
drape ▦

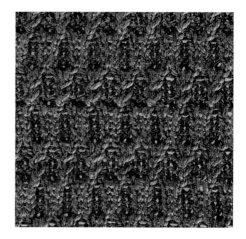

THE PATTERN

Multiple of 4 + 2

Row 1 (WS): K1, p1, k2, * p2, k2. Repeat from * to last 2 stitches, end p1, k1.

Row 2: P1, k1 tbl, p2, * k2 tbl, p2. Repeat from * to last 2 stitches, end k1 tbl, p1.

Row 3: K1, p1, k2, * p2, k2. Repeat from * to last 2 stitches, end p1, k1.

Row 4: P1, * LTP, RTP. Repeat from * to last stitch, end p1.

Row 5: K2, * p2, k2. Repeat from * to end of row.

Row 6: P2, * RT, p2. Repeat from * to end of row.

Row 7: K2, * p2, k2. Repeat from * to end of row.

Row 8: P2, * RT, p2. Repeat from * to end of row.

Row 9: K2, * p2, k2. Repeat from * to end of row.

Row 10: P1, * RTP, LTP. Repeat from * to last stitch, end p1.

Row 11: K1, p1, k2, * p2, k2. Repeat from * to last 2 stitches, end p1, k1.

Row 12: P1, k1 tbl, p2, * k2 tbl, p2. Repeat from * to last 2 stitches, end k1 tbl, p1.

Repeat rows 1-12.

MRS. HUNTER'S PATTERN

Mrs. Hunter's pattern is a traditional Irish stitch pattern. It works nicely with variegated yarns, as the wrapping-across stitches and yarn overs break up the variegation, but the motif is simple enough to not be overwhelmed by the color changes. Mrs. Hunter's pattern would be a nice border on a sweater project or a cute blanket pattern.

level
drape

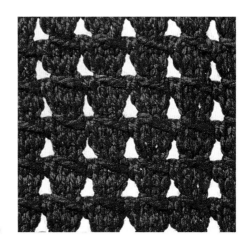

THE PATTERN

Multiple of 4 + 2

Row 1 (WS): Purl

Row 2: K1, * sl 1, k3, psso the 3 stitches just knit. Repeat from * to the last stitch, end k1.

Row 3: P1, * p3, yo. Repeat from * to the last stitch, end p1.

Row 4: Knit.

Repeat rows 1–4.

HORIZONTAL HERRINGBONE

Horizontal herringbone is a good stitch pattern for any project with a more tailored appearance. It is not a particularly elastic fabric, but would work well for jackets, vests, or scarves. Try knitting a project from side-to-side to change the appearance of the finished pattern. The wrong side of this pattern is nice, too. Note that the selvages will elongate because the slipped stitches will pull the fabric vertically. Blocking the finished work will help even out the appearance.

level ◉ ◉ ◉
drape ▥ ▥

THE PATTERN

Multiple of 4 + 3

Row 1 (RS): K3, *sl 2 wyif, k2. Repeat from * to end of row.

Row 2: P1, *sl 2 wyib, p2. Repeat from * to last 2 stitches, end p2.

Row 3: K1, *sl 2 wyif, k2. Repeat from * to last 2 stitches, end k2.

Row 4: P3, *sl 2 wyib, p2. Repeat from * to end of row.

Rows 5-12: Repeat rows 1–4 twice.

Row 13: K1, *sl 2 wyif, k2. Repeat from * to last 2 stitches, end k2.

Row 14: P1, *sl 2 wyib, p2. Repeat from * to last 2 stitches, end p2.

Row 15: K3, *sl 2 wyif, k2. Repeat from * to end of row.

Row 16: P3, *sl 2 wyib, p2. Repeat from * to end of row.

Rows 17-24: Repeat rows 13–16 twice.

Repeat rows 1–24.

Specialty

TWISTED TRIANGLES

Twisted triangles is based on a traditional Arabic knitting stitch motif. The twisted stitches give extra definition to what would appear to be a basic knit-purl pattern stitch. The pattern is reversible, although because it is the purls that are twisted, the wrong side does not have the same interesting texture. Twisted triangles would be a great pattern anywhere you would normally use Stockinette stitch or need to have an attractive wrong side.

level

drape

THE PATTERN

Multiple of 6

Row 1 (RS): * K1 tbl, p5. Repeat from * to end of row.

Row 2: * K4, p2 tbl. Repeat from * to end of row.

Row 3: * K3 tbl, p3. Repeat from * to end of row.

Row 4: * K2, p4 tbl. Repeat from * to end of row.

Row 5: * K5 tbl, p1. Repeat from * to end of row.

Row 6: * K2, p4 tbl. Repeat from * to end of row.

Row 7: * K3 tbl, p3. Repeat from * to end of row.

Row 8: * K4, p2 tbl. Repeat from * to end of row.

Repeat rows 1–8.

Specialty

LITTLE KNOTS

Little knots is a field of dainty knots against a background of Stockinette stitch. The techniques used in the Little knots pattern is similar to the Star stitch (page 26). The resulting fabric, however, looks quite different because of the Stockinette stitch background. Little knots is a pretty pattern for baby and children's sweaters. It is also nice for dressy knitted tops.

level ◉ ◉ ◉
drape ▥ ▥

THE PATTERN

Multiple of 6 + 5

Row 1 and all odd numbered rows (WS): Purl.

Row 2: Knit.

Row 4: K1, * p3tog without removing the stitches from LH needle, yo, make knot (p3tog through the same 3 stitches), k3. Repeat from * to last 4 stitches, end make knot, k1.

Row 6: Knit.

Row 8: K4, * make knot, k3. Repeat from * to last stitch, end k1.

Repeat rows 1-8.

Specialty

QUILTED LATTICE

Quilted lattice is formed by slipping stitches with the yarn held to the front of the work. The strands are later picked up when knitting a stitch, giving the fabric a quilted effect. Because the strands interrupt the plain Stockinette background, this stitch pattern works well with variegated yarn. Quilted lattice is a nice stitch pattern for sweater projects. It can work in socks as long as you remember to carry the strand loosely when slipping the stitches.

level
drape

THE PATTERN

Multiple of 6 + 3

Row 1 and all odd numbered rows (WS): Purl.

Row 2: K2, * sl 5 wyif, k1. Repeat from * to last stitch, end k1.

Row 4: K4, * insert the RH needle under the loose strand and k1, bring the stitch under the strand, k5. Repeat from * to end of row, end last repeat k4.

Row 6: K1, sl 3 wyif, * k1, sl 5 wyif. Repeat from * to 5 stitches, end k1, sl 3 wyif, k1.

Row 8: K1, * insert the RH needle under the loose strand and k1, bring the stitch under the strand, k5. Repeat from * to end of row, end last repeat k1.

Repeat rows 1–8.

FAUX CABLES ON STOCKINETTE

Faux cables on Stockinette is a pattern that has the appearance of rope cables, but it is simply a combination of k2tog decreases and knitting into the front and back of a stitch to increase. The faux cables can easily be widened. Faux cables on Stockinette can be used in any project where you would normally use Stockinette stitch. Note that the fabric will have some bias.

level ⬤ ⬤
drape ▥ ▥

THE PATTERN

Multiple of 7

Row 1 and all other odd numbered rows: Purl.

Row 2: * K3, k2tog, inc 1, k1. Repeat from * to end of row.

Row 4: * K2, k2tog, inc 1, k2. Repeat from * to end of row.

Row 6: * K1, k2tog, inc 1, k3. Repeat from * to end of row.

Repeat rows 1-6.

HERRINGBONE

Herringbone resembles an elongated chevron pattern. The knitting forms a traditional zigzag pattern by the combination of the decrease and increase. The pull of the fabric creates a scalloped cast-on edge and makes this pattern a good one to consider when using variegated yarns. Herringbone makes a tight fabric with a nice drape. It would be perfect for a dressy pullover.

level

drape

THE PATTERN

Multiple of 7 + 1

Row 1 (WS): Purl.

Row 2: * K2tog, k2, k tbl of stitch below then k tbl, k2. Repeat from * to last stitch, end k1.

Row 3: Purl.

Row 4: K3, k tbl of stitch below then k tbl, k2, k2tog, * k2, k tbl of stitch below then k tbl, k2, k2tog. Repeat from * to end of row.

Repeat rows 1–4.

Specialty

35

CLIMBING VINE TWISTED STITCH

Climbing vine twisted stitch is a series of vine motifs created by working right or left twist stitches on a Stockinette stitch background. This pattern will show up best when worked at a firm gauge in a smooth, tightly spun yarn. Climbing vine twisted stitch is a perfect overall pattern for a fine gauge knit top or a men's vest. Its grid-work look would also be attractive in accessories like hats, mittens, or socks.

level ◍ ◍ ◍
drape ▥

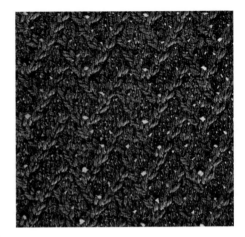

THE PATTERN

Multiple of 8

Row 1 and all odd numbered rows (WS): Purl.

Row 2: * LT, k2, LT, RT. Repeat from * to end of row.

Row 4: K1, * LT, k2, RT, k2. Repeat from * to end of row, end last repeat k1.

Row 6: * RT, LT, RT, k2. Repeat from * to end of row.

Row 8: K3, * LT, k2, RT, k2. Repeat from * to last 5 stitches, end LT, k3.

Repeat rows 1–8.

PINE TREES

Pine trees is created by slipping stitches with the yarn held to the right side of the work. The strand is then knit under to create a little tree, with each tree motif separated by a column of Garter stitch. As a result, the knitted fabric lies flat without curling. The slipped stitches makes Pine trees a suitable pattern for use with variegated yarns. It is a good pattern for blankets or accessories and would also work well in a sweater pattern—the vertical motif is slimming.

level
drape

THE PATTERN

Multiple of 8 + 1

Row 1 (WS): K2, * p5, k3. Repeat from * to last 7 stitches, end p5, k2.

Row 2: K2, * sl 5 wyif, k3. Repeat from * to last 7 stitches, end sl 5 wyif, k2.

Row 3: K2, * p5, k3. Repeat from * to last 7 stitches, end p5, k2.

Row 4: K4, * insert the RH needle under the loose strand and k1, bringing the stitch under the strand, k7. Repeat from * to end of row, end last repeat k4.

Repeat rows 1–4.

Specialty

37

TWIST STITCH BRAID

Twist stitch braid is a cable-like braid pattern created by twists that travel the stitches. Each braid is separated by Reverse Stockinette stitch, so the finished fabric resembles a rib. To best show the braids, this pattern should be knit with a tightly spun, smooth yarn at a firm gauge. Twist stitch braid can be used as an edge stitch for sweaters, hats, mittens, or gloves, or as a panel or an overall pattern in an elaborate sweater.

level ◉ ◉ ◉
drape ▥

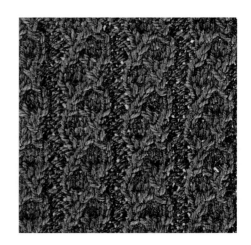

THE PATTERN

Multiple of 8 + 2

Row 1 (WS): K2, * k1, p5, k2. Repeat from * to end of row.

Row 2: P2, * k3, RT, p3. Repeat from * to end of row.

Row 3: K2, * k1, p5, k2. Repeat from * to end of row.

Row 4: P2, * LT, RT, LT, p2. Repeat from * to end of row.

Row 5: K2, * p5, k3. Repeat from * to end of row.

Row 6: P2, * p1, LT, k3, p2. Repeat from * to end of row.

Row 7: K2, * p5, k3. Repeat from * to end of row.

Row 8: P2, * RT, LT, RT, p2. Repeat from * to end of row.

Repeat rows 1–8.

WAVY COLUMNS

The Wavy columns stitch pattern is basically a rib with a traveling stitch flourish. It will pull in as you knit, but will block out to be wider. The motif would make an excellent border stitch on a sweater, hat, or mittens. It would also work well as an overall stitch for a sweater, especially one intended to fit the body more closely.

level

drape

THE PATTERN

Multiple of 8 + 3

Row 1 (WS): P3, * k3, p1, k1, p3. Repeat from * to end of row.

Row 2: K3, * p1, LT, p2, k3. Repeat from * to end of row.

Row 3: P3, * k2, p1, k2, p3. Repeat from * to end of row.

Row 4: K3, * p2, LT, p1, k3. Repeat from * to end of row.

Row 5: P3, * k1, p1, k3, p3. Repeat from * to end of row.

Row 6: K3, * p3, k1, p1, k3. Repeat from * to end of row.

Row 7: P3, * k1, p1, k3, p3. Repeat from * to end of row.

Row 8: K3, * p2, RT, p1, k3. Repeat from * to end of row.

Row 9: P3, * k2, p1, k2, p3. Repeat from * to end of row.

Row 10: K3, * p1, RT, p2, k3. Repeat from * to end of row.

Row 11: P3, * k3, p1, k1, p3. Repeat from * to end of row.

Row 12: K3, * p1, k1, p3, k3. Repeat from * to end of row.

Repeat rows 1–12.

CHECKS AND BALANCES

Checks and balances is based on an Arabic knitting pattern. It is essentially a knit-purl pattern, with the knit stitches being twisted on the right side of the work. The effect is to give more stitch definition and a more dramatic texture. The combinations of knits and purls make the edges lie flat. Checks and balances would be a suitable pattern for any project where you would normally use a knit-purl pattern—accessories, sweaters, or blankets.

level ◐ ◐ ◐
drape ▦ ▦

THE PATTERN

Multiple of 8 + 4

Row 1 (WS): K4, * p4 tbl, k4. Repeat from * to end of row.

Row 2: K tbl.

Row 3: P4 tbl, * k4, p4 tbl. Repeat from * to end of row.

Row 4: * P1, k4 tbl, p3. Repeat from * to last 4 sts, end p1, k3 tbl.

Row 5: P2 tbl, k2, * k2, p4 tbl, k2. Repeat from * to end of row.

Row 6: * P3, k4 tbl, p1. Repeat from * to last 4 sts, end p3, k1 tbl.

Row 7: K4, * p4 tbl, k4. Repeat from * to end of row.

Row 8: K tbl.

Row 9: P4 tbl, * k4, p4 tbl. Repeat from * to end of row.

Row 10: * K4 tbl, p4. Repeat from * to last 4 sts, end k4 tbl.

Row 11: P4 tbl, * k4, p4 tbl. Repeat from * to end of row.

Row 12: * K4 tbl, p4. Repeat from * to last 4 sts, end k4 tbl.

Row 13: P tbl.

Row 14: P4, * k4 tbl, p4. Repeat from * to end of row.

Row 15: P1 tbl, k3, * k1, p4 tbl, k3. Repeat from * to end of row.

there's more >

Specialty

CHECKS AND BALANCES

more >   Row 16: * P2, k4 tbl, p2. Repeat from * to last 4 sts, end p2, k2 tbl.

Row 17: P3 tbl, k1, * k3, p4 tbl, k1. Repeat from * to end of row.

Row 18: K4 tbl, * p4, k4 tbl. Repeat from * to end of row.

Row 19: P tbl.

Row 20: P4, * k4 tbl, p4. Repeat from * to end of row.

Row 21: K4, * p4 tbl, k4. Repeat from * to end of row.

Row 22: P4, * k4 tbl, p4. Repeat from * to end of row.

Repeat rows 1–22.

Specialty

KNOTTED DIAMONDS

This motif is created by working a knot stitch that pulls the fabric so that the knots appear to be the corners of an embossed diamond. The knots are worked similarly to Little knots (page 32), but the stitches are slipped before being worked together. This technique creates a more embossed look in the fabric. Knotted diamonds can be used in accessories projects or for sweaters. Since it is a small motif, it would be good for baby sweaters.

level ◍ ◍ ◍
drape ▥ ▥

THE PATTERN

Multiple of 8 + 5

Row 1 (WS): Purl.

Row 2: Knit.

Row 3: Purl.

Row 4: K5, * k3tog without removing the stitches from the LH needle, yo, k3tog through the same stitches, removing them from the LH needle, k5. Repeat from * to end of row.

Row 5: P5, * sl 3 wyif, p5. Repeat from * to end of row.

Row 6: Knit.

Row 7: Purl.

Row 8: K1, * k3tog without removing the stitches from the LH needle, yo, k3tog through the same stitches, removing them from the left hand needle, k5. Repeat from * to end of row, end last repeat k1.

Row 9: P1, * sl 3 wyif, p5. Repeat from * to end of row, end last repeat p1.

Repeat rows 2–9.

SMOCKED STITCH

Smocked stitch is named for the sewing technique it resembles. The yarn is wrapped around bunches of stitches before they are worked, and the tighter you wrap the stitches, the more smocked the fabric will appear. Smocked stitch would work well with variegated yarns, as the wrapping breaks up lengths of color. This stitch pattern is nice for adding shaping to sweaters without having to alter the stitch count, simply by virtue of the smocking pulling in. It would be the perfect pattern for the bodice of a girl's dress, too.

level

drape

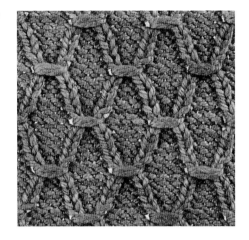

THE PATTERN

Multiple of 8 + 7

Row 1 and all odd numbered rows (WS): K1, p1, * k3, p1. Repeat from * to last stitch, end k1.

Row 2: P1, k1, * p3, k1. Repeat from * to last stitch, end p1.

Row 4: P1, S5, * p3, S5. Repeat from * to last stitch, end p1.

Row 6: P1, k1, * p3, k1. Repeat from * to last stitch, end p1.

Row 8: P1, k1, * p3, k1. Repeat from * to last stitch, end p1.

Row 10: P1, k1, p3, * S5, p3. Repeat from * to last 2 stitches, end k1, p1.

Row 12: P1, k1, * p3, k1. Repeat from * to last stitch, end p1.

Repeat rows 1–12.

TWIST STITCH WAVES

Twist stitch waves is composed of a waving series of twisted traveling stitches on a Reverse Stockinette background. Unlike many of its twisted stitch counterparts, the Twist stitch waves pattern has an attractive wrong side as well. This stitch motif would be nice for use in socks and other accessories, as well as for fine-gauge sweaters. It doesn't curl along the cast-on edge, so no additional edge stitch is necessary.

level ◉ ◉ ◉
drape ▥ ▥

THE PATTERN

Multiple of 9

Row 1 (WS): * K4, p1, k2, p1, k1. Repeat from * to end of row.
Row 2: * P1, LT, p6. Repeat from * to end of row.
Row 3: * K6, p2, k1. Repeat from * to end of row.
Row 4: * RTP, LT, p5. Repeat from * to end of row.
Row 5: * K5, p2, k1, p1. Repeat from * to end of row.
Row 6: * P1, RTP, LT, p4. Repeat from * to end of row.
Row 7: * K4, p2, k1, p1, k1. Repeat from * to end of row.
Row 8: * P2, RTP, LT, p3. Repeat from * to end of row.
Row 9: * K3, p2, k1, p1, k2. Repeat from * to end of row.
Row 10: * P3, RTP, LT, P2. Repeat from * to end of row.
Row 11: * K2, p2, k1, p1, k3. Repeat from * to end of row.
Row 12: * P4, RTP, LTP, p1. Repeat from * to end of row.
Row 13: * K1, p1, k2, p1, k4. Repeat from * to end of row.
Row 14: * P6, RT, p1. Repeat from * to end of row.
Row 15: * K1, p2, k6. Repeat from * to end of row.
Row 16: * P5, RT, LTP. Repeat from * to end of row.
Row 17: * P1, k1, p2, k5. Repeat from * to end of row.
Row 18: * P4, RT, LTP, p1. Repeat from * to end of row.
Row 19: * K1, p1, k1, p2, k4. Repeat from * to end of row.

there's more >

Specialty

TWIST STITCH WAVES

more >

Row 20: * P3, RT, LTP, p2. Repeat from * to end of row.
Row 21: * K2, p1, k1, p2, k3. Repeat from * to end of row.
Row 22: * P2, RT, LTP, P3. Repeat from * to end of row.
Row 23: * K3, p1, k1, p2, k2. Repeat from * to end of row.
Row 24: * P1, RTP, LTP, p4. Repeat from * to end of row.
Repeat rows 1–24.

INFINITY TWISTS

Infinity twists is based on a traditional French pattern that resembles the mathematical symbol for infinity. The result is beautiful twisted columns on a Reverse Stockinette stitch background. The appearance is similar to a rib stitch, but the drape is better, and the fabric doesn't pull in much. Infinity twists would be a special pattern for socks, mittens, or gloves. It would be an elegant stitch for a dressy sweater, too.

level ● ● ● ●
drape ▐▌ ▐▌

THE PATTERN

Multiple of 9 + 2

Row 1 (RS): K2, * p2, TW3 (twist 3 by knitting into 3rd, 2nd, and 1st stitch on LH needle then slip all stitches off the needle together), p2, k2. Repeat from * to end of row.

Row 2: P2, * k2, p3, k2, p2. Repeat from * to end of row.

Row 3: P2, * p2, TW3, p4. Repeat from * to end of row.

Row 4: P2, * k2, p3, k2, p2. Repeat from * to end of row.

Row 5: K2, * p2, TW3, p2, k2. Repeat from * to end of row.

Row 6: P2, * k2, p3, k2, p2. Repeat from * to end of row.

Row 7: P2, * p2, TW3, p4. Repeat from * to end of row.

Row 8: P2, * k2, p3, k2, p2. Repeat from * to end of row.

Row 9: K2, * p2, TW3, p2, k2. Repeat from * to end of row.

Row 10: P2, * k2, p3, k2, p2. Repeat from * to end of row.

Row 11: P2, * p2, k3, p4. Repeat from * to end of row.

Row 12: P2, * k2, p3, k2, p2. Repeat from * to end of row.

Row 13: K2, * p2, TW3, p2, k2. Repeat from * to end of row.

Row 14: P2, * k2, p3, k2, p2. Repeat from * to end of row.

Row 15: P2, * p2, k3, p4. Repeat from * to end of row.

Row 16: P2, * k2, p3, k2, p2. Repeat from * to end of row.

Repeat rows 1–16.

WINGS

Wings is basically a knit-purl stitch pattern with one special twist. On rows 5 and 11, a purl stitch is worked into a stitch several rows below the stitches on the needle. This maneuver pulls the center of the triangles up to form "wings." This pattern can work nicely with variegated yarn because it pulls the yarn in interesting directions. Wings is a perfect stitch pattern for sweaters, blankets, or socks.

level

drape

THE PATTERN

Multiple of 10 + 1

Row 1 (RS): Knit.

Row 2: P1, * p3, k1, p1, k1, p4. Repeat from * to end of row.

Row 3: K1, * k2, p2, k1, p2, k3. Repeat from * to end of row.

Row 4: P1, * p1, k3, p1, k3, p2. Repeat from * to end of row.

Row 5: K1, * p4, p next stitch through the stitch 3 rows below the stitch on the needle, dropping all stitches above it off, p4, k1. Repeat from * to end of row.

Row 6: Knit.

Row 7: Knit.

Row 8: P1, * k1, p7, k1, p1. Repeat from * to end of row.

Row 9: K1, * p2, k5, p2, k1. Repeat from * to end of row.

Row 10: P1, * k3, p3, k3, p1. Repeat from * to end of row.

Row 11: K1, * p4, k1, p4, p next stitch through the stitch 3 rows below the stitch on the needle, dropping all stitches above it off. Repeat from * to end of row, end last repeat k1.

Row 12: Knit.

Repeat rows 1–12.

Specialty

47

TWISTED ARCS

Twisted arcs is a combination of twisted stitches, ribbing, decreases, and yarn overs. The end result is an arching rib stitch appearance with some lacy openness. Twisted arcs is a dramatic motif that is most effective used as an overall stitch pattern. It is suitable for just about any type of project, but will look best knit in a tightly spun yarn at a firm gauge.

level ◉ ◉ ◉ ◉
drape ▥ ▥

THE PATTERN

Multiple of 10 + 1

Row 1 (WS): P1 tbl, * [k1, p1 tbl] 4 times, p2 tbl. Repeat from * to end of row.

Row 2: K1 tbl, * yo, k2tog tbl, [p1, k1tbl] 4 times. Repeat from * to end of row.

Row 3: P1 tbl, * [k1, p1 tbl] 4 times, p2 tbl. Repeat from * to end of row.

Row 4: K1 tbl, * yo, p1, k2tog tbl, [k1 tbl, p1] 3 times, k1 tbl. Repeat from * to end of row.

Row 5: P1 tbl, * [k1, p1 tbl] 3 times, p1 tbl, k1, p2 tbl. Repeat from * to end of row.

Row 6: K1 tbl, * yo, k1 tbl, p1, k2tog tbl, [p1, k1 tbl] 3 times. Repeat from * to end of row.

Row 7: P1 tbl, * [k1, p1 tbl] 4 times, p2 tbl. Repeat from * to end of row.

Row 8: K1 tbl, * yo, p1, k1 tbl, p1, k2tog tbl, [k1 tbl, p1] twice, k1 tbl. Repeat from * to end of row.

Row 9: P1 tbl, * [k1, p1 tbl] twice, [p1 tbl, k1] twice, p2 tbl. Repeat from * to end of row.

Row 10: K1 tbl, * yo, [k1 tbl, p1] twice, k2tog tbl, [p1, k1 tbl] twice. Repeat from * to end of row.

there's more >

TWISTED ARCS

more >

Row 11: P1 tbl, * [k1, p1 tbl] 4 times, p2 tbl. Repeat from * to end of row.

Row 12: K1 tbl, * yo, [p1, k1 tbl] twice, p1, k2tog tbl, k1 tbl, p1, k1 tbl. Repeat from * to end of row.

Row 13: P1 tbl, * k1, p2 tbl, [k1, p1 tbl] 3 times, p1 tbl. Repeat from * to end of row.

Row 14: K1 tbl, * yo, [k1 tbl, p1] 3 times, k2tog tbl, p1, k1 tbl. Repeat from * to end of row.

Row 15: P1 tbl, * [k1, p1 tbl] 4 times, p2 tbl. Repeat from * to end of row.

Row 16: K1 tbl, * yo, [p1, k1 tbl] 3 times, p1, k2tog tbl, k1 tbl. Repeat from * to end of row.

Row 17: P1 tbl, * [p1 tbl, k1] 4 times, p2 tbl. Repeat from * to end of row.

Row 18: K1 tbl, * yo, [k1 tbl, p1] 4 times, k2tog tbl. Repeat from * to end of row.

Repeat rows 1–18.

Specialty

49

BUTTERFLY STITCH

Butterfly stitch is created by slipping stitches with the yarn held to the right side of the work. The strands are later picked up and knit, making little butterfly motifs on a background of Stockinette stitch. Strand loosely, so that the fabric doesn't pucker. This pattern works well with variegated yarns, as it breaks up the color nicely. Butterfly stitch is a suitable pattern for use in sweaters, although the stranding causes the fabric to be less elastic.

level ● ● ●
drape ▮▮ ▮▮

THE PATTERN

Multiple of 10 + 9

Row 1 (RS): K2, * sl 5 wyif, k5. Repeat from * to last 7 stitches, end sl 5 wyif, k2.

Row 2: Purl.

Row 3: K2, * sl 5 wyif, k5. Repeat from * to last 7 stitches, end sl 5 wyif, k2.

Row 4: Purl.

Row 5: K2, * sl 5 wyif, k5. Repeat from * to last 7 stitches, end sl 5 wyif, k2.

Row 6: Purl.

Row 7: K2, * sl 5 wyif, k5. Repeat from * to last 7 stitches, end sl 5 wyif, k2.

Row 8: Purl.

Row 9: K2, * sl 5 wyif, k5. Repeat from * to last 7 stitches, end sl 5, k2.

Row 10: P4, * use the RH needle to bring the 5 strands up on to the LH needle, purl the 5 strands together with the next stitch (the center stitch of the 5 slipped stitches), p9. Repeat from * to end of row, end last repeat p4.

Row 11: K7, * sl 5 wyif, k5. Repeat from * to last 12 stitches, end sl 5 wyif, k7.

there's more >

BUTTERFLY STITCH

more >

Row 12: Purl.

Row 13: K7, * sl 5 wyif, k5. Repeat from * to last 12 stitches, end sl 5 wyif, k7.

Row 14: Purl.

Row 15: K7, * sl 5 wyif, k5. Repeat from * to last 12 stitches, end sl 5 wyif, k7.

Row 16: Purl.

Row 17: K7, * sl 5 wyif, k5. Repeat from * to last 12 stitches, end sl 5 wyif, k7.

Row 18: Purl.

Row 19: K7, * sl 5 wyif, k5. Repeat from * to last 12 stitches, end sl 5 wyif, k7.

Row 20: P9, * use the RH needle to bring the 5 strands up on to the LH needle, purl the 5 strands together with the next stitch (the center stitch of the 5 slipped stitches), p9. Repeat from * to end of row.

Repeat rows 1–20.

Specialty

SEA FOAM

Sea foam is an elaborate drop stitch pattern, being slightly complex because it offsets the dropped stitches. Dropped yarn overs form the elongated holes that make up the motif. It is an excellent stitch pattern for scarves, shawls, and blankets, but because the holes are quite large, it is not a good choice for projects intended for babies and children.

level
drape

THE PATTERN

Multiple of 10 + 6

Row 1 (RS): Knit.

Row 2: Knit.

Row 3: K6, * yo twice, k1, yo 3 times, k1, yo 4 times, k1, yo 3 times, k1, yo twice, k6. Repeat from * to end of row.

Row 4: Knit, dropping all of the yarn overs off the needles.

Row 5: Knit.

Row 6: Knit.

Row 7: K1, * yo twice, k1, yo 3 times, k1, yo 4 times, k1, yo 3 times, k1, yo twice, k6. Repeat from * to end of row, end last repeat k1.

Row 8: Knit, dropping all of the yarn overs off the needles.

Repeat rows 1–8.

Note: Do not count your stitches after rows 3 and 7, as the yarn overs will make it appear you have way too many stitches on your needles. The stitch count will return to the original number of stitches on rows 4 and 8.

BRICK WALL

Brick wall is an interesting use of combining slipped stitches with basic knits and purls. Because the slipped stitches pull the knitting, it would be a good pattern to use with a variegated yarn. This pattern tends to pull up vertically as you are knitting. It will relax with washing and blocking. Because it curls at the top and bottom edges and pulls in slightly at the sides, brick wall is best used in conjunction with an edge stitch.

level
drape

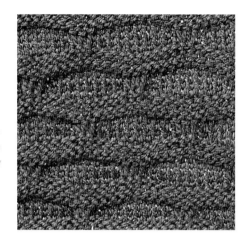

THE PATTERN

Multiple of 12

Row 1 (RS): Purl.
Row 2: Knit.
Row 3: Purl.
Row 4: * P8, sl 2 wyif, p2. Repeat from * to end of row.
Row 5: * K2, sl 2 wyib, k8. Repeat from * to end of row.
Row 6: * P8, sl 2 wyif, p2. Repeat from * to end of row.
Row 7: * K2, sl 2 wyib, k8. Repeat from * to end of row.
Row 8: * P8, sl 2 wyif, p2. Repeat from * to end of row.
Row 9: Purl.
Row 10: Knit.
Row 11: Purl.
Row 12: * P2, sl 2 wyif, p8. Repeat from * to end of row.
Row 13: * K8, sl 2 wyib, k2. Repeat from * to end of row.
Row 14: * P2, sl 2 wyif, p8. Repeat from * to end of row.
Row 15: * K8, sl 2 wyib, k2. Repeat from * to end of row.
Row 16: * P2, sl 2 wyif, p8. Repeat from * to end of row.
Repeat rows 1–16.

Specialty

53

RIBBED DIAMONDS

Ribbed diamonds is a traveling twist stitch pattern where diagonal lines create the impression of diamonds. This motif can be worked as a panel or as an overall stitch pattern. It will show best when worked in a smooth, tightly spun yarn. Ribbed diamonds would work up into a nice sock design or fine-gauge sweater.

level ◉ ◉ ◉ ◉
drape ▥

THE PATTERN

Multiple of 16 + 1

Row 1 and all odd numbered rows (WS): Purl.

Row 2: K1, * LT, RT twice, k3, LT twice, RT, k1. Repeat from * to end of row.

Row 4: K2, * LT, RT twice, k1, LT twice, RT, k3. Repeat from * to end of row, end last repeat k2.

Row 6: K1, * LT twice, RT, k3, LT, RT twice, k1. Repeat from * to end of row.

Row 8: K2, * LT twice, RT, k1, LT, RT twice, k3. Repeat from * to end of row, end last repeat k2.

Row 10: K1, * LT 3 times, k3, RT 3 times, k1. Repeat from * to end of row.

Row 12: K2, * LT 3 times, k1, RT 3 times, k3. Repeat from * to end of row, end last repeat k2.

Row 14: K1, * LT 3 times, k3, RT 3 times, k1. Repeat from * to end of row.

Row 16: K2, * LT twice, RT, k1, LT, RT twice, k3. Repeat from * to end of row, end last repeat k2.

Row 18: K1, * LT twice, RT, k3, LT, RT twice, k1. Repeat from * to end of row.

Row 20: K2, * LT, RT twice, k1, LT twice, RT, k3. Repeat from * to end of row, end last repeat k2.

there's more >

Specialty

RIBBED DIAMONDS

more >

Row 22: K1, * LT, RT twice, k3, LT twice, RT, k1. Repeat from * to end of row.

Row 24: K2, * RT 3 times, k1, LT 3 times, k3. Repeat from * to end of row, end last repeat k2.

Row 26: K1, * RT 3 times, k3, LT 3 times, k1. Repeat from * to end of row.

Row 28: K2, * RT 3 times, k1, LT 3 times, k3. Repeat from * to end of row, end last repeat k2.

Repeat rows 1–28.

TWIST STITCH BRANCHES

Twist stitch branches look like bare branches traveling across a background of Stockinette stitch. Twist stitch branches will show up best when knit with a tightly spun yarn at a firm gauge. It is a good pattern for use in socks, vests, or a stylish cardigan. It would also work well as a panel amongst other stitch patterns.

level ◍ ◍ ◍
drape ▦ ▦

THE PATTERN

Multiple of 16 + 1

Row 1 and all odd numbered rows (WS): Purl.

Row 2: K1, * RT, k5, RT, LT, k2, RT, k1. Repeat from * to end of row.

Row 4: K1, * RT, k4, RT, k2, LT, k1, RT, k1. Repeat from * to end of row.

Row 6: K1, * RT, k3, RT, k4, LT, RT, k1. Repeat from * to end of row.

Row 8: K1, * RT, k2, RT, LT, k5, RT, k1. Repeat from * to end of row.

Row 10: K1, * RT, k1, RT, k2, LT, k4, RT, k1. Repeat from * to end of row.

Row 12: K1, * RT twice, k4, LT, k3, RT, k1. Repeat from * to end of row.

Repeat rows 1–12.

TWIST STITCH LATTICE

Twist stitch lattice is an overall pattern of traveling stitches over a Stockinette stitch background. It resembles a complex cable pattern, but doesn't require a cable needle to work. Twist stitch lattice is best displayed when knit with a tightly spun yarn at a firm gauge. It would make up into a beautiful fine-gauge sweater, or a stunning afghan knit in a heavier yarn.

level

drape

THE PATTERN

Multiple of 16 + 2

Row 1 and all odd numbered rows (WS): Purl.

Row 2: K1, * LT, k4, RT. Repeat from * to last stitch, end k1.

Row 4: K2, * LT, k2, RT, k2. Repeat from * to end of row.

Row 6: K3, * LT, RT, k4. Repeat from * to end of row, end last repeat k3.

Row 8: K4, * RT, k6. Repeat from * to end of row, end last repeat k4.

Row 10: K3, * RT, LT, k4. Repeat from * to end of row, end last repeat k3.

Row 12: K2, * RT, k2, LT, k2. Repeat from * to end of row.

Row 14: K1, * RT, k4, LT. Repeat from * to last stitch, end k1.

Row 16: K8, * LT, k6. Repeat from * to last 2 stitches, end k2.

Repeat rows 1–16.

COBBLESTONES

Cobblestones is a rib-based pattern that forms gently curved squares. The fabric lies flat, and the edges scallop. The rib base of the pattern gives it elasticity. The motif is a perfect overall pattern for projects requiring a close fit, such as socks or a knitted top. Because Cobblestones has such a nice edge to it, it would also make a stunning scarf or blanket.

level
drape ▥

THE PATTERN

Multiple of 16 + 5

Row 1 and all odd numbered rows (WS): P1, * k1, p1. Repeat from * to end of row.

Row 2: K1, p1, * sl 2, k1, p2sso, [p1, k1] 5 times, p1, Dl, p1. Repeat from * to last 3 stitches, end k1, p1, k1.

Row 4: K1, p1, * sl 2, k1, p2sso, [p1, k1] 4 times, p1, Dl, p1, k1, p1. Repeat from * to last 3 stitches, end k1, p1, k1.

Row 6: K1, p1, * sl 2, k1, p2sso, [p1, k1] 3 times, p1, Dl, [p1, k1] 2 times, p1. Repeat from * to last 3 stitches, end k1, p1, k1.

Row 8: K1, p1, * sl 2, k1, p2sso, [p1, k1] 2 times, p1, Dl, [p1, k1] 3 times, p1. Repeat from * to last 3 stitches, end k1, p1, k1.

Row 10: K1, p1, * sl 2, k1, p2sso, p1, k1, p1, Dl, [p1, k1] 4 times, p1. Repeat from * to last 3 stitches, end k1, p1, k1.

Row 12: K1, p1, * sl 2, k1, p2sso, p1, Dl, [p1, k1] 5 times, p1. Repeat from * to last 3 stitches, end k1, p1, k1.

Row 14: K1, p1, * sl 2, k1, p2sso, [p1, k1] 6 times, p1. Repeat from * to last 3 stitches, end k1, p1, k1.

Row 16: K1, p1, * Dl, [p1, k1] 6 times, p1. Repeat from * to last 3 stitches, end k1, p1, k1.

there's more >

COBBLESTONES

more >

Row 18: K1, p1, k1, * p1, DI, [p1, k1] 5 times, p1, sl2, k1, p2sso. Repeat from * to last 2 stitches, end p1, k1.

Row 20: K1, p1, k1, * p1, k1, p1, DI, [p1, k1] 4 times, p1, sl 2, k1, p2sso. Repeat from * to last 2 stitches, end p1, k1.

Row 22: K1, p1, k1, * [p1, k1] 2 times, p1, DI, [p1, k1] 3 times, p1, sl 2, k1, p2sso. Repeat from * to last 2 stitches, end p1, k1.

Row 24: K1, p1, k1, * [p1, k1] 3 times, p1, DI, [p1, k1] 2 times, p1, sl 2, k1, p2sso. Repeat from * to last 2 stitches, end p1, k1.

Row 26: K1, p1, k1, * [p1, k1] 4 times, p1, DI, p1, k1, p1, sl 2, k1, p2sso. Repeat from * to last 2 stitches, end p1, k1.

Row 28: K1, p1, k1, * [p1, k1] 5 times, p1, DI, p1, sl 2, k1, p2sso. Repeat from * to last 2 stitches, end p1, k1.

Repeat rows 1–28.

Note: You will be decreasing two stitches per pattern repeat on row 14. You will return to the original number of stitches on row 16.

Specialty

CROCUSES

Like Herringbone (page 35) or the chevron stitch patterns, Crocuses uses increases and decreases to shape the knitted fabric in interesting directions. The increases and decreases that are stacked on top of each other create a scallop along the cast-on edge, but be sure to cast on loosely. Crocuses is a rather large stitch multiple, so it can be tricky to fit into just the right size of sweater. For a lacy appearance, you can work yarn overs in place of the M1 stitches.

level ● ● ●
drape ▦ ▦

THE PATTERN

Multiple of 26

Row 1 and all odd numbered rows (WS): Purl.

Row 2: * K1, M1, ssk, k4, k2tog, k3, M1, k2, M1, k3, ssk, k4, k2tog, M1, k1. Repeat from * to end of row.

Row 4: * K1, M1, k1, ssk, k2, k2tog, k4, M1, k2, M1, k4, ssk, k2, k2tog, k1, M1, k1. Repeat from * to end of row.

Row 6: * K1, M1, k2, ssk, k2tog, k5, M1, k2, M1, k5, ssk, k2tog, k2, M1, k1. Repeat from * to end of row.

Row 8: * K1, M1, k3, ssk, k4, k2tog, M1, k2, M1, ssk, k4, k2tog, k3, M1, k1. Repeat from * to end of row.

Row 10: * K1, M1, k4, ssk, k2, k2tog, k1, M1, k2, M1, k1, ssk, k2, k2tog, k4, M1, k1. Repeat from * to end of row.

Row 12: * K1, M1, k5, ssk, k2tog, k2, [M1, k2] twice, ssk, k2tog, k5, M1, k1. Repeat from * to end of row.

Repeat rows 1–12.

Needle Size Chart

Metric (mm)	US	UK/CAN
2	0	14
2.25	1	13
2.5		
2.75	2	12
3		11
3.25	3	10
3.5	4	
3.75	5	9
4	6	8
4.5	7	7
5	8	6
5.5	9	5
6	10	4
6.5	10 ½	3
8	11	0
9	13	00
10	15	000
12.75	17	
15	19	
19	35	

Abbreviations and Glossary

C3 over 4: Slip 4 stitches to the cable needle and hold to the back of the work. Knit the next 3 stitches, then purl 1 stitch from the cable needle, then knit the remaining stitches from the cable needle.

C6: Slip 2 stitches onto the cable needle and hold to the front of the work, slip 2 stitches onto a second cable needle and hold to the back of the work, k2, p2 from the second cable needle, k2 from the first cable needle.

CB2: Slip 1 stitch to the cable needle and hold to the back of the work. Knit the next stitch, then knit the stitch from the cable needle.

CB3: Slip 1 stitch to the cable needle and hold to the back of the work. Knit the next 2 stitches, then knit the stitch from the cable needle.

CB4: Slip 2 stitches to the cable needle and hold to the back of the work. Knit the next 2 stitches, then knit the stitches from the cable needle.

CB5: Slip 3 stitches to the cable needle and hold to the back of the work. Knit the next 2 stitches, then knit the stitches from the cable needle.

CB6: Slip 3 stitches to the cable needle and hold to the back of the work. Knit the next 3 stitches, then knit the stitches from the cable needle.

CB8: Slip 4 stitches to the cable needle and hold to the back of the work. Knit the next 4 stitches, then knit the stitches from the cable needle.

CF2 over 3: Slip the next 3 stitches to the cable needle and hold to the back of the work. Knit the next 2 stitches, then p1, k2 from the cable needle.

CF2: Slip 1 stitch to the cable needle and hold to the front of the work. Knit the next stitch, then knit the stitch from the cable needle.

CF3: Slip 2 stitches to the cable needle and hold to the front of the work. Knit the next stitch, then knit the stitches from the cable needle.

CF4: Slip 2 stitches to the cable needle and hold to the front of the work. Knit the next 2 stitches, then knit the stitches from the cable needle.

Yarn Chart

YARN WEIGHT SYMBOL & CATEGORY NAMES	0 lace	1 super fine	2 fine	3 light	4 medium	5 bulky	6 super bulky
TYPE OF YARNS IN CATEGORY	Fingering, 10-count crochet thread	Sock, Fingering, Baby	Sport, Baby	DK, Light Worsted	Worsted, Afghan, Aran	Chunky, Craft, Rug	Bulky, Roving

Source: Craft Yarn Council of America's www.YarnStandards.com

Specialty

CF6: Slip 3 stitches to the cable needle and hold to the front of the work. Knit the next 3 stitches, then knit the stitches from the cable needle.

CF8: Slip 4 stitches to the cable needle and hold to the front of the work. Knit the next 4 stitches, then knit the stitches from the cable needle.

Cn: Cable needle.

DI: Double increase as follows: [k1 tbl, k1] into the next stitch, then insert the left-hand needle behind the vertical strand that runs downward from between the 2 stitches just made and k1 tbl into this strand to create the third stitch.

Inc 1 pwise: Increase 1 stitch purlwise by purling into the front and the back of the next stitch.

Inc 1: Increase 1 stitch by knitting into the front and the back of the next stitch.

K: Knit.

K1b: Knit the next stitch in the row below.

K2tog: Knit 2 stitches together.

K3tog: Knit 3 stitches together.

K4tog: Knit 4 stitches together.

K tbl: Knit through the back of the loop. If the k is followed by a number, knit that many stitches through the back loop. For example, k3 tbl means knit 3 stitches (1 at a time) through the back loops.

Kwise: Knitwise.

LH: Left hand.

LT: Left twist. Knit into the back of the second stitch on the left-hand needle. Do not drop it from the left-hand needle. Knit into the front of the first stitch on the left-hand needle. Drop off both stitches from the left-hand needle. For a left twist on the wrong side of the work, simply purl the stitches instead of knitting them.

LTP: Purl through the back of the second stitch on the left-hand needle without removing it from the needle, then knit the first stitch on the left-hand needle, slipping both stitches off of the needle at the same time. If this is difficult to work, you can use a T1L1 in its place.

M1: Pick up the horizontal strand of yarn lying between the stitch just worked and the next stitch on the left-hand needle from front to back and knit into the back of it. Also referred to as M1 kwise because the new stitch is a knit stitch.

M2: Pick up the horizontal strand of yarn lying between the stitch just worked and the next stitch on the left-hand needle from front to back and knit into the back and the front of it, creating 2 new stitches.

MB (make bobble): [K1, yo, k1, yo, k1] into the next stitch on the left-hand needle. Turn work. Purl 5. Turn work. Knit 5. Turn work. P2tog, k1, p2tog. Turn work. Sl 1, k2tog, psso. Bobble is complete.

P: Purl.

P2sso: Pass 2 slipped stitches over.

P tbl: Purl through the back loop. If the p is followed by a number, purl that many stitches through the back loop. For example, p3 tbl means purl 3 stitches (1 at a time) through the back loops.

P2tog tbl: Purl 2 stitches together through the back loops. If your knitting is too tight to comfortably purl 2 stitches together through the back loops, try working an ssp in place of p2tog tbl. While it is not exactly the same decrease, it is very close.

P2tog: Purl 2 stitches together.

P3tog: Purl 3 stitches together.

Psso: Pass slipped stitch over.

Pwise: Purlwise.

RH: Right hand.

RS: Right side.

RT: Right twist. Knit into the second stitch on the left-hand needle. Do not drop it from the left-hand needle. Knit into the first stitch on the left-hand needle. Drop both stitches from the left-hand needle. For a right twist on the wrong side of the work, simply purl the stitches instead of knitting them.

RTP: Knit into the front of the second stitch on the left-hand needle without removing it from the needle, then purl the first stitch on the left-hand needle, slipping both stitches off the needle at the same time.

S5: Slip the next 5 stitches onto a cable needle (or short double-pointed needle) and hold to the front of the work. Wind the yarn counter-clockwise twice around the stitches on the cable needle, then work the stitches from the cable needle as k1, p3, k1.

Sl 1: Slip 1 stitch. When slipping stitches, it is customary to slip them purlwise unless working a decrease, when they are normally slipped knitwise. Individual instructions should indicate which direction to slip stitches.

Sl 2: Slip 2 stitches as if to k2tog.

Ssk: Working 1 stitch at a time, slip 2 stitches from the left-hand needle to the right-hand needle as if to knit. Insert the left-hand needle into the back of the 2 slipped stitches on the right-hand needle and knit the stitches together.

Ssp: Working 1 stitch at a time, slip 2 stitches from the left-hand needle to the right-hand needle as if to knit. Insert the left-hand needle into the back of the 2 slipped stitches on the right-hand needle and purl the stitches together.

Sssk: Working 1 stitch at a time, slip 3 stitches from the left-hand needle to the right-hand needle as if to knit. Insert the left-hand needle into the back of the 3 slipped stitches on the right-hand needle and knit the stitches together.

T1L1 (travel 1 stitch to the left 1 stitch): Slip 1 stitch to the cable needle and hold to the front of the work. Purl the next stitch, then knit the stitches from the cable needle.

T1L2 (travel 1 stitch to the left 2 stitches): Slip 1 stitch to the cable needle and hold to the front of the work. Knit the next 2 stitches, then knit the stitch from the cable needle.

T1R1 (travel 1 stitch to the right 1 stitch): Slip 1 stitch to the cable needle and hold to the back of the work. Knit the next stitch, then purl the stitch from the cable needle.

T1R2 (travel 1 stitch to the right 2 stitches): Slip 2 stitches to the cable needle and hold to the back of the work. Knit the next stitch, then knit the stitches from the cable needle.

T2L1 (travel 2 stitches to the left 1 stitch): Slip 2 stitches to the cable needle and hold to the front of the work. Purl the next stitch, then knit the stitches from the cable needle.

T2L2 (travel 2 stitches to the left 2 stitches): Slip 2 stitches to the cable needle and hold to the front of the work. Purl the next 2 stitches, then knit the stitches from the cable needle.

T2R1 (travel 2 stitches to the right 1 stitch): Slip 1 stitch to the cable needle and hold to the back of the work. Knit the next 2 stitches, then purl the stitch from the cable needle.

T2R2 (travel 2 stitches to the right 2 stitches): Slip 2 stitches to the cable needle and hold to the back of the work. Knit the next 2 stitches, then purl the stitches from the cable needle.

T3L1 (travel 3 stitches to the left 1 stitch): Slip 3 stitches to the cable needle and hold to the front of the work. Purl the next stitch, then knit the stitches from the cable needle.

T3L2 (travel 3 stitches to the left 2 stitches): Slip 3 stitches to the cable needle and hold to the front of the work. Purl the next 2 stitches, then knit the stitches from the cable needle.

T3R1 (travel 3 stitches to the right 1 stitch): Slip 1 stitch to the cable needle and hold to the back of the work. Knit the next 3 stitches, then purl the stitches from the cable needle.

T3R2 (travel 3 stitches to the right 2 stitches): Slip 2 stitches to the cable needle and hold to the back of the work. Knit the next 3 stitches, then purl the stitches from the cable needle.

T4L2 (travel 4 stitches to the left 2 stitches): Slip 4 stitches to the cable needle and hold to the front of the work. Purl the next 2 stitches, then knit the stitches from the cable needle.

T4R2 (travel 4 stitches to the right 2 stitches): Slip 2 stitches to the cable needle and hold to the back of the work. Knit the next 4 stitches, then purl the stitches from the cable needle.

T8B RIB: Slip the next 4 stitches onto the cable needle and hold to back of the work, k1, p2, k1 from the left-hand needle, then k1, p2, k1 from the cable needle.

T8F RIB: Slip the next 4 stitches onto the cable needle and hold to front of the work, k1, p2, k1 from the left-hand needle, then k1, p2, k1 from the cable needle.

WS: Wrong side.

Wyib: With yarn in back of work.

Wyif: With yarn in front of work.

Yo: Yarn over.

Specialty

63